Mobile ASP.NET MVC 5

Eric Sowell

Mobile ASP.NET MVC 5

ISBN-13 (pbk): 978-1-4302-5056-2

ISBN-13 (electronic): 978-1-4302-5057-9

President and Publisher: Paul Manning
Lead Editor: Gwenan Spearing
Development Editor: Douglas Pundick
Technical Reviewer: Brandon Satrom
Editorial Board: Steve Anglin, Ewan Buckingham, Gary Cornell, Louise Corrigan, James DeWolf, Jonathan Gennick, Jonathan Hassell, Robert Hutchinson, Michelle Lowman, James Markham, Matthew Moodie, Jeff Olson, Jeffrey Pepper, Douglas Pundick, Ben Renow-Clarke, Dominic Shakeshaft, Gwenan Spearing, Matt Wade, Steve Weiss, Tom Welsh
Coordinating Editor: Kevin Shea
Copy Editor: Michael Sandlin
Compositor: SPi Global
Indexer: SPi Global
Artist: SPi Global
Cover Designer: Anna Ishchenko

Distributed to the book trade worldwide by Springer Science+Business Media New York, 233 Spring Street, 6th Floor, New York, NY 10013. Phone 1-800-SPRINGER, fax (201) 348-4505, e-mail orders-ny@springer-sbm.com, or visit www.springeronline.com.

For information on translations, please e-mail rights@apress.com, or visit www.apress.com.

Apress and friends of ED books may be purchased in bulk for academic, corporate, or promotional use. eBook versions and licenses are also available for most titles. For more information, reference our Special Bulk Sales–eBook Licensing web page at www.apress.com/bulk-sales.

Any source code or other supplementary materials referenced by the author in this text is available to readers at www.apress.com. For detailed information about how to locate your book's source code, go to www.apress.com/source-code.

To my wife who for some strange reason didn't think it was a bad idea for me to completely switch career paths and to teach myself how to program ten years ago, thank you for your support and patience. You are wonderful.

And to my geek friends and coworkers who helped me the most in this programming adventure in the very beginning, Kris Pate, Jeremy Mayhew, Jeff Hamm, Shawn Lohstroh, Mark Reed, Brad Sprague, Xander Sherry, and Bryan Pierce. Without you this would have been so much harder. You answered a lot of stupid questions, gave lots of suggestions for improvement, and never told me that I couldn't figure this stuff out.

—Eric Sowell

Contents at a Glance

Contents

About the Author

Eric Sowell never planned to be a programmer but ended up being one anyway. He has been doing it for over 10 years and couldn't be happier. It has become both an exciting career and hobby. Most recently he led the team that created Match.com's mobile website and is currently the manager for mobile web application development for Match.com, where he has worked for over seven years. He is married to his great wife Kathryn, and they have three kids, all of which are glad that he has finally finished this book. He lives in Dallas, TX.

About the Technical Reviewer

Brandon Satrom (@BrandonSatrom) is the Lead Product Manager for Telerik's Cross-Platform Tools and Services, and is based in Austin, TX. An unapologetic lover of the Web, Brandon loves to talk about HTML, JavaScript, CSS, open source, and whatever new shiny tool or technology has distracted him from that other thing he was working on. Brandon loves writing and speaking and loves hanging out with and learning from other passionate developers, both online and in person. He blogs on occasion at UserInExperience.com.

Acknowledgments

In high school I developed a love for books. As a bibliophile, I thought it would be so cool if I could someday write one. At the time I knew nothing of development and would never imagine that I would at some point write a book on the topic.

This book, which is my first, got started because Gwenan Spearing of Apress e-mailed me in August of 2012. I believe she was reading the feedback about some talks I gave for aspConf and mvcConf 2 and for some reason thought she should e-mail me. Thank you so much.

This of course leads me to the technical community. Though we developers like to get in silly fights (spaces, not tabs, and single quotes in JavaScript strings, just in case you are curious) all the time, it's actually a great community to be involved with. In particular I need to thank Eric Hexter, Javier Lozano, and Jon Galloway for allowing me to be involved with them in C4MVC, mvcConf, and later aspConf. And in general I want to thank the technical community for being awesome. Thanks to the local user groups for allowing me to test out much of this material in presentations, especially my own North Dallas .NET User Group.

I had a job while writing this book, and this project did take attention away from my work on occasion. I want to thank my friend and boss, Shane Henderson, for being patient with me in this process. You are the best boss ever. Thanks for putting up with all my requests for new devices to play with (even when you don't approve them), for the flexibility to work and write, and in general for putting up with me. This book also affected my team a bit, and I want to say thank you to them. The whole mobile team at Match.com is great. Every day I look forward to coming in to work with you guys. I hope you all realize how great you are as a team, and I'm glad I got the opportunity to join you two years ago. You are an inspiration.

Thanks to my editors at Apress, Gwenan Spearing, Kevin Shea, and Douglas Pundick. You have all been very patient with me (I can be a little slow sometimes, though I'm sure you don't need me to remind you of that), and I appreciate you perseverance. You have been great.

Thanks to Brandon Satrom, my technical reviewer. We met for the first time at HTML5tx, and I knew then that you were the kind of geek that I could get along with. You gave great feedback along the way while I was writing the book, and I thank you for your encouragement.

Several friends gave feedback on chapters as I wrote them. I want to especially thank Wil Bloodworth, Mike Randrup, and Neil Duffy for reading chapters from my book. Your feedback was valuable. The book is better thanks to your efforts.

Thanks to Randall Arnold and Nokia for letting me borrow a few Windows Phones for testing. That was very helpful during the early stages of the book. A big thanks as well to Chris Koenig and Microsoft as well for giving me a Windows Phone 8 developer device to test with. Chris, you've been a friend for a while and I appreciate your continued support. You rock. And thanks to Match.com for giving us a nice supply of mobile test devices.

And finally, thanks to the family. They have all been patient as I worked on this project. The wife of course wanted to hang out more, Jonathan wanted more time playing Legos, Abby wanted more time playing with her stuffed animals, and Samuel just wanted more attention. I'm glad I can now give it.

Introduction

Some of us have been doing web development for a number of years but only in the last few were given portable, connected computers in our pockets. Though phones with web browsers are nothing new, the popularity of smartphones is making it much more tolerable, and in some cases very natural, to access the Internet on our phones. And because of the touch experience on the nicer devices, browsing on phones and tablets can often be better than on a desktop browser. Perhaps you have picked up this book because you are a web developer by trade and your own mobile usage piqued your interest in doing mobile web development. Maybe your employer wants a mobile site and you need a resource for that. Or maybe you are a hobbyist and developing for the mobile web sounds fun. Whatever the reason, I can help you.

Though I have had a mobile phone for years, I only bought a smartphone a few years ago (a Windows Phone 7 device). Now I am an iPhone user and can barely imagine not having instant access to the Internet while on the go. Fast forward a bit and I now manage mobile web development at Match.com. For the last two years I have been leading the effort to deliver a good mobile web experience to our customers. I have spent longer than that doing mobile web development and longer still doing web development for the desktop browser. Over the last few years I have had a lot of fun and learned a lot about this quickly changing topic of mobile web development. My goal is to share what I have learned with you in this book.

Who This Book Is For

This book is for the ASP.NET developer who knows how ASP.NET MVC works and is eager to learn how to use it for building mobile websites. Thorough knowledge of ASP.NET MVC is not at all required but a little is assumed. This book also assumes a little knowledge of HTML, CSS and JavaScript. You do not need any prior experience in mobile development.

What This Book Is Not

I am not here to tell you how to write native applications for iPhone, Android, or Windows Phone. Building native applications for these phones is often a fine idea. I have even tried it a bit myself. But this is not a book about writing these types of applications.

But this book is about writing cool stuff for all of those phones and more. If you want to write an app for iPhone in its native development environment, you will need to create it using Objective-C. If you want to do the same for Android, you will use Java. As for Windows Phone, you will use C# or VB.NET. One of the benefits of mobile web development is that you get to target all three and more without having to learn all of those different development platforms.

What Tools Do You Need?

To do mobile web development with ASP.NET MVC 5, you will need a copy of Visual Studio 2013. But almost nothing changed between ASP.NET MVC 4 and 5, so everything except a few things (covered in Chapter 12, "Useful Libraries for Mobile") will be the same between those two versions. If you are stuck using older versions of ASP.NET MVC and unable to upgrade, everything other than parts of Chapter 6 ("Display Modes, View Engines and Html Helpers") and Chapter 12 is still relevant. So whatever version of ASP.NET MVC you are using, this material will help you.

It is also very handy to have a wide range of mobile devices to test with. If you do not have all the mobile devices that you need, you can also use simulators or emulators. If those are not available, you can use services like Device Anywhere (http://www.keynotedeviceanywhere.com/) to test. Though you do have various options, I have found that it's much easier to test things if you have a device to use.

Why Mobile Web Development Is Awesome

There are a number of good reasons to choose the mobile Web as a development platform. First, with mobile web development, you only need one development tool set as I mentioned before. You do not need to learn Java, Objective-C, and C# to build for each major phone.

Second, this also means that you can target multiple types of devices with one codebase. This a major boost for both productivity and maintenance. Because of browser incompatibilities, it is not "write once, run anywhere." That would be fantastic. But a lot (or perhaps even most) of the code can be shared across browsers in modern smartphones.

Third, if you already have experience in web development generally, you are already on your way to working on the mobile web. Everything you learned in doing web development applies to mobile. All you need to do to be effective in mobile development is to pick up some additional skills.

Fourth, you can deploy anytime. This is actually a very big deal. Find a critical bug in a mobile website? Push a quick fix out to the server farm. Find a critical bug in a native application? Go through the relevant app store and their (sometimes) finicky process to get your change pushed out.

Fifth, no one can keep you off of their platform. For many, this may not even come up as a concern but it can be a very big deal. Anyone's application can be removed from any app store (though Apple is most notorious for this) and there is nothing you can do about it. Having a mobile website along with native applications gives you a backup strategy if a store decides to remove your application. By targeting the mobile web, you are not held captive by those who run the app stores. The only one holding you back is you.

Where Mobile Web Development Has Its Challenges

So what is not to like about mobile web development? In reality, there are several advantages to doing native mobile application development. Here are a few things to keep in mind.

First, if you ever found yourself complaining about desktop browser fragmentation, you haven't seen anything yet. On the desktop, you primarily have Internet Explorer, Chrome, and Firefox and their various versions. Since the latter two automatically update, you really only have to deal with one version of both Chrome and Firefox and a few of Internet Explorer. The mobile browser landscape is far more fragmented. Users of iOS tend to upgrade quickly, which pushes the newer, more interesting browser versions of mobile Safari more quickly. Android users are the exact opposite. They rarely upgrade and old browsers stay around for much longer. Additionally, manufacturers tweak their Android implementations and their default browsers, so you will get (seemily endless) inconsistencies at times. Along with that you also have two versions of the Windows Phone 7.x browser out as well as mobile Firefox and Opera. At the moment you may not want to forget Blackberry as it is still hanging on to some market share, which gives you another few variants of a webkit-based browser like you have on iOS and Android (though traffic from Blackberry devices is on a serious decline). And we have the recent addition of Firefox OS, though the numbers remain small for now. And that is just the browser landscape for smartphones. Fragmentation only gets worse if you start supporting older devices.

Second, native applications get more capabilities than mobile web counterparts. Native applications can register a phone for push notifications, even while the app is not running. You cannot do this with mobile websites. You can't currently upload a photo directly from a phone to a site through the browser except in iOS 6+ and Android 4+. Native applications with their native rendering also benefit from improved performance. But the good news is that as time goes on the browsers improve and get more functionality than they had before. They also become faster. But it is likely that mobile web applications will continue to trail native applications in terms of capabilities.

Third, native mobile applications also have a great story around being an acquisition tool for new customers. The native app stores can be a great channel for exposing your services to customers.

Fourth, native mobile applications already have a built-in monetization strategy through their respective app stores. If a company wants to make money on the mobile web, they have to implement payment in their web application and don't get the convenient buy for "$0.99" button that makes purchasing native applications so painless.

Ideally, the best strategy for most companies would be to target both web and native because both have their advantages. This is our strategy at Match.com. But you do not always have resources to do everything at once, so sometimes you have to weigh the advantages and disadvantages of each approach.

The Big Questions

If you have bought this book, you probably already plan on building a mobile web site. Good for you because now the adventure can begin. And it should begin with a short discussion of mobile strategy. There is more than one way to build mobile websites and your goals, circumstances, and company dynamics can really affect the direction you take. To think through this, I like to pose four questions.

First, do you plan for your mobile website to be separate from your desktop website? Some of the later questions will help you answer this one but in some cases this is easy to answer without further consideration. Let us say that you are on the mobile team for your company and another team altogether has the responsibility for making and maintaining the desktop website. In these cases it will often be best to plan on having different sites. Sharing the code and product direction may be very difficult from an organizational perspective, and having a separate site may make the most sense.

Also, if your mobile website will have very different functionality or structure than your desktop website, it is often smart to have separate sites. By having one site you can more easily share code; but if there are significant differences, you will already know that any potential sharing is going to be more difficult.

However, there are cases where having the same site is really the smart choice. If you are tasked with creating a mobile-friendly version of your company's blog, duplicating the site is likely a bad approach because responsive design techniques make this kind of task relatively easy to solve without creating a separate site. And even for more complicated sites, in the long term having two sites will often cause more hassle. As mobile devices proliferate in both number and size, desktop versus mobile becomes a hard distinction to maintain.

Second, are you trying to create a mobile web site or a mobile web app? At first glance you might think these are not that much different, but in some cases this will radically change how you approach the project.

A few examples might be helpful. If you take the previously mentioned example of a company blog, in most cases the best approach will be to use responsive web design principles to make an existing design (or new, if necessary) work well on both smartphones and desktop browsers. Other similar sites would be personal portfolios, consulting company websites or sites that are more content-oriented. This works especially well if you are targeting modern smartphones only.

On the flip side, an attempt to create a web app will definitely affect how you approach creating your mobile project. For example, when we created Match.com's mobile website for iOS and Android (those were our original target devices), we explicitly patterned our interface after our iPhone native application. This also led us to leverage a certain set of HTML5 capabilities to create a more app-like experience. From a purely code-sharing perspective, it would have been next to impossible to try and take Match.com's desktop website and try to turn it into the app that we wanted to create.

But this is often not going to be the best choice for you. Making a mobile website act like a native web app adds a great deal of difficulty to the task. Though doing this can be a fun technical exercise, this is rarely something normal users would expect, so you may be simply creating more work for yourself.

Third, are you starting something new? If you have an existing website and you are tasked with creating a mobile version, it can sometimes be very difficult to take the existing site and mobilize it. If you want to have a single site that works on both mobile and desktop, sometimes it will be easier to start another site that is built with both in mind that would eventually replace the existing desktop site, perhaps targeting a range of different devices and browsers through responsive design techniques.

If you are building something new and it is a content-heavy site (question #2 above), it is probably best to plan from the beginning for the single site to serve both purposes. But if you are creating an alternative to an existing site, sometimes it is best to plan on replacing the existing site with the new site at some point.

Fourth, who is your audience? If your audience is primarily in North America or Europe, modern smartphones like iPhone or Android will be the vast majority of your traffic in the near future. In Match's case, over 80 percent of our traffic comes from either iPhone or Android, so those were the first devices for us to target with our new mobile site. Blackberry devices, Windows Phones, and feature phones made up the remaining amount. And that made sense for us, because that is where most of our users are.

Though iOS and Android dominate US mobile traffic, itnternationally, there is a wide variety of phones outside of the iPhone/Android space. If your audience is primarily international, prepare for a very diverse device market.

So About Those Questions

I asked those four questions above because they help you think through your approach to mobile and how that corresponds to what we will discuss in this book. But for now, let us take a few examples. Say you have a blog, and you want to give users a good reading experience on their mobile devices. If your audience primarily has smartphones, section one of this book will be the primary resource for you. In many cases you will be able to use responsive web design to make a single site work fine for both smartphones and desktop browsers. For content-heavy sites like blogs, this goal is easily achievable. But if you want your blog readable by smartphones in North America and Europe as well as the feature phones of India and the keitai phones of Japan, you will find all the material in the book of useful for leveraging the server-side and developing for phones with less features.

Or perhaps you are creating an e-commerce platform. If you are a US- or European-based company, it might make sense for your business to just focus on modern smartphones. But if you want the widest reach for your project and want to handle old Blackberry devices and feature phones, you will want to learn how to target both differently (discussed in Chapter 6, "Display Modes, View Engines and Html Helpers"). And you almost surely want a different experience for both. Targeting the lowest common denominator browser capabilities to support older phones will mean ignoring the beneficial features in smartphones, which could have negative ramifications for your bottom line.

Whatever you are building, these four questions should help you think through your future mobile web efforts. Even though our mobile website is a year and a half old as of the publication this book, we are still asking ourselves these same questions and trying to decide our own direction.

ASP.NET MVC 5 and Mobile

ASP.NET MVC 5 is a great platform on which to develop mobile websites; but I want to go ahead and clarify some things that may not be so obvious from a quick glance at the project types for ASP.NET in Visual Studio 2013, as seen in this figure:

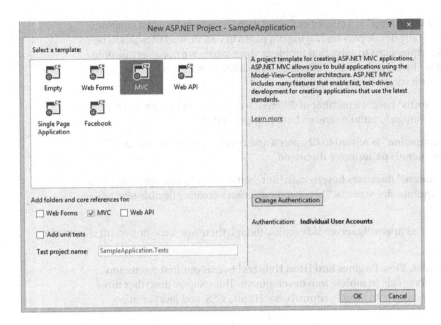

The new ASP.NET project dialog in Visual Studio 2013

As you can see, there is no "Mobile" web project. There was one in ASP.NET MVC 4 for Visual Studio 2012 and this project type pre-installed jQuery Mobile (discussed in chapter 12, "Useful Libraries for Mobile") and was probably what some thought was the default way to approach doing mobile web development simply because that was what you got when you created a "Mobile" project. But they removed this option with Visual Studio 2013.

I can't comment on why Microsoft did this because I don't know. But I do believe that this was a good choice. Though jQuery Mobile is a cool open-source project and is a good fit for some sites, it is certainly not the first place to start on mobile projects. I would strongly recommend starting with a responsive web design approach instead, which is how this book starts (as I will explain below). The good news is that the default ASP.NET MVC website templates in both MVC 4 (not the "Mobile" option) and MVC 5 are **responsive by default**. This is a better pattern to follow, so I am pleased with the changes in Visual Studio 2013.

To see a responsive approach in action, create a new ASP.NET MVC project, start it up and start shrinking and explanding your browser width. The site should flexibly adapt to the changing browser side.

Of course you might ask what relevance there is between building a mobile website and the server-side framework you use to server up your client-side assets. You can build responsive websites on any server platform, as well as basic mobile websites for older phones. Though this is true, there is quite a bit on the server you can leverage. Much of this book is about what you should use and when.

How This Book Is Structured

I've split this book into three parts, each focusing on a particular subject or area of programming. The first section is on responsive web design and comprises five chapters.

- **Chapter 1 "The Basics of Responsive Web Design"** introduces you to responsive web design by building a responsive version of the APress homepage. This chapter should give you a good overview of the basic ideas in responsive web design.

- **Chapter 2 "CSS Layout Bootcamp"** is a primer on layout with CSS with a focus on creating layouts with CSS floats. Many developers find laying out pages in CSS instead of tables to be very difficult, and this chapter aims to solve that problem, since tables are not a very flexible layout mechanism. Table-based layouts are difficult or impossible to make responsive, so we need to have an alternative way to layout web pages.

- **Chapter 3 "Flexible Layouts"** covers a number of different ways to create layouts that are responsive and flexible enough to handle screens both large and small.

- **Chapter 4 "Flexible Navigation"** is related to Chapter 3 and covers navigation as a special case. Like Chapter 3, numerous patterns are discussed.

- **Chapter 5 "Flexible Content"** discusses how to make our content flexible enough to work on both desktop-size and mobile-size screens. This chapter discusses creating flexible text, tables, video, and images.

The next section switches to discuss primarily server-side topics, though there are some important client-side discussions as well.

- **Chapter 6 "Display Modes, View Engines and Html Helpers"** begins our first discussion of how we can use the server-side in mobile web development. This chapter describes three different mechanisms we can use to flexibly control what HTML, CSS, and JavaScript get returned to the client.

- **Chapter 7 "Device and Feature Detection"** discusses how you can decide what your devices are capable of doing, which is very important for progressive enhancement and can be useful for informing how we use the techniques described in Chapter 6.

The third and final section shifts the focus again to client-side mobile web development, though Chapter 8 continues with one foot planted firmly on both the client and server-sides.

- **Chapter 8 "Mobile Performance"** shows you several techniques that are important for well-performing mobile web applications.

- **Chapter 9 "Native APIs, HTML5 and CSS3 on Mobile Today"** gives an overview of how advanced our mobile browsers are. You might be surprised to see what the average iOS, Android, or Windows Phone can do.

- **Chapter 10 "Programming for Touch"** introduces you to the very interesting world of touch-based programming. This chapter covers how to handle the various and incompatible touch programming models and ends with a very practical use case for developing with touch.

- **Chapter 11 "Advanced Touch Programming"** takes us deeper into touch development with more practical yet complex samples.

- **Chapter 12 "Useful Libraries for Mobile"** shows us a number of useful libraries for building mobile websites. Though this book is mostly about core principles and techniques, libraries can be very helpful at times.

Device Testing

"What devices should I own?" is a common question by those getting into mobile web development. "All of them" is an appropriate but not feasible answer. Here are the devices I used to test all the client-sides samples in this book, in no particular order, followed by the OS version and browsers I tested with on the devices.

1. iPhone 3G (iOS 4, Safari)

2. iPhone 4 (iOS 5, Safari)

3. iPhone 4S (iOS 6, Safari)

4. iPhone 5S (iOS 7, Safari)

5. iPad (3rd gen, iOS 6, Safari)

6. Samsung Galaxy S (SGH-I897, Android 2.1, Android Webkit)

7. Samsung Galaxy S (SGH-I897, Android 2.2, Android Webkit)

8. LG Nitro (P930, Android 2.3.5, Android Webkit)

9. Samsung Galaxy SIII (Android 4.1, Android Webkit, Chrome, Android, Opera Class, Opera Webkit)

10. BlackBerry Z10 (BlackBerry OS 10, BlackBerry browser)

11. Lumia 900 (Windows Phone 7.5, IE 9)

12. Lumia 820 (Windows Phone 8, IE 10)

13. Lumia 920 (Windows Phone 8, IE 10)

14. Samsung Slate Tablet (Windows 8, IE 10)

15. Geeksphone Keon (Firefox OS 1.0.1.0-prerelease)

16. Kindle Fire (first generation)

17. Kindle Fire HD

18. Galaxy Nexus 7 (*, Android Webkit, Chrome)

So why these devices? In some cases it is obvious. In the United States (my focus) iOS takes the largest share of mobile web traffic so testing your mobile web work on iOS is clearly the most important thing to do in almost all cases. In my experience iOS browsers tend to have fewer regressions and bugs as the newer versions were released, but it is still a good idea to test on multiple if you can. If you cannot, own a device running iOS 7. People do a great deal of web browsing on iPads as well, and if you want to support tablet traffic on your mobile site, you will need at least one iPad to test on.

Android takes the second place in mobile web traffic. Even though Android users upgrade slower than iOS users, Android 4 is still the best device to have if you can only have one. But it is on Android that you really see mobile browser fragmentation to its greatest extent, so testing on as many Android devices as possible is very important.

As for Windows Phone, it is probably best to own a Windows Phone 8 device even though at Match we still have more Windows Phone 7.5 users. Version 8 will probably surpass 7.5 in adoption at some point. The browsers are drastically different, so owning both would be good, though the small traffic you will likely get from these devices probably doesn't justify owning multiple unless you have the cash to spend or a particular affinity to Windows Phone.

It is important to have some touch device running Internet Explorer 10 at the very least just so you can test the touch APIs, whether this is a Windows 8 or Windows Phone 8 device.

Kindle and Android tablets are being sold in greater numbers, so testing on these devices is also useful.

At the moment testing a Firefox OS device is a luxury but not a necessity. Perhaps this will change in the future.

BlackBerry 10 device testing is also a luxury. The traffic for these devices is very small and BlackBerry OS' outlook is exceedingly bleak. In my experience, robust Android device testing and debugging will likely cover you for BlackBerry devices.

Downloading the code

The code for the examples shown in this book is available on the Apress website, `www.apress.com`. A link can be found on the book's information page under the Source Code/Downloads tab. This tab is located underneath the Related Titles section of the page.

The author also maintains a site for the book at `http://www.mobilemvcbook.com/`. Most of the sample code can be viewed and tested live there on the site.

Contacting the Author

Should you have any questions or comments—or even spot a mistake you think I should know about—you can contact me at `eric.sowell@gmail.com`. You can also follow me on Twitter: I go by the handle @mallioch. You can contact me there. I also maintain a site for my blog and personal projects, `http://ericsowell.com`, on which I keep up-to-date contact information.

CHAPTER 1

■ ■ ■

The Basics of Responsive Web Design

In April of 2000, John Allsopp wrote an article entitled "A Dao of Web Design" on the website A List Apart [http://alistapart.com/article/dao]. The article essentially poses the following question: Do you try to control the naturally fluid medium of the web and the variety of ways people access it? Or do you treat this natural fluidity as a strength rather than as a weakness? John's answer is simple: "Make pages which are adaptable." In many ways this is a more difficult approach to building sites for the Web. There are advantages to starting with a fixed-layout size for a page, otherwise the approach would not be so popular. But the big problem with this fixed and non-adaptive approach is that the site ends up working really well for one type of device and not particularly well for any other. Have a website designed to work on a 1024x768 display? If that layout is fixed at that width, you have created a good experience only for the desktop user. This is not adapting. This is not designing for flexibility, but it has been the norm since few were trying to target anything other than the lowest-common-denominator desktop experience.

Fast forward a decade to May of 2010, to an article written by Ethan Marcotte entitled "Responsive Web Design." Marcotte accepted Allsopp's approach and outlined the main ideas behind what is now called "responsive web design." The basic idea is that you use fluid layouts, flexible images, and media queries to design a page in such a way that it responds to its viewer and how they are viewing the site: in short, you want to "design for the ebb and flow of things" [http://alistapart.com/article/responsive-web-design]. You don't have separate designs for mobile phones, desktops, and tablets, or yet another for large-screen displays like TVs. You design in such a way that it is flexible enough for all; and you do it with techniques that already have wide browser support.

Since May of 2010, responsive web design has taken much of the web development community by storm. This adoption has been especially high for doing mobile web development. The principles of responsive web design give you a great tool for designing sites that work across a wide range of modern phones and tablets. Here are some examples:

1. We have two sizes for iPhone now as of the release of the iPhone 5 (same width but different height).

2. There are a variety of phone sizes with Android.

3. We have one phone size with Windows Phone 7 but a couple of sizes for Windows Phone 8.

4. There are many different sizes of Android tablets.

5. The Kindle Fire is now in several different sizes and resolutions.

6. The iPad now comes in two sizes (same CSS pixel resolution but different physical sizes and pixel densities).

7. Windows 8 has no specific constraints on display, so there will be a lot of variety; and the browser in tablet mode has both a full-screen and a small-screen "snapped mode" for viewing web pages.

8. Devices for both Ubuntu and Firefox OS have been announced, though it remains to be seen what range of devices they will support.

1

Go ahead and get fixed-size sites working on all those devices and try to keep your sanity. Or, instead, *take an approach that embraces the fluidity of it all and uses this fluidity as a strength instead of a weakness*. Even though responsive web design is not a mobile technique specifically, it works great for mobile technology anyway.

The techniques found in responsive web design are also future-friendly, since adoption of the technical bits is standardized and/or universally supported in recent browsers. For older browsers different techniques will have to be used, which is part of the focus of Chapter 6. But most people who want to create mobile websites focus on modern mobile browsers, in particular both Android and iPhone, since they are the undisputed dominant phones in the smartphone market today. So we will start there. This same approach will also work well on some other devices, like the Windows Phone 7.5 and 8, Blackberry 10, Firefox OS, and other mobile browsers like Opera and Firefox mobile.

This first chapter will give you an overview of responsive web design. In chapters 3 through 5 we will dive deep into the main ideas and look at a lot of examples. Even though the web design community is constantly coming out with new techniques and new standards are being implemented that would make being responsive easier (note the picture element draft, `http://www.w3.org/TR/2013/WD-html-picture-element-20130226/`), responsive web design is a very practical technique that can be used now. Working through examples will make the principles more clear as we see them used and will allow us to discuss ideas techniques can be used on a wide range of projects today.

Is This for Developers?

So who is this book for, web designers or developers? Given the start of the chapter, you would be excused in thinking that this was a chapter for designers; however, this is not the case. I am a developer, not a web designer, and I can assure you this material is for *developers*. The topic of web design is much greater than responsive web design. The technique is for making sites work across a wide range of displays and is not meant to encompass all that is web design. I will not be talking about many design ideas like color theory because I'm not qualified to do so, nor is it even necessary. We will be talking about typography, but only to the extent that it's necessary to talk about flexible sizing. We will not be talking about composition, proportion, and visual hierarchies. In other words, this book is not here to turn you into a designer. You are a developer, and it is okay if you stay that way.

But if you are a web developer, the web is your medium and your canvas; so it is valuable for you to understand how it works and what it is capable of. HTML and CSS do not belong to the designer. They are there for both web developers and web designers. In many cases, developing a more thorough knowledge of your medium is not a luxury but a necessity. At my place of employment, our designers are not web developers. We get Photoshop documents to work from. If the design has to work across multiple devices, the developers have to make that happen, not the designers. Many of you will be in the same position.

So you could say that this is a discussion of the mechanics of web design. If you are a web developer, you should know how to implement a three-column design in CSS without using tables, even if you don't have the design knowledge to navigate through all the design choices involved. Making those decisions might be someone else's job, and that's okay.

This chapter introduces you to the main ideas of responsive web design and how you can use that to make your design (or someone else's) work across a variety of screen sizes. We have a sample site that we'll use to work through some of the issues in making the design work across desktop devices and scaled down to fit nicely on common mobile devices. If you find all this discussion of floats, margins, paddings, borders, and such difficult (as many web developers do), Chapter 2 is for you. So feel free to skip ahead, but come back if you get confused.

As a bonus, understanding how responsive web design works might just make you a designer's best friend. I often wonder how many eyes glaze over when web designers start talking to developers about responsive web design. Don't be that kind of developer. Embrace your medium, and give your web designer a virtual hug.

Getting Started

Responsive web design centers around three primary ideas: flexible layouts, flexible content, and media queries. The big idea is that you can use the same HTML and CSS for both desktop and mobile browsers. In developer terms, this is like the DRY (Don't Repeat Yourself) principle in code. Mobile websites are often completely different sites than their desktop counterparts, which means everything is generally created twice. Responsive web design helps you stay DRY, making it easier to share the code, even if the "code" in this case is primarily HTML and CSS. Flexible layouts make it easier to organize the page for different sizes of device. Following flexible content practices allows the content of your site to work on multiple devices. Media queries allow you to target particular sizes and apply changes.

To see how this would work, let's jump into our sample site. As of the writing of this chapter, Apress does not have a responsive site, so we will create a responsive version of their home page. As with the other samples in this book, the source code for the sample site can be downloaded from the Apress website.

This chapter will focus on making this one page an introduction to responsive web design. The next four chapters will explain the ideas more fully and provide many more samples.

Losing that Fixed Fixation

So let's start with the home page of the site, which looks like Figure 1-1, on the left, in a desktop browser. It features a header with a horizontal menu, a large content block at the top, four columns below, and a footer. When viewed on an iPhone, the header image and text stays the same, but the menu is morphed into a centered, vertical list since it's too wide to fit on a phone. The content in the large content block below the header shifts so that it can all fit on the screen. The four-column area adapts to the device size and collapses down to a single column. The footer itself has content broken into four columns, so we collapse the content down to a single column just as we did above.

Figure 1-1. *Sample site. On the left is a screenshot from Chrome on the desktop at full screen. On the right are several screenshots from an iPhone 5 combined to show how it would look on a mobile device*

You can contrast this by looking at the current Apress site on a smartphone. There is no adaptation. Rather, the page is shrunk down so that it all fits in the screen, and you have to pinch and zoom to find what you need. It is functional, but a better approach would be to do what we are doing in our example site: adapt to the user's device and give them something easy to read and use.

The markup for the page is fairly simple, but there is a lot of it, so we'll take it a section at a time.

```
<!DOCTYPE html>
<html>
<head>
  <title>A Responsive Apress</title>
  <!--this tag is very important and will be explained at the end of the chapter -->
  <meta name="viewport" content="width=device-width" />
</head>
<body>
  <div class="page">
    <div class="header">
      <h1>apress</h1>
      <h2>For professionals by professionals</h2>

      <ul class="nav">
        <li class="nav-item"><a href="/">Home</a></li>
        <li class="nav-item"><a href="/">Alpha Program</a></li>
        <li class="nav-item"><a href="/">About Apress</a></li>
        <li class="nav-item"><a href="/">Support</a></li>
      </ul>
    </div>

    <!-- the page content goes here -->

  </div>
</body>
</html>
```

First of all, like the live Apress site, we want to set a maximum width on the main section of the site. We will start by thinking inflexibly (we'll change this below) and set the width of our content wrapper to 960 pixels and center it all horizontally. Here is our CSS for that:

```
.page {
  margin: 0 auto;
  width: 960px;
}
```

Why 960 pixels? The smallest common resolution for desktop monitors these days is still 1024x768. The number 960 is good because it's less than the maximum of 1024 pixels in width and allows for the browser border and scrollbar, when visible. It's also easily divisible, making calculations for column widths easy, since 960 is divided evenly by 2, 3, 4, 6, 8, 10, 12, and 16 (layout will be discussed further in Chapter 3). So 960 pixels is a great starting place for a fixed-width site.

Now on to the header. The only part of this section that most people would find tricky is the menu. The old-school way to lay this out would be to use an HTML table. Though this would "work" for a desktop browser, this approach is very inflexible. If you want to change the layout according to the screen size, you've now trapped yourself. By using a table, you make the layout a bit easier but only for one screen size. The savvier web developer would use a list and CSS floats to make the list lay out horizontally (with all non-layout-related styling removed).

```css
/*
  I also use a CSS reset (not listed here). If you aren't familiar with those,
I recommend checking out
  http://meyerweb.com/eric/tools/css/reset/ or check out chapter 2.
*/

.nav {
  overflow: hidden;
}

.nav li {
  float: left;
  margin-left: 17px;
}
```

The overflow value on the "nav" section keeps the size of the element from collapsing to zero, and the float applied to the list items causes them to stack to the right of the one above, with a little margin to keep them from bunching up together. For those who aren't familiar with either of these techniques, both will be discussed at length in Chapter 2.

Following the header is the main content area, which is made up of four sections. The first is the featured book, which has only a paragraph description, an image, and a link. The image is floated to the right (something we will change later), but this section poses nothing complex.

```html
<div class="featured-book">
  <p class="description">Have you got an idea for a great mobile site, or an existing site...</p>
  <img src="/content/responsivebasics/my-book-cover.png" />
  <p class="learn-more"><a href="http://www.apress.com/9781430250562">Learn More</a></p>
</div>
```

The next section is the list of links that constitutes "Our Categories" on the left side of the page. The layout of the list is not changed, but the whole section plays a part in the four-column layout that organizes this part of the page.

```html
<div class="our-categories">
  <h2>Our Categories</h2>
  <ol>
    <li><a href="http://www.apress.com/apple-mac">Apple/Mac</a></li>
    <li><a href="http://www.apress.com/at-work">At Work</a></li>
    <li><a href="http://www.apress.com/business">Business</a></li>
    <!-- more links -->
  </ol>
</div>
```

The next section, which has two of the four columns, has markup like the following:

```
<div class="products">
  <ul>

    <li class="product-item">
      <p class="product-name"><a href="http://www.apress.com/9781430243984">Pro Windows 8 Apps ...</a></p>
        <!-- other info -->
        <p>Browse other <a href="http://www.apress.com/microsoft/c">C#</a> titles</p>
      </div>
    </li>

    <li class="product-item">
      <p class="product-name"><a href="http://www.apress.com/9781430249443" title="Dashboards...</a></p>
        <!-- other info -->
        <p>Browse other <a href="http://www.apress.com/office/office">Office</a> titles</p>
      </div>
    </li>
    <!-- two more items -->

  </ul>
</div>
```

These items will be arranged into two of our four columns, the two columns in the middle. Finally we have our rightmost column of content, which contains secondary, somewhat miscellaneous bits of information.

```
<div class="secondary">
  <div class="secondary-item">
    <h2>Companion eBooks</h2>
    <p>Why limit yourself to one format? If you've purchased the print edition of most Apress
titles....</p>
    <p class="more"><a href="http://www.apress.com/companion/customer/view/">Buy a Companion
eBook</a></p>

  </div>

  <!-- more items -->
</div>
```

So how would we arrange these into four columns? We would take our total allowable width (960 pixels, which we set above), divide that width into sizes appropriate for our three sections, and float them. In other words, it could look a lot like this:

```
.our-categories {
  float: left;
  padding: 0 25px;
  width: 150px;
  /* total width with padding, 200px */
}
```

```
.products {
  float: left;
  padding: 0 20px;
  width: 480px;
  /* total width with padding, 520px */
}

.secondary {
  float: left;
  width: 240px;
  /* total width, 240px */
}
```

Each section is floated left and the total width of the sections is 960 pixels, so the three sections line up side by side. For those not comfortable with CSS layouts using floats, Chapter 2 will explain how all of this works in detail. With the CSS above, we would see Figure 1-2.

Figure 1-2. *Three-column layout*

Next we need to arrange the product items in the middle section so that they form two columns. To implement this, we follow a similar procedure and set the width of the items and float them. The CSS below does this nicely.

```
.product-item {
  float: left;
  margin: 10px 10px;
  width: 220px;
}
```

After we implement these CSS changes, we get what we want: the four-column layout in Figure 1-3.

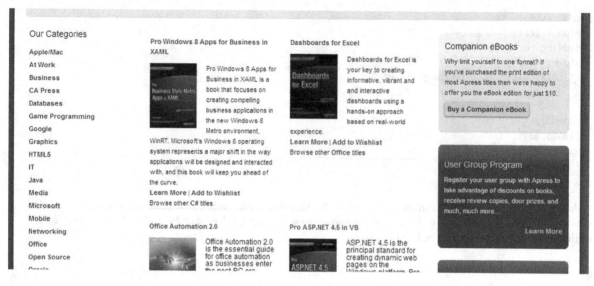

Figure 1-3. *Four-column layout*

Our last section is the footer, which is a four-column nested list of links. We will use the same techniques as above and float these lists.

```
<div class="footer">
  <h2>Quick Links</h2>
  <ul>
    <li>Interact with Us
      <ul>
        <li><a href="#">Contact Us</a></li>
        <li><a href="#">Customer Support</a></li>
        <li><a href="#">User Groups</a></li>
        <li><a href="#">Write For Us</a></li>
      </ul>
    </li>
    <li>Company Information
      <ul>
        <li><a href="#">About Us</a></li>
        <li><a href="#">Press Room</a></li>
      </ul>
    </li>
    <li>Trade Resources
      <ul>
        <li><a href="#">Sales and Distribution</a></li>
      </ul>
    </li>
```

```
      <li>Legal
        <ul>
          <li><a href="#">Terms &amp; Conditions</a></li>
          <li><a href="#">Privacy Policy</a></li>
        </ul>
      </li>
    </ul>
</div>
```

As you can see from the markup, each "column" is a list item, a direct descendent of the uppermost unordered list element, so we will target these elements. The footer's width is not the expected 960 pixels in width but 956 pixels in width so that the background image can be sized to be just inside the total width of the content. But not to worry, since 956 is divisible by four.

```
.footer > ul > li {
  float: left;
  line-height: 20px;
  width: 239px;
}
```

This gives us what we see in Figure 1-4, our footer.

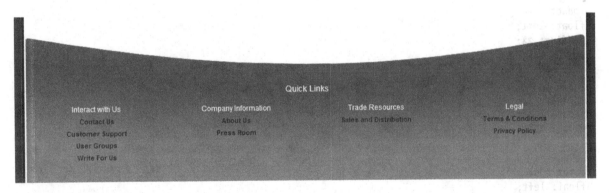

Figure 1-4. *The footer, laid out as four columns*

The problem is that a fixed layout like you see above, whether it uses HTML tables for layout or not, works poorly on small devices. We need a better way to handle both desktop browsers and smaller mobile device browsers: the solution is to stop thinking in terms of fixed sizes. Fixed sizes are nice because they give you a consistent palette for your layout and design. This makes it easier to create a site design for a particular size browser but makes it harder to design for every other size. So instead of fearing the variability, learn to *embrace* it. Think of the browser's flexibility to render at different sizes and take advantage of that. This is what responsive design is about.

A Flexible Layout

So let's apply responsive principles to make this page more flexible. Instead of a fixed width for the container and the various content sections, we will set a maximum width for the container and percentages for the columns.

```
.page {
  margin: 0 auto;
  max-width: 960px;
}

.our-categories {
  float: left;
  padding: 0 2%;
  width: 16%;
}

.products {
  float: left;
  padding: 0 2%;
  width: 46%;
}

.product-item {
  float: left;
  padding: 2%;
  width: 46%;
}

.secondary {
  float: left;
  width: 25%;
}

.footer > ul > li {
  float: left;
  width: 23%;
}
```

Now if you were to view the site in your browser and change the size lower than 960px, you would see the page flexibly scale down to fit the new size and back up again if the browser window is made wider. This is handy. Text on the web is inherently flexible unless we purposefully constrain it, like we were doing before. Now we let the text change and flow with the size of their containing DOM elements.

Flexible Content

Though text is flexible on the web by default, images are a bit more problematic. On this page there is one image we need to deal with so that it works well on both larger desktop monitors and smaller phone screens: the one in the header. In this particular case the image is too big for phones around 320 pixels in width, which includes many phones, most notably the iPhone. Viewing our site right now gives us this unsightly view in Figure 1-5.

Figure 1-5. Inflexible image. Ouch!

With our new more flexible layout, we can see some problems with these if we change the browser window size.

Clearly, this will not do. The word "apress" is too close to the border of the background, and the yellow subheading juts out in a rather unfortunate manner. We also need to do something about the menu and the following text but that will come below. Fortunately, the fix for the image can be easily applied.

```
.header img {
    max-width: 95%;
}
```

And after reloading the browser, we are greeted with a much more pleasant sight!

So what is going on here? This image is contained within a `div` whose width is constrained by the size of the browser window. As the browser window size changes, the containing `div` changes and the image scales up or down to fit. In this case I use a maximum width of 95 percent, so it should fill all the space that it can; but if it's too big to fit, it will scale down and leave a little buffer between it and its containing `div`. You could supply lower percentage values, and it would also work fine.

Flexible content is one of the most difficult things when implementing responsive web design. There will be much more to say about flexible images and other types of content in Chapter 5.

CSS Media Queries

We have discussed two of the three elements of responsive web design, a flexible layout and flexible content. The last element, media queries, takes our flexibility to a whole new level. Our page is more flexible than it used to be, but we still have some issues. The most significant of these is the menu. The CSS for the menu is as follows:

```
.nav {
  border-top: solid 1px #333;
  overflow: hidden;
}

.nav li {
  float: left;
  margin-left: 17px;
}
```

In normal lists, items would stack vertically. The float: left bit changes that behavior and causes the list items to "float" up to the left, effectively making a vertical list go horizontal. This works great until the DOM element holding the list gets resized smaller than the width of all the list items combined. This will cause the last item to wrap, appearing on the next line. If the browser is sized smaller, another list item will wrap and so on. You can see this unsightly affect in Figure 1-6 above.

Figure 1-6. *An image as flexible as its container*

When an element in the site (whether it's content or some structural/navigational piece like this menu) does not work well at given size, CSS media queries are a very useful tool. Media queries allow you to query the device context so you know what's going on and can respond appropriately. By far the most common media query I use is the query for width, though you can query other properties like height, orientation, aspect ratio, and resolution. For this site, I'll use a media query to see if the device has reached a certain breaking point; if it has, I'll change the layout. In this case, my menu breaks around 425 pixels in width, so I'll add a media query to change the menu from a horizontally stacking menu to a vertically stacking menu. The most important changes are in bold.

```
@media screen and (max-width: 425px) {

  .nav li {
    border-top: solid 1px #333;
    float: none;
    margin: 0;
    padding: 12px 0;
    text-align: center;
  }
}
```

The "media query" part of this is in the first line of that CSS. This query checks two things: first, it makes sure the media type is screen (as opposed to print, projection, braille, et al.), and then it checks that the screen is 425 pixels in width *or lower*. If either one of these is false (either you are printing something, for example, or the browser window is 426+ pixels wide), the CSS nested in the media query is ignored. But if both are true, the CSS nested in the media query is applied. The great thing about media queries is that the styling follows the normal rules of CSS and is additive when placed after the other styling rules. The previous CSS is still applied to the elements, so you only need to put in style rules that you want to add. For example, the padding for the .nav item is still the same as it was when it was set earlier in the style sheet. This can be assumed in the media query. These style rules can also override previous styles, as is the case for the float value for .nav .li. To change the list back to its normal, vertical-stacking behavior, the previous float needs to be turned off, and you do that by setting float: none.

■ **Note**   Media in CSS refers to how the document is to be presented. As web developers, we most commonly assume that the media we are targeting is the screen, but other media types include braile (for tactile feedback devices), projection (for viewing on a projector), and speech (used for speech synthesizers). To target all media types, "all" can be used. Since responsive web design is primarily a visual technique, we will be focusing on the screen.

Another place on this page that media queries can be used effectively is with the multi-column section at the bottom of the page. Though we have made our layout and our content flexible and everything can be scaled down, at a certain point the scaling becomes too great and readability is compromised (and doesn't look good, either). In this case, removing the columns and going for a single-column approach for the bottom pieces makes sense around the 600-pixel mark, so I added this media query to override the previous CSS and add some styling to make things better in this resolution.

CSS media query to turn the three-column layout into a single-column layout

```
@media screen and (max-width: 600px) {
  .featured-book .description {
    float: none;
    width: 96%;
  }

  .featured-book img {
    float: none;
  }
```

```
  .our-categories li {
    width: 50%;
  }

  .products {
    float: none;
    width: 96%;
  }

  .product-item {
    float: none;
    width: 90%;
  }

  .secondary {
    width: 100%;
  }

  .secondary-item {
    border-radius: 0;
    width: 92%;
  }

  .footer > ul > li {
    float: none;
    width: 100%;
  }
}
```

Media queries give you a lot of power because any CSS can be put in a media query. And because any CSS can be put in a media query, you can use media queries to make slight changes to a design or radically change the entire look and feel of a site (though this is usually not a good idea). But *you can*. Media queries give you tremendous capabilities for tailoring a site's design or layout to a particular screen size.

The Viewport Meta Tag

The last basic thing you need for doing responsive design for mobile is to add a viewport meta tag. The term "viewport" refers to the size of the screen that is viewing the page. In very basic terms, the viewport meta tag tells the device how to render the site with respect to the screen size of the device. As was said above, responsive design isn't just an approach for developing for mobile, but it is useful for handling a wide range of screens. But for mobile, you almost always want a viewport meta tag. Here are several samples.

```
<meta name="viewport" content="width=device-width" />
<meta name="viewport" content="width=device-width, initial-scale=1" />
<meta name="viewport" content="width=device-width, initial-scale=1, minimum-scale=1,
maximum-scale=1" />
<meta name="viewport" content="width=device-width, initial-scale=1, user-scalable=no" />
```

Though the term "viewport" and how it is relevant for defining web standards predates the iPhone, Apple introduced this meta tag to control the viewport on the iPhone. The other mobile browsers have followed, and it seems to have universal support in modern mobile browsers. After enough browsers adopted the tag, it was standardized by the W3C and should be considered standard practice in your mobile development work. Let's take our sample site above and how it fares in actual mobile browsers both with and without the viewport tag, as well as with various options set.

This first screenshot is of the site if it has no viewport tag, whether we are using a fixed-width design (like an explicit `width: 960px` as we had before) or a responsive design. Why it works this way is an interesting question. Let's start by defining the term "viewport." The viewport for a page is the area visible to the user in the browser. If you take a wide, fixed-width site and view it in a mobile browser, your viewport will be just a small window into the total page when zoomed in like the second view in Figure 1-7. If zoomed out, it may look like the first view in Figure 1-7. Because the site has a fixed width, the content size cannot be changed; only your zoom level can change. So the viewport, or the viewable area, can differ from the total area the page can take up.

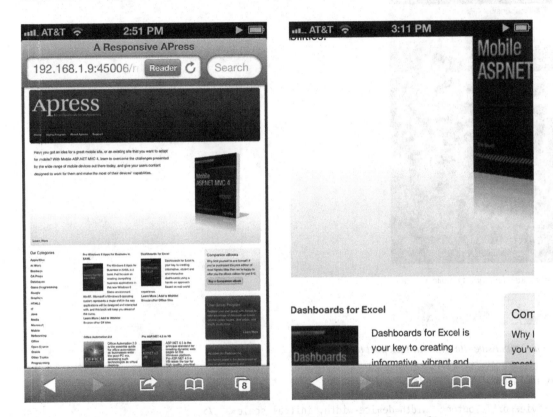

Figure 1-7. *Our mobile site without a viewport meta tag, default view, and zoomed in*

The strange thing is that a responsive design that *can* be resized *will not* be resized if there is no viewport meta tag. Why? When Apple launched the iPhone with its browser, they couldn't assume that lots of websites would scale down. Actually, you would assume the opposite. So instead of automatically scaling the viewport down to 320 pixels in width, they instead defaulted to showing things at a width of 980 pixels. As mentioned above, that's right around the popular desktop resolution that web designers generally target. This is why a responsive website without a viewport meta tag is treated as if the width is 980 pixels, even though the site can support the smaller size.

So if the mobile browsers assume a width slightly under 1,000 pixels (it varies somewhat), how do you tell the browser to not behave that way? You use the viewport meta tag. Take the following meta tag for example:

```
<meta name="viewport" content="width=device-width" />
```

The setting tells the viewport that the width of the browser should be the width of the device, not the *default* width of the browser. If you are using an iPhone, the device width is 320 pixels, so any of the media queries that get applied at sizes down to 320 pixels will be applied. In the examples above there are three max-width media queries for 425, 600, and 800 pixels respectively in our sample site above. All three would be applied because the iPhone's size in portrait orientation is smaller than both. In Figure 1-8 we see our site with the media query applied. As you can see, it is what we want. This is why I said above that the viewport meta tag is something you almost always want to set when developing for mobile. Without it our responsive CSS above would have been for naught.

Figure 1-8. *Our responsive site with our viewport meta tag*

Let's try another one of our sample viewport tags.

```
<meta name="viewport" content="width=device-width, initial-scale=2" />
```

Notice the value of two in the initial scale setting. This viewport yields the result we see in Figure 1-9.

Figure 1-9. Our site with a viewport meta tag with a zoom value of two applied

In this case the site is set to be of the proper width (the device width) but the initial view is zoomed by a factor of two. Though this is not something most will want to do, it's an option for those who need it.

The last options I want to talk about are these two variations of the viewport meta tag.

```
<meta name="viewport" content="width=device-width, initial-scale=1, minimum-scale=1,
maximum-scale=1" />
<meta name="viewport" content="width=device-width, initial-scale=1, user-scalable=no" />
```

These two viewport tags are functionally equivalent. From a visual standpoint, either one will give you the same view of the site in Figure 1-8. The difference is that these settings disallow zooming. As a general rule this should be discouraged because it creates potential usability problems (those with poor eyesight cannot zoom in to view the text if it's too small), but there may be cases where it makes sense. One positive side effect is that some browsers will remove the 300ms delay on the browser click event with this viewport setting. For more information on why mobile browsers act that way, see Chapter 10 on programming for touch. But just in case you need to disable zoom, this is an option you can set in the viewport meta tag.

Incompatibilities

Though viewport meta tags and media queries have great support on iPhone and Android devices, this does not mean they always work the same. Question: what should happen when you switch a phone to landscape mode? The answer is different between iOS and Android. Let's assume we have the following media queries:

```
@media screen and (max-width: 400px) {
  /* css for our first media query */
}
```

```
@media screen and (max-width: 500px) {
  /* css for our second media query*/
}
```

Assuming your Android device is the same screen size as the iPhone 4S (320 pixels wide, 480 pixels tall), only one of our media queries above gets triggered in landscape mode, the second media query. It has a max-width check of 500 pixels, and since the screen is less than 500 pixels in width, this media query kicks in. But the media query set at 400 pixels max-width does not kick in because the width is now 480 pixels. This is also the behavior on Windows Phone and Firefox OS.

For iOS, if the page has either of the first two viewport meta tags and you view the page in landscape, both media queries will be applied. If an iPhone 4S is used, the width *should* be 480 pixels, and one of the media queries should be applied. If an iPhone 5 is used, the width *should* be 568 pixels, and neither of the media queries should be applied because the viewport is wider than our largest max-width media query. But in both cases, both media queries are applied and the page is zoomed to show exactly the same width of page as when in portrait orientation. It's almost as if the device is acting like it is 320 pixels wide. And that is exactly what is going on. If you put the following script in the page with a media query tag that only specifies width (like the first one we discussed above), you see that the inner width of the browser is actually 320 pixels wide.

How to get the inner width of the window with JavaScript

```
<script type="text/javascript">
  window.addEventListener('resize', function () {
    console.log('inner width', window.innerWidth);
  });
</script>
```

So that's why both media queries are applied. But if you set the minimum and maximum scaling to one in a viewport meta tag, iOS begins to behave like Android. In other words, add this:

```
<meta name="viewport" content="width=device-width, initial-scale=1, minimum-scale=1,
maximum-scale=1" />
```

So if it is important for your site to make iOS behave like Android, you will need to turn off scaling. Note that setting "user-scalable=no" does not have the same effect as setting the scale values.

Retina Screens

You might be wondering about the iPhone retina screens. With the iPhone 4, Apple doubled the resolution of the iPhone. Previously, it was 320x480 in resolution. Retina screens are 640x960 on the iPhone 4 and iPhone 4S, and 640x1136 on the iPhone 5. Do we need to have separate media queries for these widths? Fortunately, no (in most cases).

For these retina screens, you actually need to think in terms of device pixels versus CSS pixels. Device pixels refer to how many are actually on the screen. Retina screens in portrait orientation are 640 device pixels wide. However, as far as CSS is concerned, the screen is 320 pixels in width. This is fantastic, because media queries for width will work the same on screens of different pixel densities. And if they hadn't implemented the retina screens in this way, all sites that were previously targeting 320 pixels in width would suddenly be half the size on the new phones. So making retina screens behave in this manner was important.

Though this is generally a desirable behavior, there are scenarios where you do want to pay attention to different pixel densities. Ever since the iPhone 4 was released, the retina screen has been both praised for its awesomeness and caused angst because most images for the web were not prepared for the 326 ppi displays of the new devices. This is why many images still look fuzzy on them. Even though this is a problem easily solved, it is not easily solved *well*.

There are ways of querying the pixel ratio of the device though there are inconsistencies in the browsers. This will be discussed in Chapter 5 in more detail. That is the first scenario.

The second scenario relates to text size. Let's compare the third generation iPad (9.7 inch display, 2048x1536 resolution, 264 ppi) and the iPad mini (7.9 inch display, 1024x768 resolution, 163 ppi). In the case of the larger iPad, even though it has a resolution of 2048x1536, it is 1024x768 in CSS pixels, so the two devices will respond to all the exact same width-based media queries. This also means that text for both will be sized the same as far as CSS is concerned but will actually be *smaller* on the iPad mini because the screen is smaller. Unfortunately, this means small text will be even smaller, so you might have readability problems on the iPad mini.

Both of these scenarios can be handled. In Chapter 5 you will learn more about making your content work across different screen resolutions and pixel densities.

Summary

Responsive web design is a great technique for giving you flexibility in the browser. This approach is built on three key ideas: flexible layouts, flexible content, and CSS media queries. The great thing about it is that it gives you a relatively easy way to handle different display sizes: from the browser on an iPhone up to the browser in a widescreen HD TV.

But the approach is not without its weaknesses. For example, responsive non-textual content can be problematic, and there are differing ideas on the best way to solve this. Displaying tabular data on smaller devices can also be difficult. These problems and others will be discussed in chapters 3, 4, and 5. Responsive design also does not help you with older phones, so you will need some sort of adaptive rendering approach, which will be discussed in Chapter 6. But for modern browsers, desktop and mobile, it's a fantastic tool for creating sites.

One thing that many developers will find difficult with responsive design is that it's absolutely necessary to drop those old table-based layout patterns that the web development world used to follow. They are simply not flexible enough. But many do not understand float-based positioning and often abandon that approach after frustration sets in. Fortunately, learning how to do layout using floats is pretty easy once you have a few ideas. And this is the topic we now turn to.

CHAPTER 2

■ ■ ■

CSS Layout Bootcamp

"I tried to use CSS for my layouts but gave up and used tables instead." This is a common sentiment. If you have been in web development long, you've probably heard this. You might have even said this yourself, I know I have many times. But it doesn't need to be this way. Once you understand a few things about how browsers lay out elements, CSS layouts become doable. Eventually they actually become easy.

On the one hand, doing CSS-based layouts is about web development, both mobile and desktop. It has nothing to do in particular with mobile web development. But if you are going to do responsive layouts, it is important because table elements you might use for a full-size website layout are going to make mobile development much harder.

First Steps

The first thing to keep in mind is that browsers come with default styling. In some ways this is very helpful, but I've found that default styling can get in the way when trying to do precise CSS layouts. Some developers use what are called "CSS resets" to reset all of the browsers' styling to a baseline so as to remove cross-browser inconsistencies. The basic idea of a CSS reset is something like the first part of the following CSS selection:

```css
html, body, div, span, applet, object, iframe,
h1, h2, h3, h4, h5, h6, p, blockquote, pre,
a, abbr, acronym, address, big, cite, code,
del, dfn, em, img, ins, kbd, q, s, samp,
small, strike, strong, sub, sup, tt, var,
b, u, i, center,
dl, dt, dd, ol, ul, li,
fieldset, form, label, legend,
table, caption, tbody, tfoot, thead, tr, th, td,
article, aside, canvas, details, embed,
figure, figcaption, footer, header, hgroup,
menu, nav, output, ruby, section, summary,
time, mark, audio, video {
  margin: 0;
  padding: 0;
}

div, span, li
{
  font-family: Helvetica;
}
```

As you can see, it goes through all the HTML elements and "resets" any default margins and paddings. Using a CSS reset is highly recommended. Some prefer to use CSS normalizers, which attempt to normalize the CSS instead of resetting everything to nothing. This is a fine approach as well, though CSS resets make things a bit easier for me. To use a CSS reset properly, put the reset as the first CSS imported into the page. Later styles that you supply will override the reset.

This is an example of a simple page without the reset and the same page with the margin and padding reset above. This screenshot was taken in Chrome on Windows 7, though what you see in this screenshot in Figure 2-1 is similar to what you would see in Internet Explorer or Firefox. The gray bar at the top is a part of Chrome, not a part of the page; this was included so you could see exactly how much spacing is put in the top of the document by default.

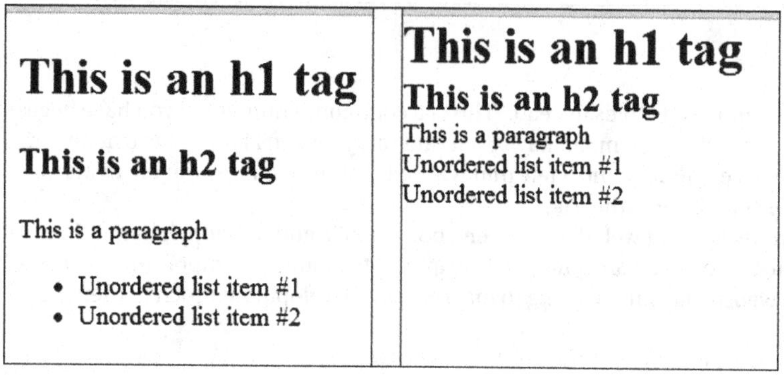

Figure 2-1. *Default browser styling versus using a CSS reset*

By default, browsers include margin and padding on many elements like those above, including the body of the document. Without the default margin and padding the spacing between each element is determined by its actual width and height. Removing default margin and padding makes calculating sizes for things easier and makes the task of this chapter much simpler: this is because margin and padding contribute to height and width calculations, as you will see below.

The above is the base styling for all the rest of the styling in this chapter. The first part is a selection from Eric Meyer's CSS reset (http://meyerweb.com/eric/tools/css/reset/). His reset is normally more elaborate, but the entire thing is not needed here.

As a short note on terminology, I am going to use the word "container" a lot. This always refers to the DOM element that contains another element. Let's say we have a span inside a div. The div is the "container" of the span. If any element is in the root of the body element, body is its container.

Finally, you will notice that the width is included in each screenshot in the chapter. The exact width of the window will be important in many of our examples. This is calculated with the following script:

```
window.onload = function () {

    var pageWidth = document.getElementById('pageWidth');
    pageWidth.innerHTML = window.innerWidth;

    window.addEventListener('resize', function () {
        pageWidth.innerHTML = window.innerWidth;
    });
}
```

The Basic Rules

Let's start with a few fundamentals before we work with layouts. Now that we have our setup, we can begin. I will explain how layout with CSS works by enumerating the most important points as rules. This will help us succinctly state how the browsers work, as well as give us points of reference we can use later.

Display: Block, Inline, and Inline Block

The first fundamentals to discuss are how display: block, display: inline and display: inline-block work. Here we see all three in Figure 2-2.

```
<span style="border: solid 1px red;">I am a span</span>
<div style="border: solid 1px blue">I am a div</div>
<span style="border: solid 1px green; display: inline-block;">I have display: inline-block</span>
```

```
Page width: 400


I am a span
I am a div
I have display: inline-block
```

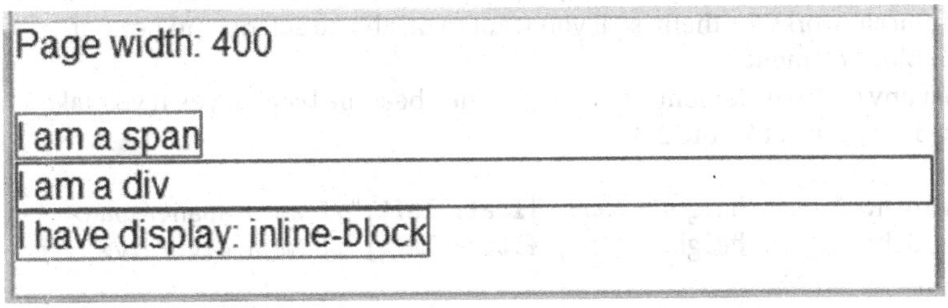

Figure 2-2. *Three values of display exemplified, inline, block, and inline-block*

First of all, spans are by default "inline" for their display value and divs are block, so these values do not need to be specified. And an element's behavior can be changed. As you can see, the last element has a style value to override its default display value.

Note how they behave. Inline elements take up only the width of the content in them. The text of "I am a span" is only so wide, so the first span takes up exactly that much space. Other examples of elements that are inline include b, i, strong and em. Block elements take up the entire horizontal space of their container, like the div above. Other examples of elements that are block by default are p and li. Inline-block elements are most like inline elements but you get more capabilities. Note the following in Figure 2-3.

```
<span style="border: solid 1px red; width: 250px; height: 40px;">I am a span</span>
<div style="border: solid 1px blue; width: 250px; height: 40px;">I am a div</div>
<span style="border: solid 1px green;
  display: inline-block;
  width: 250px;
  height: 40px;">I have display: inline-block</span>
```

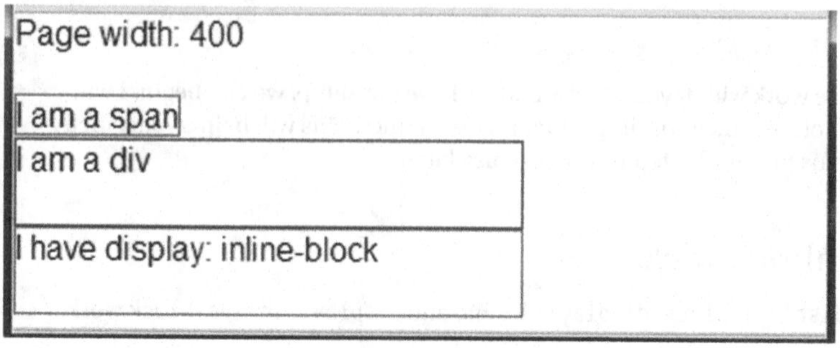

Page width: 400

I am a span

I am a div

I have display: inline-block

Figure 2-3. *Width and height applied to inline, block and inline-block elements*

Inline elements will not respond to width and height styling, but block elements will. Inline block elements will act like inline elements by default in that their initial size will be determined by the size of their content but are like block elements in that their width and height values can be set by CSS. Though padding seems to work fine with inline elements, it appears that only left and right margin works for them, so if you want to be able to set top and bottom margins, you will have to use inline-block or block elements.

An interesting thing happens if you float any of these elements. Essentially, they become block-level. If you take the same markup as before and add float: left, you get Figure 2-4.

```
<span style="border: solid 1px red; width: 250px; height: 40px; float: left;">I am a span</span>
<div style="border: solid 1px blue; width: 250px; height: 40px; float: left;">I am a div</div>
<span style="border: solid 1px green;
  display: inline-block;
  width: 250px;
  height: 40px;
  float: left;">I have display: inline-block</span>
```

Page width: 400

I am a span

span 252px × 42px

I have display: inline-block

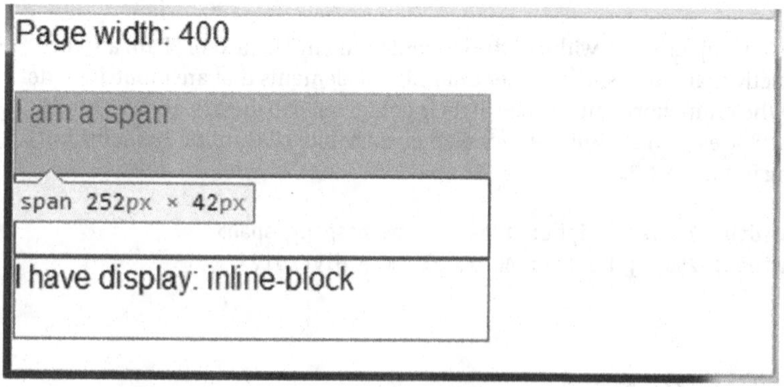

Figure 2-4. *Inline, block, and inline-block elements when they are floated*

Inline and block elements are quite old and have universal support. Inline-block is generally well supported on recent browsers. Internet Explorer 6 and 7 exhibit some quirky behavior but in some cases will be just fine, and in others you will need to resort to some hacks. If you are dealing with more recent browsers, you should be safe.

Let's boil down these ideas into our first three rules:

■ **CSS Rule #1**   Inline elements are as wide as their content, and their dimensions cannot be set with CSS.

■ **CSS Rule #2**   Block elements span the width of their container by default but can have their dimensions set with CSS.

■ **CSS Rule #3**   Inline-block elements by default are as wide as their content, but their dimensions can be set with CSS.

Floats

If there's anything that people find conceptually difficult in CSS, it's the concept of floats. I was confused about them for the longest time. But hopefully the following will help you if you are not clear on how they work. Float exists to change how an element behaves in the normal flow of a page. By default, elements flow one after another in a page and top down in the order of the markup in the source file.

The basic purpose of floating is to take an element and cause it to float within the content after it. In other words, CSS floats change the flow of the document. Imagine, if you will, an image floating in a group of words. The floating image displaces the words around it, causing them to flow around the image. Here in Figure 2-5 is an example of an image floated left in a paragraph.

```
<p><img src="peanut.jpg" style="float: left;" />This is Peanut. Peanut was made for me by my daughter...
Though we mourn the loss of the sock, the addition of Peanut to the family is definitely worth it.
</p>
```

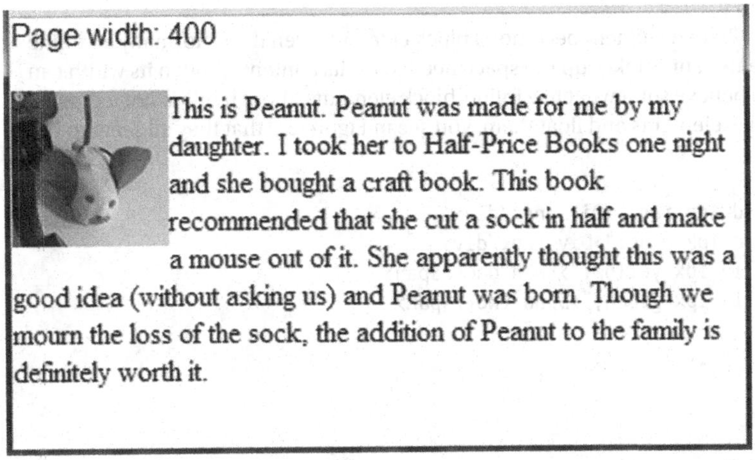

Figure 2-5. *Image floated left in a paragraph element. The text could use some margin from the image, but this is just meant to illustrate how floated elements work*

Here in Figure 2-6 is the same markup with `float: right` and then no float with the same markup.

Page width: 400

This is Peanut. Peanut was made for me by my daughter. I took her to Half-Price Books one night and she bought a craft book. This book recommended that she cut a sock in half and make a mouse out of it. She apparently thought this was a good idea (without asking us) and Peanut was born. Though we mourn the loss of the sock, the addition of Peanut to the family is definitely worth it.

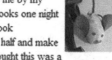

Page width: 400

This is Peanut. Peanut was made for me by my daughter. I took her to Half-Price Books one night and she bought a craft book. This book recommended that she cut a sock in half and make a mouse out of it. She apparently thought this was a good idea (without asking us) and Peanut was born. Though we mourn the loss of the sock, the addition of Peanut to the family is definitely worth it.

Figure 2-6. On the left, the image has float: right applied. On the right, no float is applied

As you can see from the above images, the picture that is floated left will have the surrounding content flow around it to the right, and the picture floated right will have the surrounding content flow to its left. If the image is not floated, it acts like an img tag normally would, as an inline element. In terms of the DOM and how floated elements work, the floated element stays in its position (in a sense) but is also removed from the normal flow of the document. In the float examples above, the image stays in its position in the DOM but floats to the left or right depending on the float value used. So if something is floated, the content that follows it will flow around it.

The flowing behavior only applies if there is enough horizontal width for the elements to flow. In the above example, the larger the image, the less words would be able to float horizontally beside it. If the image was too large, no words would flow around it. So for a float behavior to be useful, it must allow enough horizontal space for the elements that would follow and float around it.

We should also note at this point that a floated element becomes a block element, even if it is normally an inline element like img. But note that a floated element only takes up the space needed for its content (though its width can be set with CSS). In this sense they seem to behave somewhat like inline-block elements, though this is not technically accurate. If you take a series of mixed-display elements and float them, you see in Figure 2-7 that they all seem to be acting like content-sized block elements.

```
<div style="float: left; border: solid 1px red;">Div one</div>
<div style="float: left; border: solid 1px blue;">Div two</div>
<span style="float: left; border: solid 1px yellow;">Span one</span>
<span style="float: left; border: solid 1px green;">Span two</span>
```

Page width: 400

Div one Div two Span one Span two

Figure 2-7. Two divs and two spans, all floated

This leads us to our next rule.

■ **CSS Rule #4**   If an element is floated, it takes on the characteristics of a block element regardless of its CSS display setting and the content that follows it flows around it.

So to reiterate, this means that floated elements can have their width set, which is something very important for layouts using floats. So if you explicitly set the width of the elements, you get Figure 2-8.

```
<div style="float: left; border: solid 1px red; width: 90px;">Div one</div>
<div style="float: left; border: solid 1px blue; width: 90px;">Div two</div>
<span style="float: left; border: solid 1px yellow; width: 90px;">Span one</span>
<span style="float: left; border: solid 1px green; width: 90px;">Span two</span>
```

Page width: 400

Div one   Div two   Span one   Span two

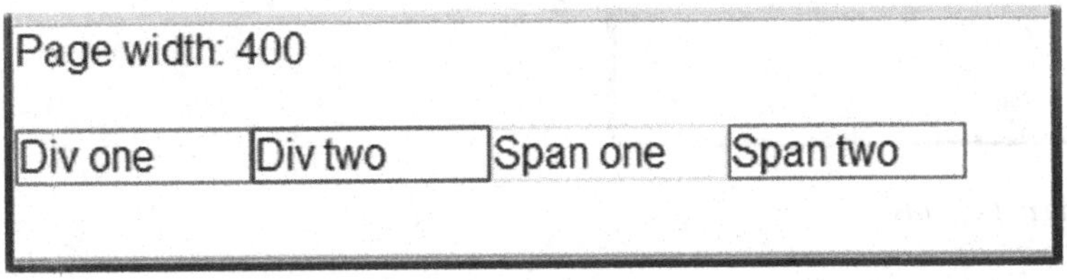

Figure 2-8. Two divs and two spans, all floated, with width values

So why do you need to care about width? Let's say you have two divs with more content than the above example and float them. You may see something you do not expect, as in Figure 2-9.

```
<div style="float: left; border: solid 1px red;">This is some text. It is too wide.</div>
<div style="float: left; border: solid 1px blue;">This is some text. It is too wide.</div>
```

Page width: 400

This is some text. It is too wide.
This is some text. It is too wide.

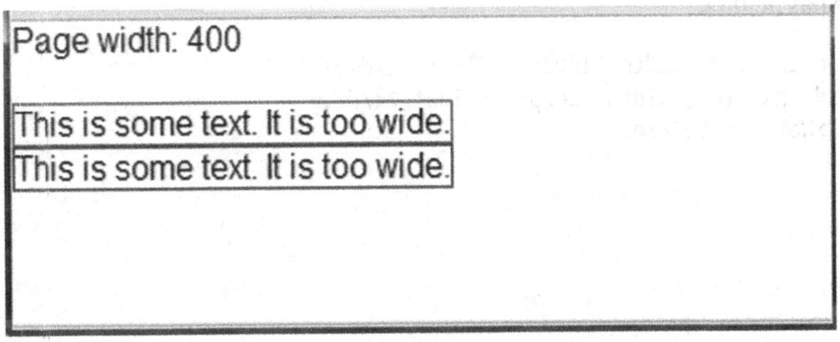

Figure 2-9. Divs too wide to float

Both elements are actually floated, but they are too wide to float next to each other. This gives us our next rule.

■ **CSS Rule #5**   Two elements cannot float next to each other if the width of the two is greater than the available width of the container.

This means that if you are trying to float two things side by side and one wraps when you don't think it should, something is probably wider than you expect. This is exactly why many people recommend always setting an explicit width on floated items, whether that width is set in pixels, ems, or percentages. If this content happened to by dynamic (perhaps out of a CMS), any float logic may fail to apply because the dynamically changed content is too wide. So if we set the width of each piece of content to 198 pixels, things will line up as we expect. Though you might expect 200 pixels to be the correct width (since our page is 400 pixels wide), it needs to be a bit narrower. We'll discuss calculating width shortly in the section entitled "Calculating Width." Figure 2-10 has our floated elements with their width set.

```
<div style="float: left; border: solid 1px red; width: 198px;">This is some text. It is too wide.</div>
<div style="float: left; border: solid 1px blue; width: 198px;">This is some text. It is too wide.</div>
```

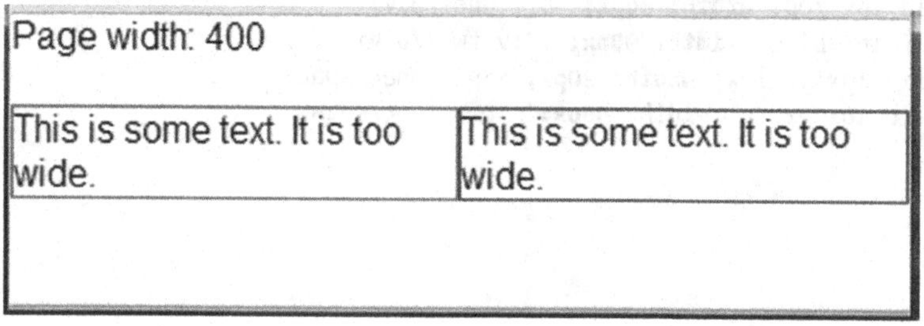

Figure 2-10. *Two divs arranged side-by-side with floats*

So then we have our next rule.

■ **CSS Rule #6**   Always set an explicit width for floated elements so they will behave consistently.

Another thing that frequently frustrates would-be masters of floats is the concept of clearing floats. Floats not only affect themselves but content around them, so *you can clear floats to tell the browser to start ignoring the floats and return back to "normal" layout mode.* Take the following example. Let us say you have three divs, the first two are floated and have widths set but the last one has neither.

```
<div style="float: left; border: solid 1px red; width: 100px;">Float 1</div>
<div style="float: left; border: solid 1px blue; width: 100px;">Float 2</div>
<div style="border: solid 1px green;">Not floated</div>
```

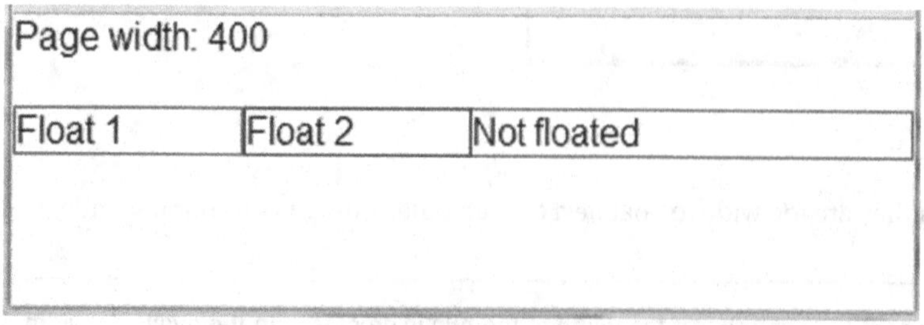

Figure 2-11. *Floated elements affecting a non-floated element*

Given a 400-pixel container, you might assume that the first two appear side by side but the last would appear below them. Unfortunately, if you thought that, you would be wrong, as you can see in Figure 2-11.

Remember the very first discussion of floats? Floated elements make other elements float around them. In this case we have two floated elements. Since they do not take up the entire horizontal space available to them, the next piece of content will try to flow around them. This "not floated" text is not floated (obviously) but rather it is wrapping around the elements that are above it, since it is wide enough to fit next to them. If the element was larger (if the width was set or the content was wider), this would not be the case. So if we want that third element to appear below the two floated elements (no matter its actual width) we need to clear the floats. If we do that, we get what we expect in Figure 2-12.

```
<div style="float: left; border: solid 1px red; width: 100px;">Float 1</div>
```

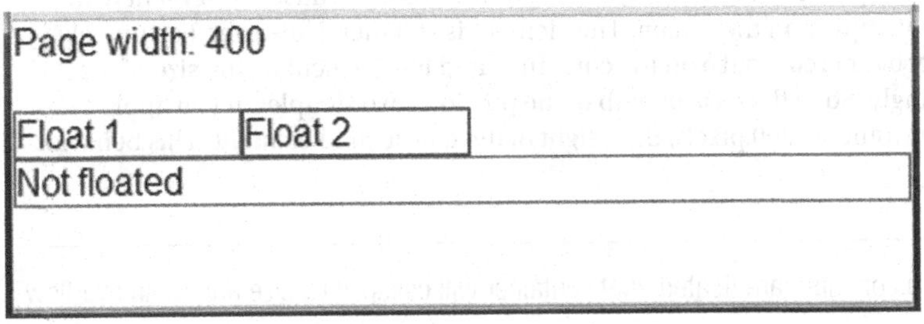

```
Page width: 400

Float 1        Float 2
Not floated
```

Figure 2-12. *Example of clearing a float*

```
<div style="float: left; border: solid 1px blue; width: 100px;">Float 2</div>
<div style="border: solid 1px green; clear: left;">Not floated</div>
```

Since the floats we want to clear are left floats, we use clear: left. If the floats are right, we could use clear: right. You could also clear floats of either type with clear: both. So the CSS clear property tells the browser to stop applying the logic of floats to elements around them. This is very important to remember, so we should make it one of our rules.

■ **CSS Rule #7**   Clear your floats when you are done with them so that the float behavior gets turned off.

Collapsing Containers

Another interesting characteristic of floated elements is that their containers often collapse. And by collapse, I mean that sometimes containers will have zero height. Above we said that floated elements are removed from the normal flow of the document. In the case of Peanut (see Figure 2-4), the floated element (an img) was in a paragraph and the paragraph did *not* collapse. The reason it did not is that the paragraph had content in it (the text of the paragraph) other than the floated element (the image). Although the floated element affected how the content is arranged in the paragraph, the height of the paragraph was actually determined by the height of the text content in it. To clarify, what would be the height of the container in the following?

```
<div id="theContainer">
    <div style="height: 100px; float: left; width: 100px;">Div #1</div>
    <div style="height: 200px; float: left; width: 100px;">Div #2</div>
    <div style="height: 50px; width: 100px; display: inline-block;">Div #3</div>
</div>
```

If you said "50 pixels," then you are correct. The first two div elements are floated and so are taken out of the document flow and do not directly affect the height of their container. The third element is not floated, so the container calculates its height based on its own "normal" child element, so the container is 50 pixels tall. Here is another very similar example:

```
<div id="theContainer" style="background-color: #808080;">
    <div style="height: 100px; float: left; width: 100px;">Div #1</div>
    <div style="height: 200px; float: left; width: 100px;">Div #2</div>
    <div style="height: 50px; float: left; width: 100px;">Div #3</div>
</div>
```

In this case the height of the container is 0 pixels. No one will see background color, because an element with a background color but with 0 height will not appear on the screen. The element is still there, however. Fortunately, there is a trick for cases like this. You can set overflow: auto on the container, and it will calculate the size of the floats in it and determine its height accordingly. So in the case of both of the previous two samples, if you apply overflow: auto to the container, its height would be 200 pixels, the height of the tallest child element. This behavior gives us our last float-related rule.

■ **CSS Rule #8**   If all the child elements of a container are floated, that container will collapse its size unless an overflow value is set.

Coming to grips with floats was the biggest conceptual challenge for me in CSS, but these rules cover the most important behavior of floats, especially in regard to layout.

Calculating Width

Calculating width is the last of our CSS layout fundamentals. Soon we will be creating CSS-based layouts easily; but to do so, we need to be able to determine how big an element will be. Many would assume that the width of an element is equivalent to the value assigned in the CSS width property. The truth is far more complicated: width value only applies to the width of the content. *It is important that you make a distinction between the width of a bit of content versus the total width of an element.* The width of content will either be the width of the content calculated by its actual size or set with the CSS width property. The total width of an element equals left margin + left border + left padding +

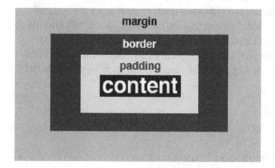

Figure 2-13. Calculating width includes the content, padding, border, and margin

content width + right padding + right border + right margin (see Figure 2-13). When we refer to "total width" from here on, we mean this larger width, because that's what really matters for positioning with CSS.

Back in Figure 2-10, we had two floated, side-by-side elements with a CSS width of 198 pixels and a border in a container the size of 400 pixels. Now you probably know why the elements needed to be that width and no larger. The border had a width of 1 pixel, which added 2 pixels of total width because the border was on both sides of the element. So the total width of each was actually 200 pixels, even though the element was set to a width of 198 pixels with CSS. The lesson here is that if you are going to create layouts that have multiple elements side by side, you have to pay close attention to the total width of the elements so that the extra bits of width elements get from padding, border and margin do not throw off your layout.

Box-Sizing

Every element in HTML is essentially a box. Some people refer to HTML's "box model." The box model is how the browser determines the size of the box, or the total size of the element as we have been calling it.

There is a CSS property called "box-sizing" with pretty wide support for what we are going to use it for (border-box) that you can use to change how elements calculate the size of their box/total width. This CSS property has three values: content-box, padding-box, and border-box. If the first option is specified, the width property in CSS will only affect the content. In other words, the default sizing of an element is content-box, which is what we have been discussing. The padding-box option makes the CSS width property affect both the content and the padding. So if you set a width of 100 pixels on an element, it will force the width of the element to be 100 pixels including both content *and padding*, unlike before. The third option, border-box, makes the CSS width property apply to the content width, the padding and the border but not the margin. How about some examples? Take a look at Figure 2-14.

```
<style>
  .box {
    border: solid 5px #000;
    padding: 5px;
    width: 250px;
  }

  .content-box {
    -moz-box-sizing: content-box;
    -webkit-box-sizing: content-box;
    box-sizing: content-box;
  }

  .padding-box {
    -moz-box-sizing: padding-box;
    -webkit-box-sizing: padding-box;
    box-sizing: padding-box;
  }

  .border-box {
    -moz-box-sizing: border-box;
    -webkit-box-sizing: border-box;
    box-sizing: border-box;
  }
</style>

<div style="width: 270px; background-color: #CCC;">270 pixels wide</div>
<div class="box content-box">content box</div>
<div style="width: 260px; background-color: #CCC;">260 pixels wide</div>
<div class="box padding-box">padding box</div>
<div style="width: 250px; background-color: #CCC;">250 pixels wide</div>
```

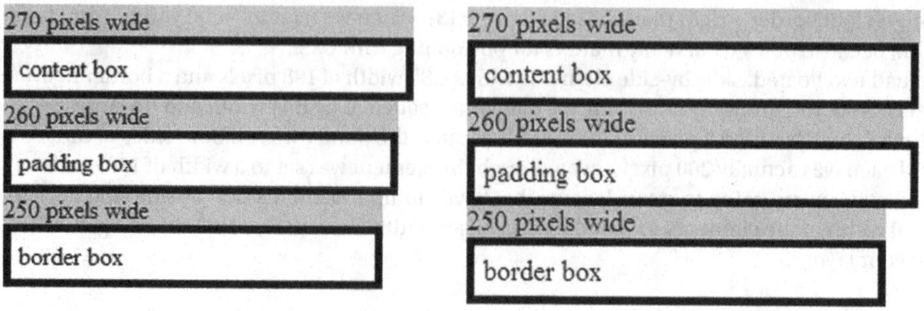

Figure 2-14. Box-sizing examples from desktop Firefox (left) and Chrome (right)

```
<div class="box border-box">border box</div>
```

For reference in the screenshots, each example box has a reference box above set to the width that they should be if the property was implemented. The first example uses the default box model for the web, content-box. In this case total width is left margin + left border + left padding + content + right padding + right border + right margin, which comes out to a total width of 270 pixels.

In the second example, the padding is included in the content width, so the total width is left margin + left border + content + right border + right margin, which comes out to a total of 320 pixels.

In the third example, the padding and border are included in the content width, so the total width is left margin + content + right margin, which comes to a total of 310 pixels.

Which should you use? Because of almost non-existent (as of early 2013) browser support for padding-box, at this point that option is not very feasible. The third has really good support as long as you do not intend to target Internet Explorer 7 or earlier. To get widest support, use –moz-box-sizing: border-box and –webkit-box-sizing: border-box prefixes along with the unprefixed CSS setting.

One method that some are recommending is to apply a box-sizing rule universally in a site. You could easily do it like this:

```
*
{
  -moz-box-sizing: border-box;
  -webkit-box-sizing: border-box;
  box-sizing: border-box;
}
```

This actually works great for mobile with the exception of HTC Android browsers. For whatever reason, there is a bug in every HTC Android browser that I have tried (all Android 2.2 and 2.3) when this rule is applied to text inputs. When the input is not in focus, the input looks normal. But when focused, the default border of the input disappears and leaves the cursor hanging in the air. If this bug does not bother you, then feel free to use this since mobile support is quite good on modern mobile browsers. Though I like the idea in many ways, the rest of our discussion will not be using this rule. HTC has lots of Android phones on the market, and I would rather not be triggering this bug. So from now on we are back to default, where sizing is determined by total margin, total border, total padding, and content size.

■ **CSS Rule #9**   Width is determined by the following formula unless you change the box-sizing: left margin + left border + left padding + content width + right padding + right border + right margin.

Laying Out a Page in CSS

Now we finally get to the primary discussion of the chapter, which is how you can lay out a page effectively using CSS. We are going to accomplish two tasks to help us apply the rules above. The first task will be to create a page with a header and a two-column content area, one of which will be a sidebar. It will also have a footer. The other task will be to create a horizontal menu out of an unordered list, a very common task for a web developer. For both of these tasks we will have a fixed width to keep this simple as we learn the rules. In the next chapter we will discuss how to turn both of these fixed-width layouts into fluid, responsive layouts.

Creating a Page with a Sidebar

The page we will create is a page with a header, a sidebar (on the left), a main content area (on the right) and a footer. It is conceptually a two-column layout. All the rules discussed can be just as easily applied to create a three or four column layout. But to keep it simple, we will stick with two columns and the page will look a lot like Figure 2-15.

Figure 2-15. *Basic layout of a page with a sidebar—a very common page layout*

The most basic HTML I would use to build this structure would look like the following:

```
<div id="page">
  <div id="header">
    Header content
  </div>
  <div id="sidebar">
    Sidebar content
  </div>
  <div id="content">
    Main content
  </div>
  <div id="footer">
    Footer content
  </div>
</div>
```

The various bits of content for the page would go into each of these containers, and this content would have its own styling. But this shell would define the areas where our content belonged. The only superfluous element is the root element with the id of "page." This is not actually needed, but we can use it to constrain the size of all of the child elements. Let's start with the CSS to give us some basic colors and to setup the header and footer.

```
#page {
  width: 960px;
}

#header {
  background-color: #bdbdbd;
  height: 100px;
  width: 100%;
}

#sidebar {
  background-color: #d2d2d2;
}

#content {
}

#footer {
  background-color: #bdbdbd;
  height: 30px;
  width: 100%;
}
```

By constraining the container (the div with the id of "page") to 960 pixels we get two benefits. First, all elements that should span the entire page area can just be set to a size of 100 percent and everything will fit correctly. Second, we can easily center the content in the browser by setting the CSS margin setting to margin: 0 auto if we are so inclined. Now the entire page acts as a unit.

The next thing to do is to setup our two columns in the middle: the sidebar and the main content area. We will set the sidebar to a little less than a third of the content's size. We will follow rule #5 and #6 above and set our width to make sure there is enough space for both elements when floated. We will also follow rule #7 and clear the floats so the footer appears below the sidebar and content areas.

```
#sidebar {
  background-color: #d2d2d2;  float: left;
  width: 200px;
}

#content {
  float: left;
  width: 760px;
}
#footer {
  background-color: #bdbdbd;
  clear: both;
  height: 30px;
  width: 100%;
}
```

The sample in Figure 2-16 works well in getting us our two-column layout, but we have some issues. The first issue is that there is no spacing. The text could use some padding so it doesn't lie too close to the edges of its container, and a little text layout adjustment makes sense as well. The second issue is that one column is obviously shorter than we want. We will solve these problems one at a time.

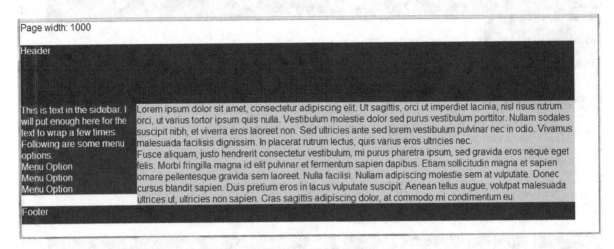

Figure 2-16. *CSS for creating a two-column content body, sidebar, and content area*

Adding Some Padding

Let us make some simple padding and spacing changes and see if this improves things. I'll start with adding 20 pixels of padding to the content area and see what I get in Figure 2-17.

```
#content {
  float: left;
  padding: 20px;
  width: 760px;
}
```

Figure 2-17. *Adding padding messed up our nice two-column layout*

This is not what we wanted. We just wanted more padding between the text and its container. If there is anything that frustrates developers who still have problems with float-based layouts, it is this kind of problem. But if you go back to our rules above, this makes sense. And the good news is that this is easily avoidable!

Once again, two floated elements will only float up next to each other if there is enough horizontal space for both to fit (rule #5). In this case there is not enough space, so the second block wraps under the first. Second, we need to remember our rules about width calculation (rule #9). Total element width is made up of the content width plus all surrounding margin, border, and padding. So by adding 20 pixels of padding to each side of the element, we have increased the size of the column on the right from 760 pixels to 800 pixels. The size of the sidebar is 200 pixels, which puts us at a width of 1000 pixels, which will not fit in the 960-pixel-width page container. Fortunately, this means the fix is easy. Instead of the above CSS, use the following:

```
#content {
    background-color: #E5D9CF;
    float: left;
    padding: 20px;
    width: 720px;
}
```

So now that we remember that any margin, border, and padding added to the elements must be subtracted from the width of the elements, spacing things out is quite easy. So we can make some changes and our content is less crammed.

```
#sidebar {
  background-color: #d2d2d2;
  float: left;
  padding: 20px;
  width: 160px;
}

#sidebar p {
    font-size: .8em;
    line-height: 1.4em;
}

#sidebar ol {
    margin: 10px 0 0 20px;
}

#sidebar li {
    font-size: .8em;
    font-weight: bold;
    list-style-type: none;
    margin: 8px 0;
}

#content {
  background-color: #e6e6e6;
  float: left;
  padding: 20px;
  width: 720px;
}

#content p {
    line-height: 1.4em;
    margin: 0 0 20px 0;
}
```

What you see in Figure 2-18 works great and will work for many layouts. But it can be improved, and next we will discuss how this can be done.

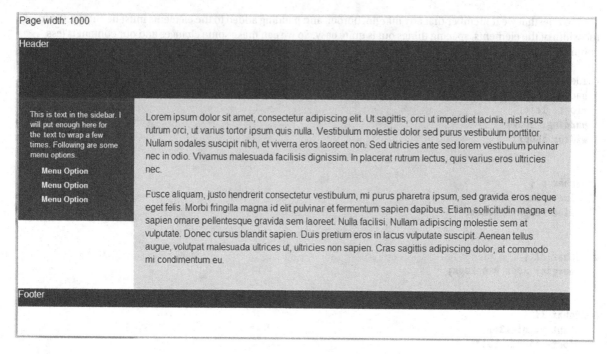

Figure 2-18. *Now with padding to give our content some space to breathe*

Consistent Columns

We are left with the height problem of our two columns. We want both columns to extend all the way to the footer, but this is not happening because the default height value of elements is determined by their content. If we were using a `table` to lay out this content, we wouldn't have this problem because the whole row would be sized the height of the largest cell. In my experience, once you understand the "gotchas" for calculating width, this is the only negative to doing float-based layouts.

But we can solve this. To do so, we could explicitly set the height of each column via CSS, perhaps `height: 200px`. But this is problematic. What if the user increases the browser's text size? What if you are using this as a template for other pages with different content? This is a solution to consider *only if you can assume your content will be inflexible*. But we will not. Here are two solutions to this problem.

Display Like a Table without a Table

First, you could try removing the float layout and use `display: table-cell` on both columns. The display value tells elements of the page to act as if they were table elements. So if you want two divs to act like two cells in a table row, set this as the display property. Following is the same CSS from above with the new display values set. Note that the float had to be removed for this to work.

```
#sidebar {
  background-color: #403d3a;
  display: table-cell;
  color: #FFF;
  padding: 20px;
  width: 160px;
}
```

```
#content {
    display: table-cell;
    background-color: #E5D9CF;
    padding: 20px;
    width: 720px;
}
```

When this is suggested, many bring up the rather obvious fact that we are trying to avoid the inflexibility of the `table` element but still using sizing mechanisms that are named after tables. The problem with using tables for layout is primarily two-fold. First, they are rather inflexible, and this is going to be a big problem when we get to the next chapter and try to change the layout of things based on screen size. Second, using a table to express layout keeps the markup from being semantically accurate. When you do this, you're mixing presentation and data. But CSS *is* about presentation. Putting presentation-related code there makes sense. To complain (as some do) that using `display: table-cell` gets us back where we started misses the point of *why* using the `table` element for layout was bad. So I think this is fine, and you can use this without having to worry too much about the CSS Float Police. But using the strategy has a drawback in that this display mode is not supported in Internet Explorer 6 and 7. If you're not supporting those browsers (and if you're just building a mobile site for relatively new smartphones, you probably aren't), you may have good enough mobile browser support to use this technique.

Faux Columns

Another technique is called "faux columns" and is very old. The great thing about aging techniques like this is that they should work on just about any browser that has CSS support for floats, which is certainly Android and iOS, as well as many others. This technique is at least as old as Dan Cederholm's 2004 "A List Apart" article by the same name (http://alistapart.com/article/fauxcolumns), which introduced the technique. The only negative thing about this approach is that it achieves the effect by using a background image instead of pure CSS.

This technique is called "faux" columns because the floated elements appear to be columns of equal height even though they really are *not*. The first thing to do is wrap our two elements in another element that we can attach a background image to. Next create a background image of the desired proportions (960 pixels in width, 1 pixel in height) with the column design that you want and set that as a background image of the new containing element and then have it repeat vertically. In this particular example, you want the solid colors of the columns to appear to extend to the maximum height of both, so you would use an image with those colors. The dark brown color takes up about 180 pixels on the left and the tan color the remaining pixels on the right. In other words, do this to get what we see in Figure 2-19.

```
<div id="contentWrapper">
    <div id="sidebar">
        <p>This is text in the sidebar...</p>
            <ol>
                <li>Menu Option</li>
                <li>Menu Option</li>
                <li>Menu Option</li>
            </ol>
    </div>
    <div id="content">
        <p>Lorem ipsum dolor...</p>
    </div>
</div>
```

```
#contentWrapper {
  background-image: url(fixed-faux-column-background.jpg);
  background-repeat: repeat-y;
  overflow: auto;
}
```

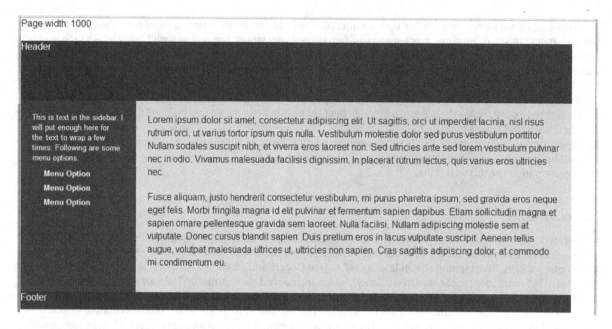

Figure 2-19. *The page after implementing faux columns*

So we see how to set a background image and repeat it vertically. No surprise there. The more important thing to point out is the overflow: auto setting. Recall above (rule #8) that a container that contains only floated elements will have no height because the floated elements are taken out of the normal page layout flow. Without this CSS property applied, the outer div is 0 pixels tall, so you never see the background. Setting overflow: auto tells the browser to calculate that space taken up by the floated elements, which gives you the appropriate size for setting the background image. So even though the two columns do not technically stretch to the bottom, it looks as though they do. And the total height of the area will be determined by the tallest of the two columns, which will stretch the container and maintain the illusion of equal-sized columns.

Whether you choose to not deal with the column problem or to solve it one of these ways, you have options. Though laying out columns is admittedly a bit awkward in CSS, it's a solvable problem as long as you know the rules.

Creating a Horizontal Menu in CSS

Another very common design element on the web is the horizontal menu. Like the multi-column layout above, many find styling these difficult. Here we will take what we have learned and create a horizontal menu using several of the techniques above. Figure 2-20 shows what it will look like when it is finished.

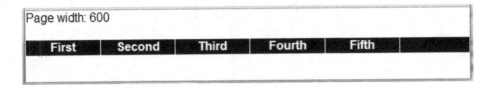

Figure 2-20. *A horizontal menu*

It is generally considered a best practice to use a list for a menu since a menu is nothing more than a list of links (even if you use the new HTML5 nav element). In our case, we will use an unordered list.

```
<ul>
  <li><a href="first.htm">First</a></li>
  <li><a href="second.htm">Second</a></li>
  <li><a href="third.htm">Third</a></li>
  <li><a href="fourth.htm">Fourth</a></li>
  <li><a href="fifth">Fifth</a></li>
</ul>
```

Before we jump in to changing the default layout of lists, we should understand why a list is displayed like it is by default. If you have a list with a few items in it (if it is a ul like the list above, you will see a bulleted list), the list items do not stack up on top of each other because of their list-ness. They stack up because the li element is a block-level element. You may recall from above that block-level elements (that is, those that are by default display: block), will take up the entire horizontal width of their container (rule #2), forcing the next element to appear below instead of to the side. So you need to augment this behavior if you want to turn this vertical list into a horizontally stacking menu.

Laying Out the Menu Using Floats

Let's try using floats. Since we want to float the list items, the first thing to do is set a width on them (rule #6) and then apply a value of float: left to the list items to have them stack up to the left. We want a black background spanning the entire menu, so we can't put a background on the list items since they do not reach all the way across the screen. So we will set the background color of the containing ul and set its overflow: auto value so it doesn't collapse (rule #8). The following is our resulting CSS, including some extra style to handle text colors and borders. I hope you agree that this is fairly easy once you learn the rules.

```
<style type="text/css">

  ul {
    background-color: #000;
    overflow: auto;
  }

  li {
    border-right: solid 1px #FFF;
    float: left;
    list-style-type: none;
    text-align: center;
    width: 100px;
  }
```

```
a {
    color: #FFF;
    font-weight: bold;
    text-decoration: none;
}
```

```
</style>
```

Laying Out the Menu Using Display: Inline-block

Inline-block should also work well for making the menu horizontal because they can stack horizontally and their width can be set (rule #3), so setting both display and width gets us our basic layout. Unlike floats, inline-block elements do not escape the document flow, so the containing ul does not need to have its overflow value tweaked. You can often accomplish the same design using inline-block as you can using float, which is the case here.

Though you may not see it, because our background color is black, there is actually a space between the menu items given the markup. So the menu items take up more horizontal space using this method than with using floats. This is because there are spaces between them in the DOM. Unlike floated elements, they *are* in the normal flow, so spaces between them in the HTML markup cause this behavior. The easiest way to solve this is to remove the spaces in the DOM by lining the elements directly up against each other. You can also set the font size on the ul to 0 but then reset the font size on the li. For this example I will just ignore the issue and let the spaces remain. And remember that you have to set the background color on the container and not the items: this is because the list items do not span the entire width of the container, just like the float example above.

```
ul {
    background-color: #000;
}
```

```
li {
    border-right: solid 1px #FFF;
    display: inline-block;
    list-style-type: none;
    text-align: center;
    width: 100px;
}
```

```
a {
    color: #FFF;
    font-weight: bold;
    text-decoration: none;
}
```

Summary

So you have seen two examples of how to do layout with CSS without using a single HTML table. Once you know the rules, doing layouts with pure CSS is not nearly as daunting a task as many think it is. However, this is a book on mobile, so we should not stop here. Our 960-pixel layouts above might work on larger tablets but will fail spectacularly on smaller devices, so we need fluid layouts that adapt to the size of the screen. You saw briefly how to do that in Chapter 1. Chapter 3 will give you more examples and work through common issues in responsive layouts.

CHAPTER 3

■ ■ ■

Flexible Layouts

There are three basic concepts in responsive web design, creating flexible layouts, creating flexible content, and using media queries to handle problems caused by major differences in screen size. Though flexible content is arguably much more important, flexible layouts with media queries are the poster child of responsive web design, and this is the subject of this chapter. Without a flexible layout, it's difficult if not impossible to have flexible content. So this is a good starting point for digging into responsive web design. In the next chapter we will focus specifically on creating flexible navigation, something closely related to flexible layouts. We discussed both briefly in Chapter 1, but here we will discuss these topics in depth and give several more examples. In Chapter 5 we will discuss flexible content in depth.

To make sure that the following work on a wide range of devices, all samples were tested on the devices listed in the introduction.

Setting up a New Responsive ASP.NET MVC Site

Let's start by setting up a responsive ASP.NET MVC site. If you create an ASP.NET MVC 4 "Internet Site" you get a site that already uses media queries to transform its layout for mobile devices. But since you are learning, you want to create a site using the "Basic" template (which I will name "RWDSample"). With this template we get a starter CSS file (/Content/Site.css) and a Layout page (/Views/Shared/_Layout.cshtml).

This site template comes with no controller classes or views, so we create a very simple home controller as follows:

```
using System.Web.Mvc;

namespace RWDSample.Controllers
{
  public class HomeController : Controller
  {
    public ActionResult Index()
    {
      return View();
    }
  }
}
```

We then create a simple view. In it we will paste the html we used in Chapter 2 to show the page width along with the necessary JavaScript. It should look like this:

```
@{
    ViewBag.Title = "Index";
}
```

43

```
<script type="text/javascript">
window.onload = function () {

   var pageWidth = document.getElementById('pageWidth');
   pageWidth.innerHTML = window.innerWidth || document.body.clientWidth;

   window.addEventListener('resize', function () {
     pageWidth.innerHTML = window.innerWidth;
   });
}
</script>
<div>Page width: <span id="pageWidth"></span></div>
```

The layout contains one very useful thing by default: a viewport meta tag. It also comes with references to jQuery and Modernizr, neither of which we will need at this point. If you are following along with a new project, you can remove those.

And finally, we are going to open up the CSS file and paste in the same reset and font changes from Chapter 2 to reset the padding and margins on all elements.

```
html, body, div, span, applet, object, iframe,
h1, h2, h3, h4, h5, h6, p, blockquote, pre,
a, abbr, acronym, address, big, cite, code,
del, dfn, em, img, ins, kbd, q, s, samp,
small, strike, strong, sub, sup, tt, var,
b, u, i, center,
dl, dt, dd, ol, ul, li,
fieldset, form, label, legend,
table, caption, tbody, tfoot, thead, tr, th, td,
article, aside, canvas, details, embed,
figure, figcaption, footer, header, hgroup,
menu, nav, output, ruby, section, summary,
time, mark, audio, video {
  margin: 0;
  padding: 0;
}

div, span, li
{
  font-family: Helvetica;
}
```

If you use other ASP.NET MVC 4 templates you simply need to replace the default code and CSS with what you see above. The same goes for ASP.NET MVC 5. We are now ready to begin.

Revisiting the Three-Column Layout

Let's start by revisiting the idea of creating a three-column layout. We need some simple HTML markup and the following should do fine.

```
<div id="content">
    <div class="column">This is the first...</div>
    <div class="column">This is the second...</div>
    <div class="column">This is the third...</div>
</div>
```

Our immediate goal is to turn the content into a responsive three-column layout that becomes a one-column layout on smaller screens. Though there are a number of options available for doing this (see Chapter 2), we will use floats because doing a layout in this manner has the broadest support in modern browsers. As an example of this approach, you can look at the CakePHP site (Figure 3-1). Sure it's not the web framework you are using now, but it does give you a good example of a three-column responsive design.

Figure 3-1. *A good example of a three-column responsive site*

Making Our Three-Column Layout Flexible

To turn our markup into a flexible three-column layout, this is all the CSS that you really need to produce the result in Figure 3-2.

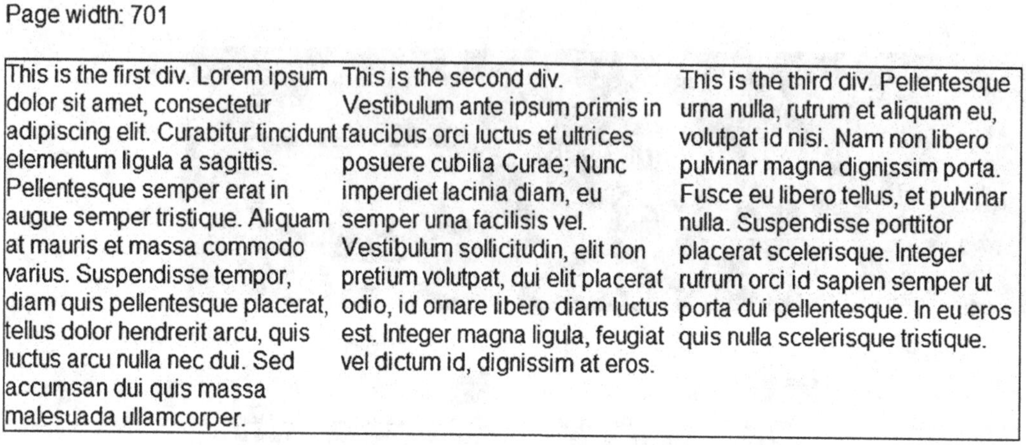

Page width: 701

This is the first div. Lorem ipsum dolor sit amet, consectetur adipiscing elit. Curabitur tincidunt elementum ligula a sagittis. Pellentesque semper erat in augue semper tristique. Aliquam at mauris et massa commodo varius. Suspendisse tempor, diam quis pellentesque placerat, tellus dolor hendrerit arcu, quis luctus arcu nulla nec dui. Sed accumsan dui quis massa malesuada ullamcorper.

This is the second div. Vestibulum ante ipsum primis in faucibus orci luctus et ultrices posuere cubilia Curae; Nunc imperdiet lacinia diam, eu semper urna facilisis vel. Vestibulum sollicitudin, elit non pretium volutpat, dui elit placerat odio, id ornare libero diam luctus est. Integer magna ligula, feugiat vel dictum id, dignissim at eros.

This is the third div. Pellentesque urna nulla, rutrum et aliquam eu, volutpat id nisi. Nam non libero pulvinar magna dignissim porta. Fusce eu libero tellus, et pulvinar nulla. Suspendisse porttitor placerat scelerisque. Integer rutrum orci id sapien semper ut porta dui pellentesque. In eu eros quis nulla scelerisque tristique.

Figure 3-2. A flexible three-column layout with no margins or padding

```
.content {
  border: solid 1px #000;
  overflow: auto; /* keeps the floats of the columns from collapsing the parent. See chapter 2. */
}

.column {
  float: left;
  width: 33.333333%;
}
```

Creating Space

I added a border to make the size of the content clear. No matter how wide or narrow the screen, this simple CSS gives you a three-column elastic layout. The only problem is that it has serious readability issues since the text in each column has no margin or padding to separate it from the nearby column(s). Let's keep in mind our rule about calculating width in Chapter 2 (that total width equals margins + borders + padding + content) and some margins. If we add a margin of 3 percent to each of the columns, this has to be subtracted from the width of the content. And since margin appears on both the left and right sides of the content, you have to remember to subtract it twice. The width is no longer 33.333333% but 27.333333%. You can see the results in Figure 3-3.

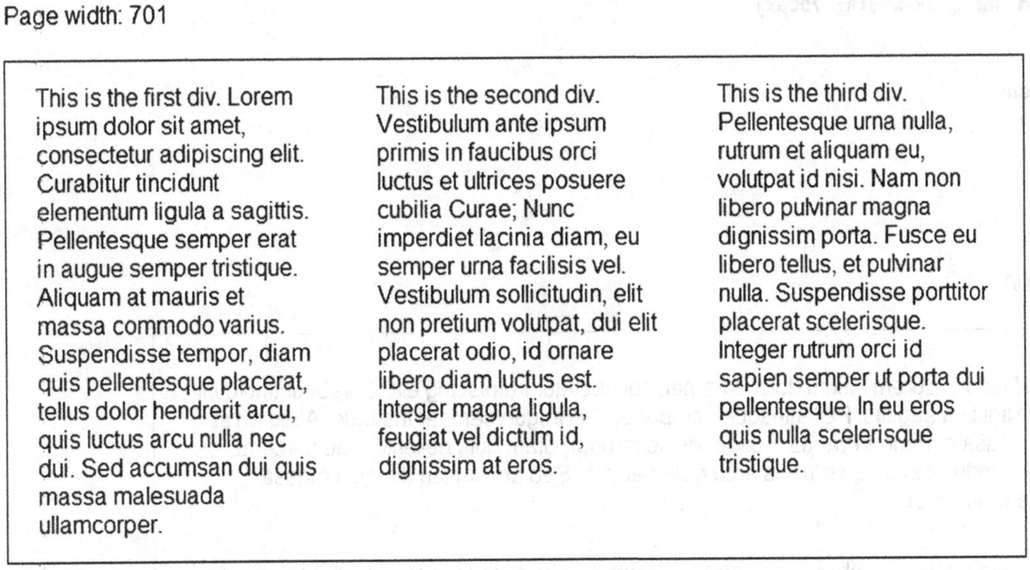

Page width: 701

This is the first div. Lorem ipsum dolor sit amet, consectetur adipiscing elit. Curabitur tincidunt elementum ligula a sagittis. Pellentesque semper erat in augue semper tristique. Aliquam at mauris et massa commodo varius. Suspendisse tempor, diam quis pellentesque placerat, tellus dolor hendrerit arcu, quis luctus arcu nulla nec dui. Sed accumsan dui quis massa malesuada ullamcorper.

This is the second div. Vestibulum ante ipsum primis in faucibus orci luctus et ultrices posuere cubilia Curae; Nunc imperdiet lacinia diam, eu semper urna facilisis vel. Vestibulum sollicitudin, elit non pretium volutpat, dui elit placerat odio, id ornare libero diam luctus est. Integer magna ligula, feugiat vel dictum id, dignissim at eros.

This is the third div. Pellentesque urna nulla, rutrum et aliquam eu, volutpat id nisi. Nam non libero pulvinar magna dignissim porta. Fusce eu libero tellus, et pulvinar nulla. Suspendisse porttitor placerat scelerisque. Integer rutrum orci id sapien semper ut porta dui pellentesque. In eu eros quis nulla scelerisque tristique.

Figure 3-3. Flexible three-column layout that is much easier to read

```
.content {
  border: solid 1px #000;
  overflow: auto;
}

.column {
  float: left;
  margin: 15px 3%; /* the top and bottom margins don't need to be as flexible */
  width: 27.333333%;
}
```

Though this is a very flexible layout, it would not look right on a smaller screen. The columns would be too narrow, and readability would be greatly compromised. To solve this, we add a media query to change the layout once the screen size gets too small. It could look like Figure 3-4:

```
#content {
  border: solid 1px #000;
  overflow: auto;
}

.column {
  float: left;
  margin: 15px 3%;
  width: 27.333333%;
}
```

```
@media screen and (max-width: 700px)
{
  .column {
    float: none;
    margin: 4%;
    width: 92%;
  }
}
```

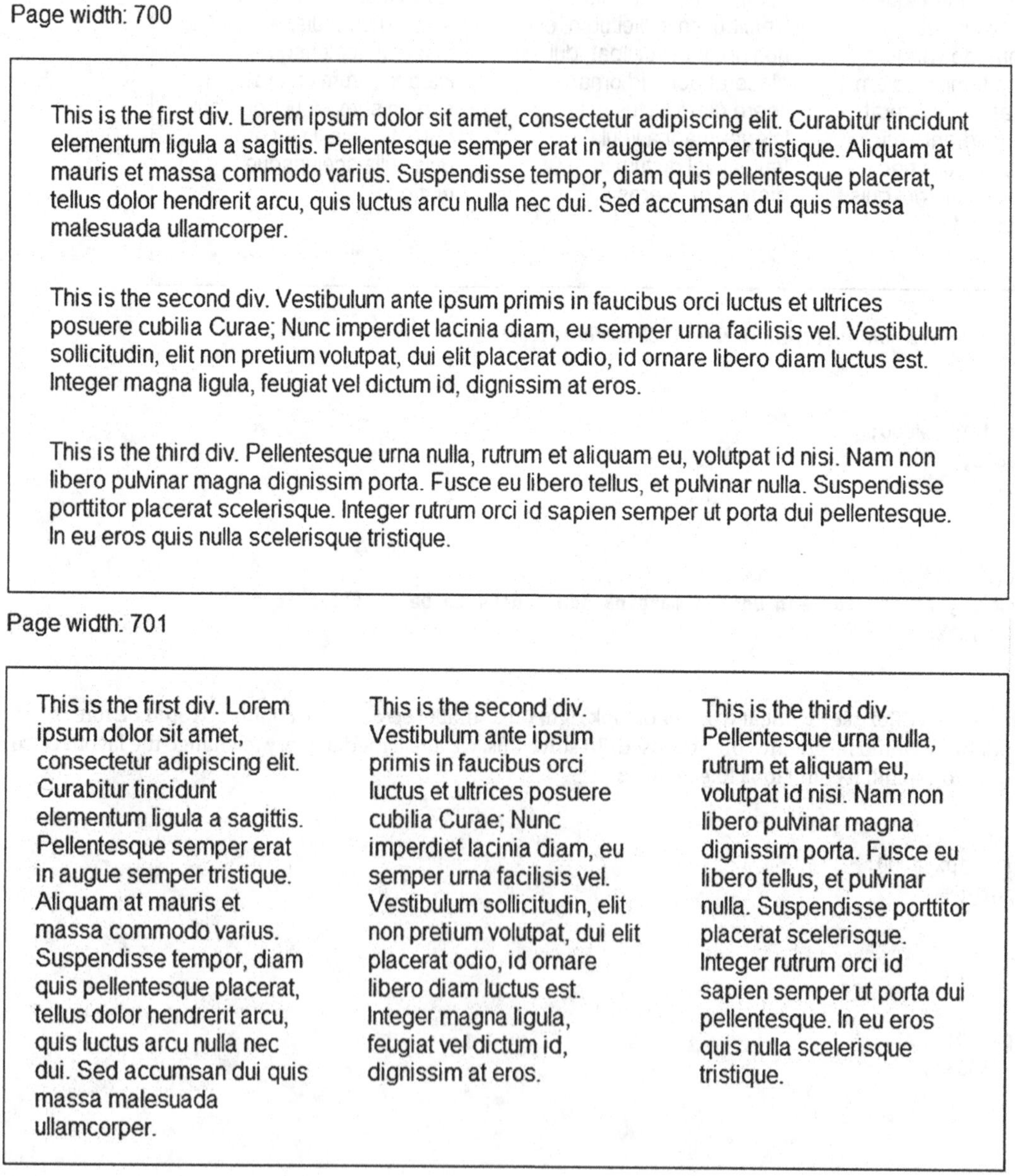

Page width: 700

This is the first div. Lorem ipsum dolor sit amet, consectetur adipiscing elit. Curabitur tincidunt elementum ligula a sagittis. Pellentesque semper erat in augue semper tristique. Aliquam at mauris et massa commodo varius. Suspendisse tempor, diam quis pellentesque placerat, tellus dolor hendrerit arcu, quis luctus arcu nulla nec dui. Sed accumsan dui quis massa malesuada ullamcorper.

This is the second div. Vestibulum ante ipsum primis in faucibus orci luctus et ultrices posuere cubilia Curae; Nunc imperdiet lacinia diam, eu semper urna facilisis vel. Vestibulum sollicitudin, elit non pretium volutpat, dui elit placerat odio, id ornare libero diam luctus est. Integer magna ligula, feugiat vel dictum id, dignissim at eros.

This is the third div. Pellentesque urna nulla, rutrum et aliquam eu, volutpat id nisi. Nam non libero pulvinar magna dignissim porta. Fusce eu libero tellus, et pulvinar nulla. Suspendisse porttitor placerat scelerisque. Integer rutrum orci id sapien semper ut porta dui pellentesque. In eu eros quis nulla scelerisque tristique.

Page width: 701

This is the first div. Lorem ipsum dolor sit amet, consectetur adipiscing elit. Curabitur tincidunt elementum ligula a sagittis. Pellentesque semper erat in augue semper tristique. Aliquam at mauris et massa commodo varius. Suspendisse tempor, diam quis pellentesque placerat, tellus dolor hendrerit arcu, quis luctus arcu nulla nec dui. Sed accumsan dui quis massa malesuada ullamcorper.

This is the second div. Vestibulum ante ipsum primis in faucibus orci luctus et ultrices posuere cubilia Curae; Nunc imperdiet lacinia diam, eu semper urna facilisis vel. Vestibulum sollicitudin, elit non pretium volutpat, dui elit placerat odio, id ornare libero diam luctus est. Integer magna ligula, feugiat vel dictum id, dignissim at eros.

This is the third div. Pellentesque urna nulla, rutrum et aliquam eu, volutpat id nisi. Nam non libero pulvinar magna dignissim porta. Fusce eu libero tellus, et pulvinar nulla. Suspendisse porttitor placerat scelerisque. Integer rutrum orci id sapien semper ut porta dui pellentesque. In eu eros quis nulla scelerisque tristique.

Figure 3-4. *A basic three-column responsive layout*

By specifying "max-width: 700px" in my media query, I limit the CSS in the media query to only apply when the screen is 700 pixels or smaller. This width is entirely arbitrary, and any value can be chosen. Some might be tempted to design their media queries around device sizes, such as 320 pixels (iPhone in portrait orientation) or 480 pixels (iPhone 4S and previous in landscape orientation). This obviously works but I think makes the whole task generally harder because you will probably want to support devices of varying size (and if you support Android phones or tablets, you will have to). I strongly recommend sizing according to the constraints of the content, *not the device*. In my experience if you think device first, you end up having to write more CSS in media queries. Thinking in terms of devices is actually approaching this whole problem backward. A bit of content is sized incorrectly because the viewport is too small for that content, not because you are viewing it on a 320-pixel-wide iPhone specifically. So if you fix it for a 320-pixel-width phone, what happens when another device comes along at 340 pixels in width? What about 350 pixels in width? If you are thinking "device first," you solve for a subset of devices. *If you think "content first," you solve for all devices.*

Adding Borders

Everything so far has been rather straightforward, involving just a little basic math to calculate our percentages. Unfortunately, adding borders is a bit tricky because you can't set border width using percentages, so you have to combine percentages and pixels. If you add a one-pixel border as seen in the following CSS, you have problems.

```css
#content {
  border: solid 1px #000;
  overflow: auto;
}

.column {
  border: solid 1px #000; /* this will cause our design to break :( */
  float: left;
  margin: 15px 3%;
  width: 27.333333%;
}

@media screen and (max-width: 400px)
{
  .column {
    float: none;
    margin: 4%;
    width: 92%;
  }
}
```

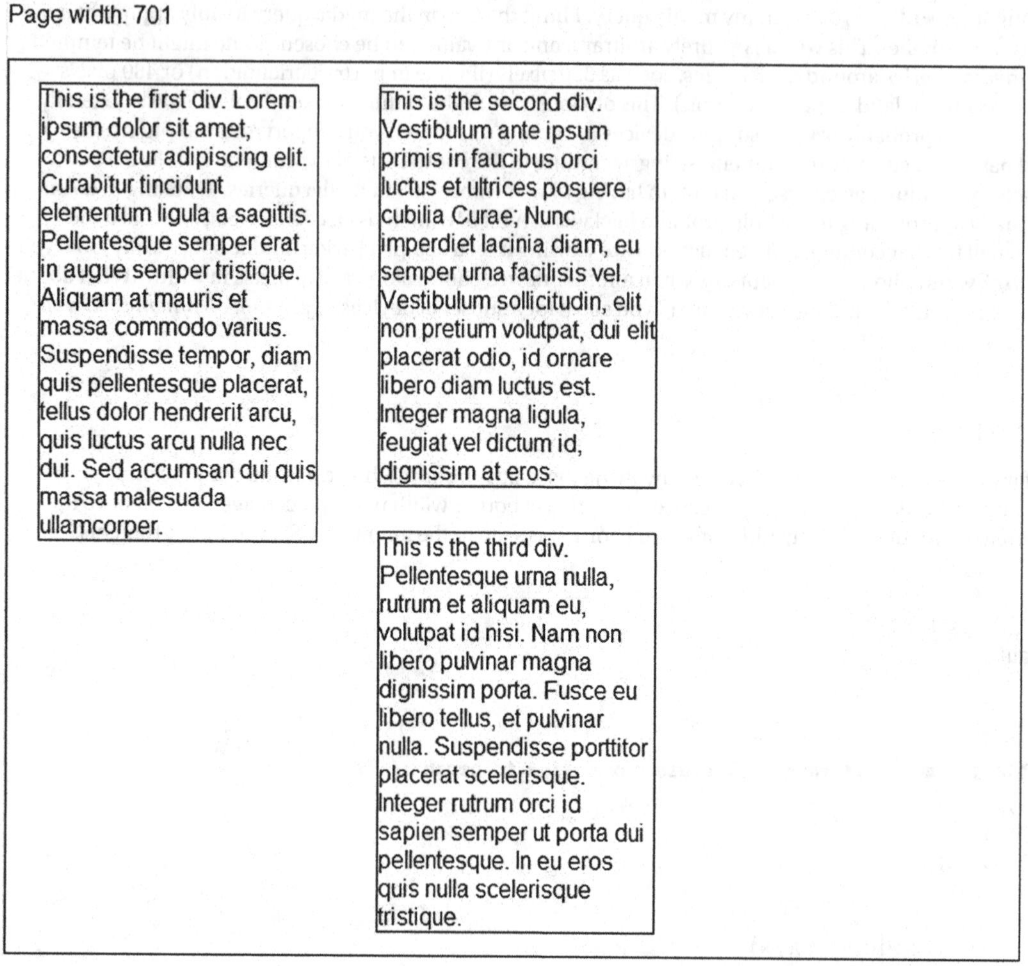

Page width: 701

Figure 3-5. *Broken three-column responsive layout. The borders are making the columns too wide*

If we think through our sizing, what should the total width of our three columns be? The content width, margin, and padding added together is 99.999999%, so if the viewport, for example, is sized at 960 pixels the combined width should be 959.999990 pixels. I would presume each browser might round that up or down; but since that is below the maximum width of 960 pixels, the floated columns fit fine and nothing has to wrap down to fit. But if a one-pixel border is added for each element, the total width of the three is now 965.999990 pixels (we added two pixels to each). Since that is larger than the maximum size of the container, the last element must wrap.

Fortunately, this can be solved in several ways. The easiest way to do so would be to replace the border setting with `outline: solid 1px #000`, which does not add to the total width of the element unlike border. The CSS `outline` property has good support, though it is not supported as widely as the `border` property (which is universally supported). If the outline is supported well enough in devices that you want to support, then this is a very easy way to solve this problem.

Another way to solve this involves using a little more math. What would happen if we set the column width to 27 percent instead of 27.333333 percent? With the margin and padding included, the total width taken up without the borders would be around 950.4 pixels, leaving us with space enough for 9.6 pixels worth of border. This is plenty of space for our six pixels of border. Unfortunately the available width depends on the width of the screen. Ninety-nine percent of 600 pixels is 594, which means right about there our design is going to break. Where exactly the layout breaks will probably depend on the browser. You could solve this by creating a new media query around that size to shrink down the columns a bit more to allow for the borders at smaller sizes: but as you can imagine, this could get messy. But it should work.

Finally, you could solve this by not using CSS borders at all but rather the "faux columns" technique discussed in Chapter 2. This technique involves an extra image download but allows you to avoid browser incompatibilities and annoying math calculations.

Since it has good support on mobile and is the easiest option, we will use the outline property to get the desired effect here. And because we now need a space between border and content, let's add some padding.

```
#content {
  border: solid 1px #000;
  overflow: auto;
}

.column {
  outline: solid 1px #000; /* yay for easy stuff! */
  float: left;
  margin: 15px 3%;
  padding: 2%;
  width: 23.333333%; /* adding padding requires us to restrict the width */
}

@media screen and (max-width: 700px)
{
  .column {
    float: none;
    margin: 4%;
    width: 88%; /* because the padding above will still be applied, we need to shrink this too. */
  }
}
```

In Figure 3-6 we have our finished, flexible, and responsive three-column layout. It includes outlines to delineate the content sections and good padding and margins.

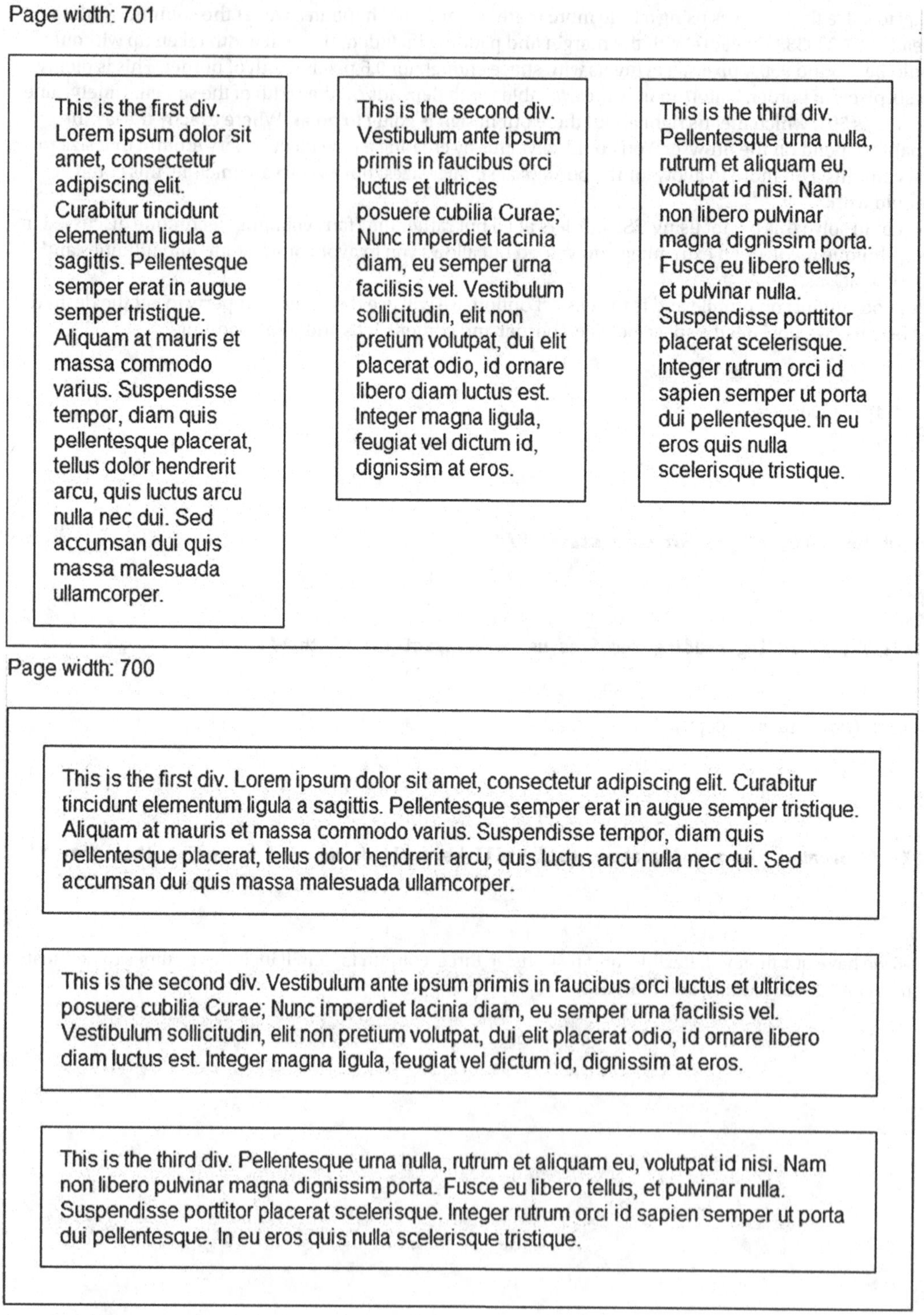

Page width: 701

This is the first div. Lorem ipsum dolor sit amet, consectetur adipiscing elit. Curabitur tincidunt elementum ligula a sagittis. Pellentesque semper erat in augue semper tristique. Aliquam at mauris et massa commodo varius. Suspendisse tempor, diam quis pellentesque placerat, tellus dolor hendrerit arcu, quis luctus arcu nulla nec dui. Sed accumsan dui quis massa malesuada ullamcorper.

This is the second div. Vestibulum ante ipsum primis in faucibus orci luctus et ultrices posuere cubilia Curae; Nunc imperdiet lacinia diam, eu semper urna facilisis vel. Vestibulum sollicitudin, elit non pretium volutpat, dui elit placerat odio, id ornare libero diam luctus est. Integer magna ligula, feugiat vel dictum id, dignissim at eros.

This is the third div. Pellentesque urna nulla, rutrum et aliquam eu, volutpat id nisi. Nam non libero pulvinar magna dignissim porta. Fusce eu libero tellus, et pulvinar nulla. Suspendisse porttitor placerat scelerisque. Integer rutrum orci id sapien semper ut porta dui pellentesque. In eu eros quis nulla scelerisque tristique.

Page width: 700

This is the first div. Lorem ipsum dolor sit amet, consectetur adipiscing elit. Curabitur tincidunt elementum ligula a sagittis. Pellentesque semper erat in augue semper tristique. Aliquam at mauris et massa commodo varius. Suspendisse tempor, diam quis pellentesque placerat, tellus dolor hendrerit arcu, quis luctus arcu nulla nec dui. Sed accumsan dui quis massa malesuada ullamcorper.

This is the second div. Vestibulum ante ipsum primis in faucibus orci luctus et ultrices posuere cubilia Curae; Nunc imperdiet lacinia diam, eu semper urna facilisis vel. Vestibulum sollicitudin, elit non pretium volutpat, dui elit placerat odio, id ornare libero diam luctus est. Integer magna ligula, feugiat vel dictum id, dignissim at eros.

This is the third div. Pellentesque urna nulla, rutrum et aliquam eu, volutpat id nisi. Nam non libero pulvinar magna dignissim porta. Fusce eu libero tellus, et pulvinar nulla. Suspendisse porttitor placerat scelerisque. Integer rutrum orci id sapien semper ut porta dui pellentesque. In eu eros quis nulla scelerisque tristique.

Figure 3-6. *Finished three-column responsive layout*

What about Older Browsers?

Responsive web design is a great technique for building sites that work for both mobile and desktop browsers. Though media queries are supported on all recent releases of popular desktop browsers and all browsers in recent smartphones, there are still older devices out there without support.

Thinking about our layout above, a mobile browser without media query support visiting the page would have a very poor experience. Because the media query makes the design usable on a smaller screen, the media query fix would not get applied if the browser does not support media queries. But if a desktop browser without support visited (such as old Internet Explorer), the experience would probably be fine since the browser window would likely be large enough. If we want the website to work on both mobile and desktop this is not acceptable because the site becomes unusable for one of the two.

Let's turn this around and rethink our approach a bit. What if we switched the CSS around and put the CSS for making columns in the media query instead?

```
#content {
  border: solid 1px #000;
  overflow: auto;
}

.column {
  outline: solid 1px #000;
  float: none;
  margin: 10px 0;
  padding: 0;
  width: 100%;
}

@media screen and (min-width: 400px)
{
  .column {
    float: left;
    margin: 2%;
    padding: 2%;
    width: 25.333333%;
  }
}
```

In this case a browser without media query support will get a page without columns. In the case of the mobile device without media query support, you get exactly what you want. In the case of an old desktop browser, you get something that is not ideal; *but it is usable*, which is most important. In desktop and mobile browsers with media query support, (the vast majority), you get exactly what you want. What you are left with is an approach that is both backward-compatible and forward-compatible because it works on older systems and is exactly what you want on newer and future browsers.

Note that the switch in approach required us to change the media query from max-width to min-width, because the logic has now been reversed.

This is one form of *progressive enhancement*, a very useful technique. Contrary to the thinking of many, *sites do not have to look the same in every browser*. This used to be the status quo but it is far too much work for practically no benefit. Instead, make the site work in the older browsers and work *great* in the newer browsers that you want to support, even if it may look different when viewed in desktop Internet Explorer and in mobile Safari on the iPhone.

A Two-Column Layout

As you might expect, a two-column layout would follow the same principles as the three-column layout. But to keep it interesting, we will put another constraint on ourselves. We want the columns to be aligned with the outside of our content element, instead of having margins around separating them as we did above, like you see here in Figure 3-7.

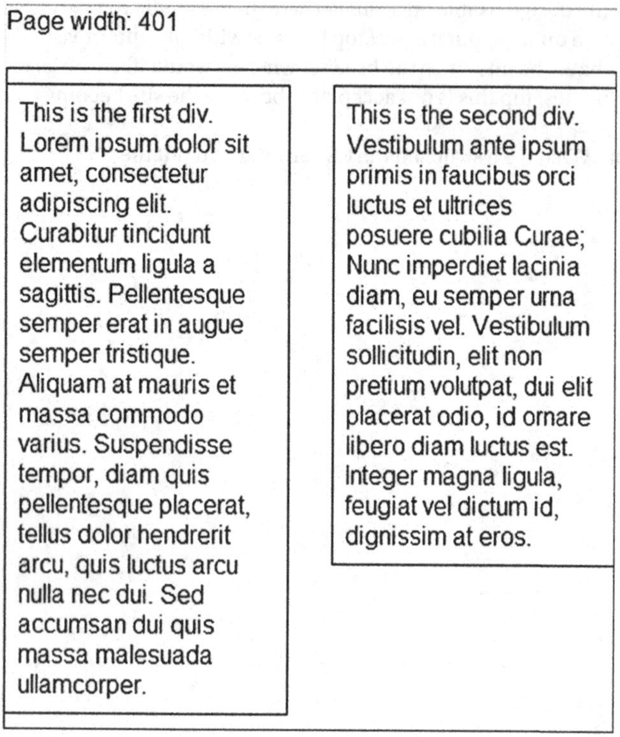

Page width: 401

This is the first div. Lorem ipsum dolor sit amet, consectetur adipiscing elit. Curabitur tincidunt elementum ligula a sagittis. Pellentesque semper erat in augue semper tristique. Aliquam at mauris et massa commodo varius. Suspendisse tempor, diam quis pellentesque placerat, tellus dolor hendrerit arcu, quis luctus arcu nulla nec dui. Sed accumsan dui quis massa malesuada ullamcorper.

This is the second div. Vestibulum ante ipsum primis in faucibus orci luctus et ultrices posuere cubilia Curae; Nunc imperdiet lacinia diam, eu semper urna facilisis vel. Vestibulum sollicitudin, elit non pretium volutpat, dui elit placerat odio, id ornare libero diam luctus est. Integer magna ligula, feugiat vel dictum id, dignissim at eros.

Figure 3-7. *Two columns with each column aligned to the outside of the page*

First we will trim down our columns to two:

```
<div class="content">
  <div class="column"></div>
  <div class="column"></div>
</div>
```

Now it is time for the CSS. Two things are in order. First, we will start with the CSS to create the two columns in large-screen mode. Second, we put in CSS to change it to a single column when the screen is 400 pixels in width or less.

```
.content {
  border: solid 1px #000;
  overflow: auto;
}
```

```
.column {
  outline: solid 1px #000;
  float: left;
  margin: 10px 0;
  padding: 0;
  width: 50%;
}

@media screen and (max-width: 400px)
{
  .column {
    float: none;
    width: 100%;
  }
}
```

This works great but we need some padding and margins and we need to add it so that the columns align with the outside. We add a padding of 2 percent to separate the text a bit from the edge of the columns. Creating the margin in the middle is a bit trickier. What we want to do is apply a margin to one of the elements but not the other to move the right column over to the right side of the #content container. We could add a class to the second column to target it specifically or we can use CSS selectors. One option would be to use the adjacent selector and put this in a media query. For those who may not be familiar with it, the adjacent selector is useful for targeting an element only when it is adjacent to another element.

```
.content {
  border: solid 1px #000;
  overflow: auto;
}

.column {
  outline: solid 1px #000;
  float: left;
  margin: 10px 0;
  padding: 2%;
  width: 42%;
}

/* The column on the right, because it is adjacent to the column on the left,
will get this CSS setting applied. */
.column + .column {
  margin-left: 8%;
}

@media screen and (max-width: 400px)
{
  .column {
    float: none;
    width: 96%;
  }

  .column + .column {
    margin-left: 0;
  }
}
```

So each column has a width of 46 percent (width of 42 percent + padding of 2 percent on each side), leaving an 8 percent separation between the columns. If the column separation is too large, you can increase the width and decrease the margin on the right-most column. As you can see in Figure 3-8, this is a relatively easy way to create a two-column layout.

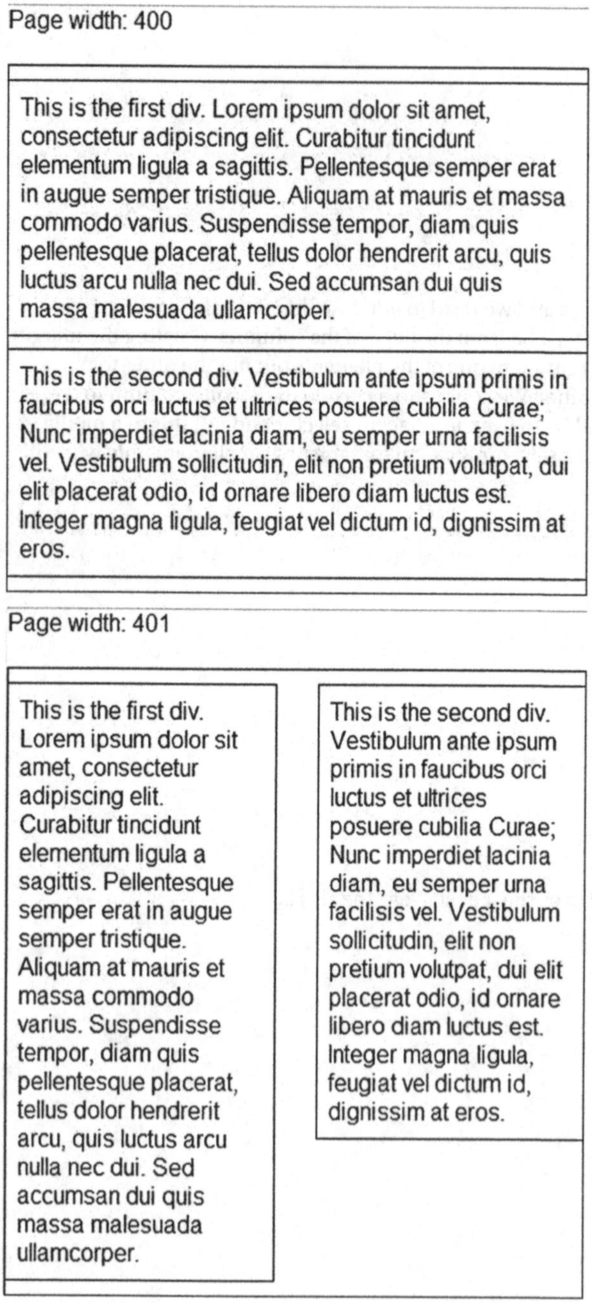

Page width: 400

This is the first div. Lorem ipsum dolor sit amet, consectetur adipiscing elit. Curabitur tincidunt elementum ligula a sagittis. Pellentesque semper erat in augue semper tristique. Aliquam at mauris et massa commodo varius. Suspendisse tempor, diam quis pellentesque placerat, tellus dolor hendrerit arcu, quis luctus arcu nulla nec dui. Sed accumsan dui quis massa malesuada ullamcorper.

This is the second div. Vestibulum ante ipsum primis in faucibus orci luctus et ultrices posuere cubilia Curae; Nunc imperdiet lacinia diam, eu semper urna facilisis vel. Vestibulum sollicitudin, elit non pretium volutpat, dui elit placerat odio, id ornare libero diam luctus est. Integer magna ligula, feugiat vel dictum id, dignissim at eros.

Page width: 401

This is the first div. Lorem ipsum dolor sit amet, consectetur adipiscing elit. Curabitur tincidunt elementum ligula a sagittis. Pellentesque semper erat in augue semper tristique. Aliquam at mauris et massa commodo varius. Suspendisse tempor, diam quis pellentesque placerat, tellus dolor hendrerit arcu, quis luctus arcu nulla nec dui. Sed accumsan dui quis massa malesuada ullamcorper.

This is the second div. Vestibulum ante ipsum primis in faucibus orci luctus et ultrices posuere cubilia Curae; Nunc imperdiet lacinia diam, eu semper urna facilisis vel. Vestibulum sollicitudin, elit non pretium volutpat, dui elit placerat odio, id ornare libero diam luctus est. Integer magna ligula, feugiat vel dictum id, dignissim at eros.

Figure 3-8. *A two-column responsive layout*

A Ten-Column Layout with Header and Footer

There are some sites where the subject matter might lend itself to small chunks of data instead of larger columns. This is also a good case for us to tackle because it shows us that we can push what we've learned to potentially ridiculous extremes. And since we have such power over our medium, we might as well abuse it for fun.

Since this is really just an extension of the same rules in the above two examples, we will add in some new factors. First, let's use some real content to prove that this actually works. Second, in terms of layout, we want a header and footer. For large monitors, we want to support ten columns. We also want the layout to switch to five columns wide when the screen is less than 800 pixels in width, two columns wide when less than 500 pixels and one column wide at 400 pixels and lower. We will also have no max width value on the container to allow this to grow to the full width of the browser, whatever the size. Finally will also put a border and rounded corner around the items. This last bit makes things much more difficult since outline-radius is barely supported by browsers, so we have to use borders and border-radius. As you know from the discussion on borders so far, border values are specified in pixels instead of percentages, which will make this layout more difficult.

We will start with a portion of our markup.

```
<div class="header">
  <h1>Things I Enjoy</h1>
</div>
<div class="items">
  <div class="item">
    <img src="~/content/images/bacon_500.jpg" />
    <p>Bacon</p>
  </div>
  <!-- 9 more items -->
</div>
<div class="footer">
  &copy; Eric Sowell, 2013
</div>
```

Because we want to assume no media query support for older browsers, we will start with a basic single-column layout. The total width of each should not be more than 100 percent, so we set a max-width of 90 percent with a margin of 5 percent on each side. This allows the content to grow to fill the screen for every variation of device size below 400 pixels (Figure 3-9).

Stuff I Felt Like Putting in This Demo

Bacon

CSS

Figure 3-9. Our page viewed on a small screen

```
.item {
  border: solid 1px #777;
  border-radius: 5px;
  float: left;
  margin: 0 5% 10px 5%;
  max-width: 90%;
  overflow: hidden;
  text-align: center;
}

.item img {
  margin-top: 2.5%;
  max-width: 95%;
}

.item p {
  min-height: 3em;
  text-align: center;
  font-size: .9em;
}
```

Now that we have this in place, we can work our way up in screen size. At 400 pixels in width, we are going to switch to two per screen, which means changing the max-width and margin for the item. This total width of 49.4 percent was determined through testing on different devices. The extra space is left in because of the border (Figure 3-10).

Figure 3-10. *Our page viewed at a little over 400 pixels*

```
@media screen and (min-width: 400px) {
  .item {
    max-width: 47.4%;
    margin: 5px 1%;
  }
}
```

Next we handle 500 pixels in width, which has five items across (Figure 3-11).

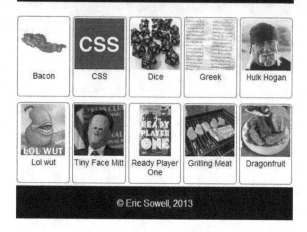

Figure 3-11. *Our page viewed at a little over 500 pixels*

```
@media screen and (min-width: 500px) {
  .item {
    max-width: 18.6%;
    margin: 5px .5%;
  }
}
```

And finally, when the screen is 800 pixels in width or wider, we switch to the ten-column layout shown in Figure 3-12.

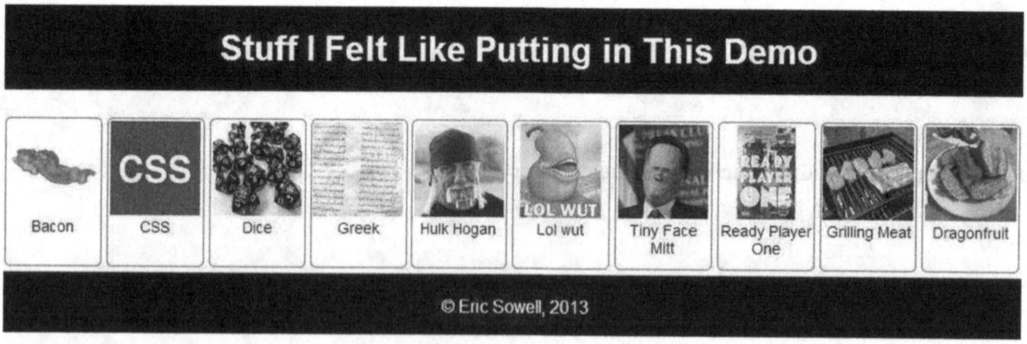

![Stuff I Felt Like Putting in This Demo - large screen view]

Figure 3-12. *Our page viewed on a large screen*

```
@media screen and (min-width: 800px) {
  .item {
    max-width: 9.2%;
    margin: 5px .25%;
  }
}
```

Because the items are floated, you need to make sure the footer has floats cleared, otherwise it would float up text to the bottom-rightmost item in the list.

```
.footer {
  clear: both;
}
```

Everything else not specified here is colors and text-alignment. If you want to see the rest you can check out the source code. See the introduction for the location.

Summary

Flexible layouts allow you to use the same site to handle multiple screen sizes. By using flexible containers and media queries, we can create two-column, three-column, ten-column, or more layouts that easily adapt to the devices that view them. Sites often need flexible navigation as well, which is something you will learn about in the next chapter.

CHAPTER 4

■ ■ ■

Flexible Navigation

In the last chapter we discussed creating a responsive, flexible layout and worked through several patterns. But none of them had the one element that you find on virtually every website: the navigation menu. Even though responsive navigation uses some of the tricks of responsive layout, it has its own problems and patterns, so I wanted to discuss it separately. One big difference between the patterns here and those in the last chapter is that JavaScript can start playing a major part, though this will bring in its own challenges. Note that all samples assume the basic CSS reset that was used at the beginning of Chapter 2. The samples were all tested on our standard device testing set as listed in the introduction.

All of the following patterns have one thing in common: on mobile, we are trying to hide/move/minimize the navigation to get the user to the content as soon as possible, yet still have the navigation within easy reach. On desktop monitors, it is usually trivial to accommodate both navigation and content in a single glance. On mobile devices, this is often much more difficult.

Making the Horizontal Menu Vertical

In the first chapter on the basics of responsive web design we used one easy pattern, which simply involved taking the horizontal navigation and turning it vertical again, which you can see in Figure 4-1. This was achieved with some simple CSS for removing the floats and applying a little formatting.

Figure 4-1. *Making a horizontal menu vertical for smaller screens*

Because that was described in Chapter 1, we won't go into much detail about that now. But here is a review. You may recall that our menu was implemented as an unordered list like this:

```
<ul class="nav">
  <li class="nav-item"><a href="/">Home</a></li>
  <li class="nav-item"><a href="/">Alpha Program</a></li>
  <li class="nav-item"><a href="/">About Apress</a></li>
  <li class="nav-item"><a href="/">Support</a></li>
</ul>
```

The CSS for making the unordered list lay out horizontally was as follows.

```
.nav {
  overflow: hidden;
}

.nav li {
  float: left;
  margin-left: 17px;
}
```

After reading Chapter 2, this CSS should make sense. The list items are all floated, which causes them to stack horizontally instead of vertically. They are also given a left margin for a little spacing as well. The list itself has `overflow: hidden` applied to keep its height from collapsing because all its child elements are floated.

But this menu has a problem on smaller screens because the floated elements will start wrapping to the next line. To accommodate this, we change the menu to a vertical list on smaller screens.

```
@media screen and (max-width: 425px) {
  .nav li {
    float: none;
    margin: 0;
    padding: 12px 0;
    text-align: center;
  }
}
```

This CSS change is wrapped in a media query so it only applies to screens that are 425 pixels or smaller. In this media query we remove the floats and margins as well as add some vertical padding to space the elements out.

You'll find that this is the simplest approach for handling single-level navigation menus. This approach has one significant negative to it, however, which is that it forces the user to scroll to see the content that was presumably the focus all along. The longer the menu, the longer the user would have to scroll. The following patterns handle this problem better.

Moving the Menu to the Bottom

This pattern solves the navigation-first problem by moving the menu to the bottom, with a link at the top that takes you to the menu so you don't have to scroll all the way down past the content to get to it. You can see an example of this in Figure 4-2. Fortunately, this pattern is also very easy to implement, and you will learn two separate ways of implementing it. Both implementations work well, but the first is a bit easier to understand, so we'll start there.

Figure 4-2. *Showing the menu up top on wide screens, below on smaller screens*

The core idea of the pattern is that on larger screens the menu is shown near the top; but on smaller screens the menu is shown at the bottom. So that the user doesn't have to scroll all the way down the screen to get to the menu, a link to the menu is shown at the top.

We start with our basic markup with the most important bits highlighted.

```
<div id="content">
  <a id="menuLink" href="#menu">Menu</a>
  <header>
    <h1>Responsive Navigation</h1>
  </header>
  <nav id="navTop">
    <ul>
      <li><a href="#">First Link</a></li>
      <li><a href="#">Second Link</a></li>
      <li><a href="#">Third Link</a></li>
    </ul>
  </nav>
  <div id="primary">
    <p>Lorem ipsum dolor sit amet...</p>
  </div>
  <div id="sidebar">
    <p>Vestibulum ante ipsum primis...</p>
  </div>
```

```
   <nav id="navBottom">
     <a name="menu"></a>
     <ul>
       <li><a href="#">First Link</a></li>
       <li><a href="#">Second Link</a></li>
       <li><a href="#">Third Link</a></li>
     </ul>
   </nav>
</div>
```

The CSS for creating the basic layout is as follows:

```
#content {
  max-width: 960px;
  margin: 0 auto;
  outline: solid 1px #000;
  overflow: auto;
}

header {
  border-bottom: solid 1px#EEE ;
  padding: 15px;
}

nav {
  background-color: #000;
  clear: both;
  overflow: auto; /* keeps the ul from collapsing (see chapter 2) */
  padding-left: 15px;
}

li {
  border-right: solid 1px #777;
  float: left;
  list-style-type: none;
  padding: 3px 5px;
  width: 100px;
}

li a {
  color: #FFF;
  text-decoration: none;
}

#primary {
  float: left;
  padding: 3%;
  width: 60.66666%;
}
```

```
#sidebar {
  background-color: #EEE;
  float: left;
  padding: 3%;
  width: 27.33333%
}

#menuLink {
  background-color: #000;
  color: #FFF;
  min-height: 35px;
  padding: 15px 15px 0 0;
  text-align: right;
  text-decoration: none;
}

#navBottom, #menuLink {
  display: none; /* Both the menu link and the nav in the bottom are hidden by default. */
}
```

To handle the navigation layout for smaller devices, the following media query is used, which will be applied when the screen is 500 pixels or smaller.

```
@media screen and (max-width: 500px) {
  nav {
    padding: 0;
  }

  #navTop { /* This hides the topmost menu. */
    display: none;
  }

  #menuLink { /* This will show the link at the top, which will skip the user to the bottom menu. */
    display: block;
  }

  #navBottom { /* By default the bottom menu is hidden. This shows it. */
    display: block;
  }

  /* All the rest of the CSS changes are concerned with switching to a single-column layout. */
  li {
    border-bottom: solid 1px #555;
    float: none;
    padding: 10px 0;
    text-align: center;
    width: auto;
  }
```

```
li a {
  display: block;
  height: 100%;
}

#primary, #sidebar {
  float: none;
  width: 94%;
}
}
```

So with simple markup and relatively straightforward CSS, the effect we want is achieved. But before we discuss the strengths and weaknesses of this approach, let us see another way to implement a similar pattern. This approach creates one visual difference, reversing the position of the header text and the menu in the widescreen design. It looks like Figure 4-3.

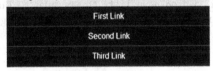

Figure 4-3. *Our second implementation of putting the menu at the bottom of smaller screens*

Why the difference? This implementation removes the duplicated menu, putting it only at the bottom. To achieve this effect, here are the CSS changes you need to make:

```
nav { /* take the nav from its default position and stick it at the top of the screen. */
  position: absolute;
  top: 0;
}

header { /* since the nav is now at the top, bump the header down to make room for it */
  margin-top: 30px;
}

@media screen and (max-width: 500px) {
  header { /* the extra margin in the header is no longer needed to accommodate the navigation. */
    margin-top: 0;
  }

  nav { /* reset to default behavior, which pops the menu back to where it belongs in the layout. */
    position: static;
    top: auto;
  }
}
```

Even though the nav is located at the bottom of the page, you use CSS to move it to the very top for all wide screens. Using absolute positioning, it's easy to put it at the very top of the page. You could also position it below the header by setting a fixed height on the header, but this is easiest. But when the screen is 500 pixels or smaller, the media query kicks in and puts the nav back to where it belongs by default, putting the navigation back at the bottom.

Both work fine, though the first suffers from duplicate HTML and the second is just a bit more complicated. Both will also work on devices without media query support because the default styling puts the navigation at the top, which is a good default.

Turning the Menu into a Select

Another way to deal with a potentially large navigation menu is to get rid of it entirely and turn it into an HTML select element (aka, a drop-down list). One popular .NET developer blog (http://www.hanselman.com) used this approach in the previous design of his blog, as seen in Figure 4-4.

Figure 4-4. *Scott Hanselman's blog*

This approach is easy to implement and works with few caveats. The markup is very similar to the above. Note the addition of the select.

```
<nav id="navTop">
  <ul>
    <li><a href="#">First Link</a></li>
    <li><a href="#">Second Link</a></li>
    <li><a href="#">Third Link</a></li>
  </ul>
  <select id="selectNav"></select>
</nav>
```

Note that there is nothing in the select. We will use a little JavaScript to fill that. The following CSS can be added to the above to give us all the styling implementation that we need:

```
#selectNav { /* By default, hide the select. */
  display: none;
}

/* When the screen gets too small, hide the main nav and show the select */
@media screen and (max-width: 500px) {
  #navTop ul {
    display: none;
  }

  #selectNav {
    display: block;
    width: 100%;
  }
}
```

So how do we fill that select? We will use a short script with some jQuery to make this easier, though you could obviously do something similar without it.

```
$(document).ready(function () {

  var nav = $('#selectNav');
  //We need to create an option in the select for every anchor tag in the
  //   nav, so we use the jQuery each function.
  $('nav li a').each(function() {

    var anchor = $(this);

    //This creates a DOM object and adds the specified attributed to
    //   the element.
    var option = $('<option />', {
      value: anchor.attr('href'),
      text: anchor.text()
    });

    nav.append(option);
  });
```

```
nav.change(function () {
  window.location = $(this).find("option:selected").val();
});
});
```

When the page is loaded, the select menu is created from the links in the navigation. If the screen is over 500 pixels in width, the select is hidden and the main navigation is visible. If the screen size is 500 pixels or smaller, the main navigation is hidden and the select is shown. When an option from the select is selected, the select's change event is fired and the window location changes, loading the new page. You can see this approach in Figure 4-5.

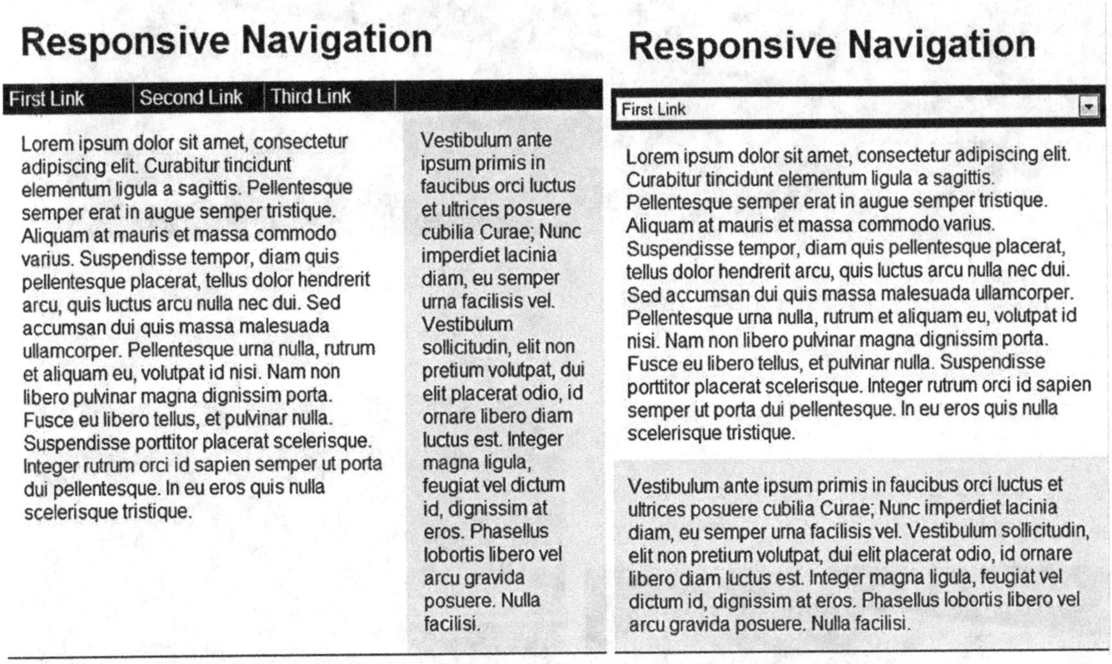

Responsive Navigation

First Link	Second Link	Third Link

Lorem ipsum dolor sit amet, consectetur adipiscing elit. Curabitur tincidunt elementum ligula a sagittis. Pellentesque semper erat in augue semper tristique. Aliquam at mauris et massa commodo varius. Suspendisse tempor, diam quis pellentesque placerat, tellus dolor hendrerit arcu, quis luctus arcu nulla nec dui. Sed accumsan dui quis massa malesuada ullamcorper. Pellentesque urna nulla, rutrum et aliquam eu, volutpat id nisi. Nam non libero pulvinar magna dignissim porta. Fusce eu libero tellus, et pulvinar nulla. Suspendisse porttitor placerat scelerisque. Integer rutrum orci id sapien semper ut porta dui pellentesque. In eu eros quis nulla scelerisque tristique.

Vestibulum ante ipsum primis in faucibus orci luctus et ultrices posuere cubilia Curae; Nunc imperdiet lacinia diam, eu semper urna facilisis vel. Vestibulum sollicitudin, elit non pretium volutpat, dui elit placerat odio, id ornare libero diam luctus est. Integer magna ligula, feugiat vel dictum id, dignissim at eros. Phasellus lobortis libero vel arcu gravida posuere. Nulla facilisi.

Responsive Navigation

First Link	▼

Lorem ipsum dolor sit amet, consectetur adipiscing elit. Curabitur tincidunt elementum ligula a sagittis. Pellentesque semper erat in augue semper tristique. Aliquam at mauris et massa commodo varius. Suspendisse tempor, diam quis pellentesque placerat, tellus dolor hendrerit arcu, quis luctus arcu nulla nec dui. Sed accumsan dui quis massa malesuada ullamcorper. Pellentesque urna nulla, rutrum et aliquam eu, volutpat id nisi. Nam non libero pulvinar magna dignissim porta. Fusce eu libero tellus, et pulvinar nulla. Suspendisse porttitor placerat scelerisque. Integer rutrum orci id sapien semper ut porta dui pellentesque. In eu eros quis nulla scelerisque tristique.

Vestibulum ante ipsum primis in faucibus orci luctus et ultrices posuere cubilia Curae; Nunc imperdiet lacinia diam, eu semper urna facilisis vel. Vestibulum sollicitudin, elit non pretium volutpat, dui elit placerat odio, id ornare libero diam luctus est. Integer magna ligula, feugiat vel dictum id, dignissim at eros. Phasellus lobortis libero vel arcu gravida posuere. Nulla facilisi.

Figure 4-5. Our implementation of turning the navigation menu into an HTML select

This approach is great in that it can handle menus of any size and make them all tiny. Even multi-level menus can be handled by using the optgroup tag in the select, though the JavaScript would get a bit more complicated. This is exactly how multiple levels of navigation hierarchy are handled on Scott Hanselman's blog above. His primary navigation gets switched out for a select at 720 pixels.

The obvious strength in this approach is that it minimizes the navigation effectively. Devices will also have a native selection control when the user chooses the select, which is nice. The negative is that it requires JavaScript. If the browser has media query support but JavaScript is turned off, small devices will get no navigation menu unless you put the work in to handle that situation.

Creating Accordion-Style Navigation at the Top

Another useful pattern involves keeping the menu at the top but hiding it. This is the approach that http://www.microsoft.com took in its responsive design, seen in Figure 4-6. At around 550 pixels their menu switches from horizontal to hidden with a menu icon to press to reveal the menu. The menu is also animated as it opens and closes, a nice touch.

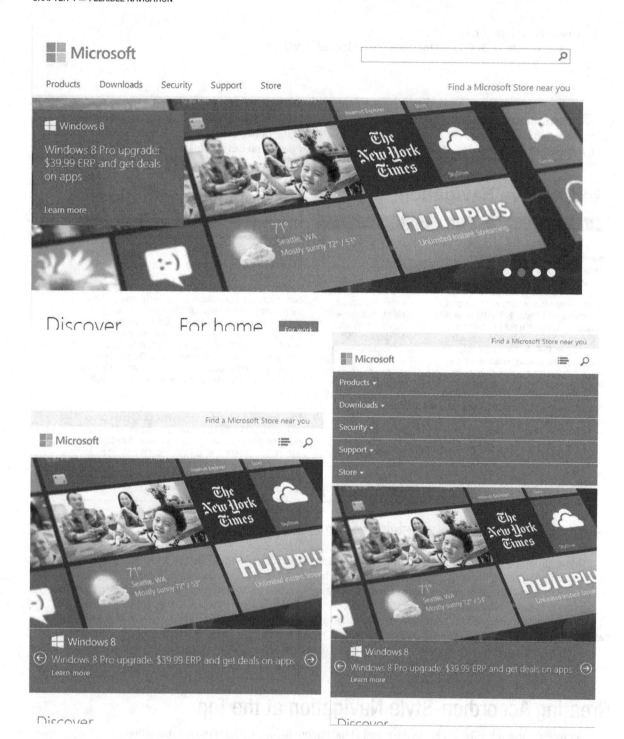

Figure 4-6. *The first image shows the Microsoft home page as viewed in a desktop browser, the second two in a smaller browser. Note that the menu in the smaller browser screenshot is collapsed in the image on the left and expanded in the image on the right*

Let's discuss how we would implement a similar menu. Like the last pattern, I am going to use JavaScript to make this work, but I will use it as little as possible (and less than the `microsoft.com` site uses). As for our implementation, the larger screen size will look like the screen you are by now familiar with though the smaller screen will look like Figure 4-7:

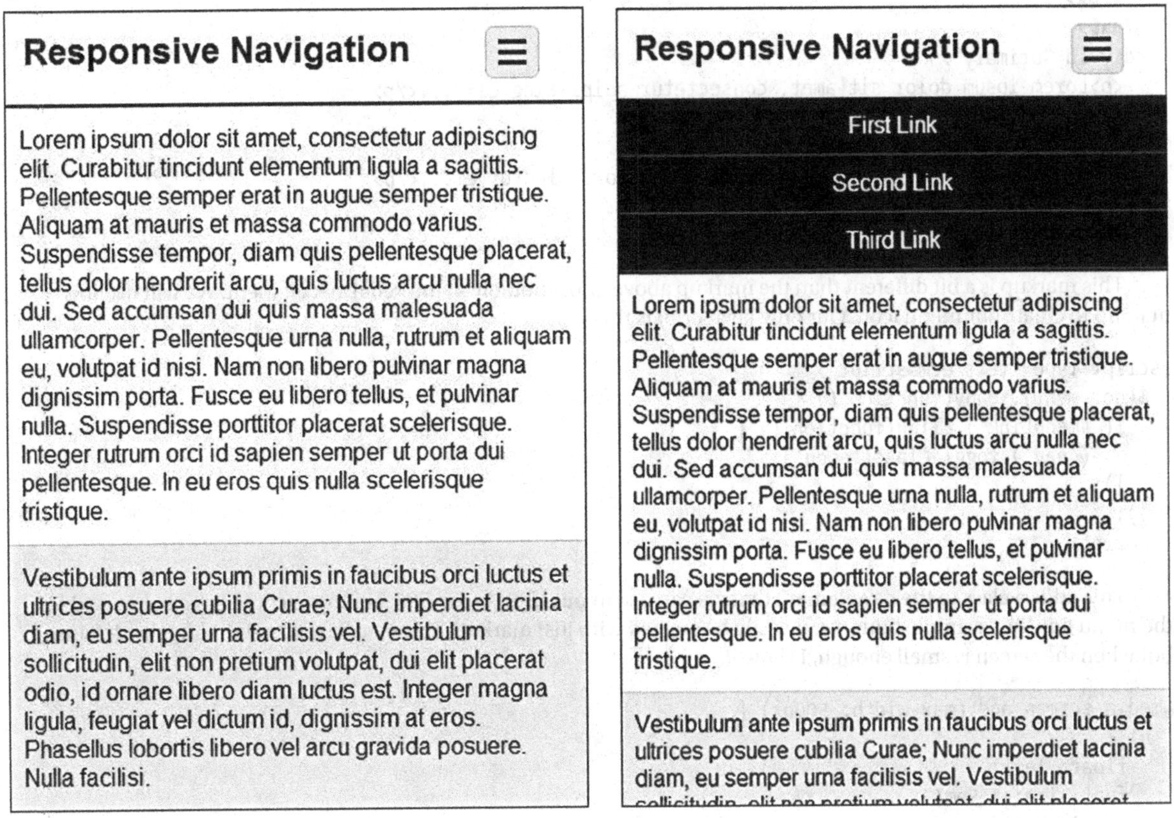

Figure 4-7. *An accordion-style menu*

We start with our markup:

```
<div id="content">
  <header>
    <h1>Responsive Navigation</h1>
    <div id="menuLink">
      <span class="menuBarGroup">
        <span class="menuBar"></span>
        <span class="menuBar"></span>
        <span class="menuBar"></span>
      </span>
    </div>
  </header>
```

```
  <nav>
    <ul>
      <li><a href="#">First Link</a></li>
      <li><a href="#">Second Link</a></li>
      <li><a href="#">Third Link</a></li>
    </ul>
  </nav>
  <div id="primary">
    <p>Lorem ipsum dolor sit amet, consectetur adipiscing elit...</p>
  </div>
  <div id="secondary">
    <p>Vestibulum ante ipsum primis in faucibus orci luctus et...</p>
  </div>
</div>
```

This markup is a bit different than the markup above, most notably in the menuLink element. We will use this markup to create our menu icon. Our only JavaScript is this.

```
<script type="text/ecmascript">
  $(document).ready(function () {
    $('#menuLink').click(function () {
      $('nav').toggleClass('open');
    });
  });
</script>
```

This adds a class to the nav element that we can use in our CSS. As for CSS, an image could have been used for the menu link, but a simple button can easily be created with just markup. This menuBarGroup is hidden by default, but when the screen is small enough, I show it.

```
@media screen and (max-width: 500px) {
  h1 {
    float: left;
    font-size: 1.5em;
    margin-bottom: 15px;
    max-width: 80%;
  }

  #menuLink {
    display: block;
    float: right;
    width: 40px;
  }

  .menuBarGroup {
    background-color: #eee;
    border: solid 1px #ccc;
    border-radius: 5px;
    display: block;
    overflow: auto;
    padding: 8px 8px 4px 8px;
    width: 19px;
  }
```

```
.menuBar {
  background-color: #000;
  display: block;
  height: 3px;
  margin-bottom: 4px;
  width: 19px;
  }
}
```

To fit the menu link beside the heading, I float both the menuLink and h1 elements beside each other. This gives us a simple menu icon.

As for the menu itself, the styling looks like the following. (The lines in bold are those that create the transition effect.)

```
@media screen and (max-width: 500px) {

  nav {
    height: 0;
    overflow: hidden;
    -webkit-transition: all .5s ease;
    -moz-transition: all .5s ease;
    -o-transition: all .5s ease;
    transition: all .5s ease;
  }

  nav.open {
    height: auto;
    min-height:40px;
    max-height:400px;
  }
}
```

The styling for the list items is like that in the first example in the chapter. The only difference is how we are styling the containing nav element. When the screen is 500 pixels or less, by default, the nav element is given a height of 0, effectively hiding the menu items. When expanded, the height is changed to auto, which will size the nav by the actual height of all its child elements.

To create the animation of expanding/shrinking navigation, I used CSS3 transitions. To get this to work, the first obvious addition will be the rules for transitioning. All properties are transitioned (only height differs in this case, but in my experimentation using all here worked better due to buggy height transitioning, discussed a bit more below), the transition lasts for half a second and an "ease" timing function is used to determine how the intermediate steps in the animation are calculated. Appropriate browser-specific prefixes are used to target older devices/browsers that may not implement the final, non-prefixed standard notation. One is not included for Internet Explorer because you either have transition (IE 10) or you don't (< IE 10), so a prefix would bring no benefit. Browsers that do not support transitions will simply snap the menu open and closed as the open class is added/removed from the nav element, giving you good backward compatibility. For more information on CSS transitions, see Chapter 9, "Native APIs, HTML5 and CSS3 on Mobile Today".

The remaining CSS in bold above is required, but its function is probably not obvious to most. First, an overflow of hidden is set on the nav element because otherwise a scrollbar appears in the element as the animation progresses. After all, the content will not fit in the containing element at first because there isn't enough room, so a desktop browser will by default add a scrollbar. Hiding the overflow solves this problem.

Second, you cannot animate height from 0 to auto. You can either animate to a set height (which means you need to pay close attention to the actual height of the navigation and when it changes, update the CSS) or you can set a min- and max-height value, in which case the transition will work. But even this is tricky. When the open class is added to the nav, the animation will move forward. When the class is removed, it will move backward. In the backward animation, it will start at the min-height and animate from there. This is only very noticeable when the min-height is significantly smaller than the actual size of the element. So it is best to set the min-height close to the actual height and the max-height close to the actual height, which is only slightly less work than actually figuring out the exact pixel height of the nav element. It is your choice how you want to handle the animation as both work. Alternatively, you could handle the animation entirely with JavaScript.

Creating Off-Canvas Flyout Navigation

Our last pattern hides the navigation off-screen. Facebook and Google popularized this pattern on their mobile sites, though their implementations are not responsive. Figure 4-8 shows what Facebook's looks like:

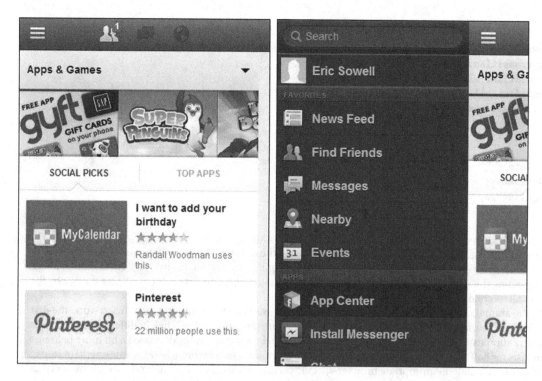

Figure 4-8. *Facebook's off-canvas navigation*

Our implementation will be responsive (of course). Since we are using old but well-supported CSS tricks for layout, this implementation works for all our targeted devices. The basic idea behind this pattern is that the menu is hidden, but it slides into place whenever the user clicks on the navigation button. When the menu slides into place, the content slides off the right-hand side of the screen. If the navigation button is clicked a second time, the menu slides back off and the content resumes its normal position. Sound easy? Figure 4-9 shows what our final result will look like.

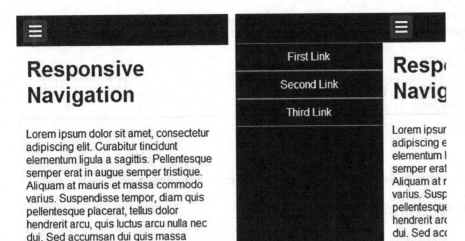

Figure 4-9. *Implementing off-canvas navigation*

Our HTML has to be a little different than the markup we had before, so here it is:

```
<div class="pageWrapper">
  <div class="contentWrapper">
    <div id="menuLink">
      <span class="menuBarGroup">
        <span class="menuBar"></span>
        <span class="menuBar"></span>
        <span class="menuBar"></span>
      </span>
    </div>
    <header>
      <h1>Responsive Navigation</h1>
    </header>
    <nav>
      <ul>
        <li><a href="#">First Link</a></li>
        <li><a href="#">Second Link</a></li>
        <li><a href="#">Third Link</a></li>
        <li><a href="#">Fourth Link</a></li>
      </ul>
    </nav>
    <div class="content">
      <div class="primary">
        <p>Lorem ipsum dolor sit amet, consectetur adipiscing elit...</p>
      </div>
      <div class="secondary">
        <p>Vestibulum ante ipsum primis in faucibus orci luctus et...</p>
      </div>
    </div>
  </div>
</div>
```

The important addition is highlighted. I'll explain why we need this extra containing div shortly. Note that the nav is nested within contentWrapper. As for the JavaScript, it's just like as in the previous sample.

```
<script type="text/ecmascript">
  $(document).ready(function () {
    $('#menuLink').click(function () {
      $('body').toggleClass('open');
    });
  });
</script>
```

The CSS for general formatting is similar to that above, so we will only concern ourselves with the new styling.

```
@media screen and (max-width: 400px) {

  nav {
    background-color: #000;
    height: 100%;
    position: absolute;
    top: 0;
    left: -70%;
    width: 70%;
  }

  nav ul {
    margin-top: 45px;
  }

  nav li {
    border-right: none;
    border-bottom: solid 1px #777;
    border-top: solid 1px #777;
    float: none;
    padding: 10px 0;
    text-align: center;
    width: 100%;
  }

  .contentWrapper {
    -webkit-transition: all .5s ease;
    transition: all .5s ease;
    position: relative;
  }
}
```

First let's discuss the styling relevant before the user clicks the button. The nav element is positioned absolutely, left 70 percent of the width of the screen. Since the nav element is also 70 percent in width, this hides it just off the screen. The styling for the ul and li is important to how things look but not important for the core layout, so we can skip discussing that. To open up the navigation, a class is added to the body, at which point the following is relevant.

```
@media screen and (max-width: 400px) {

  .open .contentWrapper {
    left: 70%;
  }

  .pageWrapper {
    overflow-x: hidden;
  }
}
```

At this point the contentWrapper element slides over from the left 70 percent. The nav element, which is already positioned 70 percent left of the contentWrapper, now slides into view. If you've been keeping track of the math, at this point the nav plus contentWrapper is actually 140 percent the width of the device. Unless we do something the page will now have scrollbars if it's on a desktop browser. If on a mobile browser, the page can now be wiggled (technical terminology) left and right. To solve this problem we have the pageWrapper element whose overflow-x value is set to hidden, which allows the contentWrapper to slide to the right without affecting actual page width. Note that -x must be specified, since we want the user to be able to scroll down the screen.

This responsive navigation technique can also benefit from some CSS transitions, so this was added to the contentWrapper. The simple transition declaration will animate the move from left: 0 to left: 70 percent for devices that support transitions. For those that do not, the element will snap into place and the transition statements are ignored.

Summary

We have now covered five different flexible and responsive navigation solutions. There are more patterns to follow, and new ones are being pioneered all the time. You can see that the techniques involved are not much different than what we used to create flexible layouts, which is a good thing. Now it is time to deal with content. If the layout and navigation are flexible, the content has to be flexible as well.

CHAPTER 5

■ ■ ■

Flexible Content

Now we have reached our discussion on flexible content, perhaps the most important part of a responsive web design. If the content of your website does not work well on a wide range of devices, having flexible layout and navigation is of little value. After all, layout and navigation exist to present the *content* of your site.

Once again, techniques for being responsive are advancing, so what you see here should be considered a starting place or a way to get you thinking, not *the only way* of making the content of your site responsive. Unlike before, we will be primarily concerned with flexibility in two different ways, both flexibility of size on screen (like before) but also size in bytes transferred in the case of images. It is easy to create a responsive design for a site that delivers the same content to both mobile and desktop. Unfortunately, this often means that you will be delivering more to the mobile device than it actually needs, which is bad for devices with slower bandwidths. So now you'll learn about flexible content and see how you can solve this problem.

In order to support mobile, some sites remove content because dealing with mobile can sometimes be difficult. I consider this to be cheating. If something can be cut to streamline for mobile, consider cutting it for desktop as well, since it is obviously not that important. Mobile users don't expect to visit a site on mobile and lose functionality or content. Responsive web design is about making the same content work on both mobile and desktop, so we will avoid all techniques that remove content to make mobile "work," because that's not making mobile work as it should. So when I say flexible content, I don't mean that we should remove content. We should make it adapt.

The quickest way to cut the bandwidth requirements of our mobile sites may be to remove content; but as I said above, this is usually a bad idea. Because many people only access the web on a mobile device, removing content on mobile may keep some who visit the site from ever seeing the content they need. You can't assume that the visitor to your site will use a desktop in conjunction with their mobile device while using your site. You can't even assume that they *own* one. Instead, whenever possible, keep the same content and make it flexible but watch the bandwidth usage. Most of this chapter is centered around flexible content in terms of fitting everything on any screen, but the section on flexible images will also cover ways to save the visitor to your site from downloading too much.

In this chapter, we'll break up common content into different types of content. The first, easiest, and most important will be text followed by tables, video, and images.

Flexible Text

Text on the web has always been flexible and is the easiest type of content to deal with in a responsive manner. As the container of a text changes size, text conveniently and automatically breaks between words causing wrapping, which allows text to adapt well to different screen sizes. And unlike some other content types, in most cases we will want to show the same text to mobile and desktop users because text is bandwidth-friendly. But this doesn't mean we should ignore text while thinking responsively. Let's start by setting up some ground rules on how text sizing works on the Web and then move on to how best to tweak it.

The default font size for mobile and desktop browsers is 16 pixels. Confirming this is easy. I created a page to show off the following markup and tried it on every device and browser I could find. The result can be seen in Figure 5-1.

```
<h1>Font size not set</h1>
<h1 style="font-size: 32px;">Font size set to 32px</h1>

<h2>Font size not set</h2>
<h2 style="font-size: 24px;">Font size set to 24px</h2>

<p>Font size not set.</p>
<p style="font-size: 16px;">Font size set to 16px.</p>
```

Font size not set

Font size set to 32px

Font size not set

Font size set to 24px

Font size not set.

Font size set to 16px.

Figure 5-1. My default text size test page viewed on an iPhone 4S running iOS 6

The test is fairly straightforward. If the text sizes for any of those three elements that had no CSS ever differed from those that did, then that browser would not default to the specified size. But they all did, so until a browser comes out that changes this, we can make the following three assumptions: default text is sized at 16 pixels, h2 tags are sized at 1.5 times the size of default text, and h1 tags are sized as two times the size of default text. So by default, all the browsers size text according to a set of standard proportions. As we change the size of the text we will maintain these ratios, though you can always change them for your own sites.

Table 5-1. *Default Browser Font Sizes*

Tag	Default Size
h1	32 pixels
h2	24 pixels
h3	19 pixels
h4	16 pixels
h5	13 pixels
P	16 pixels

Em

Next let's discuss a different unit of measurement, one that we should generally be using when sizing text instead of pixels, and that is the "em". The em is a better measurement for thinking about text. Unlike pixels, it is a relative unit of measurement. Applying a value of 1.1em to the font size of an element increases the size by 10 percent, whatever the starting font size is. This means that em-sized elements can depend on the sizes of other elements. This will give us some nice abilities that we will exploit below. I also bring this up at this point because it's a unit that web designers generally prefer and, if we reinterpret our data above, actually makes for easier numbers. Let's talk about that a bit more.

Historically the em comes from printing, where an em as a unit of measure is equal to the width of the capital letter M in any given typeface. When it comes to browsers, 1 em is equal to the default font size of the browser. So in our examples above, the default size of a p element is 1 em, an h2 element is 1.5 ems and an h1 element 2 ems. When expressed in ems, the pattern of the sizes is more obvious but that's not surprising because typography geeks are more likely to talk in ems and not in pixels. Given the "coincidence" here, I presume that this was something the browser makers thought as well.

Because ems are generally the preferred unit for designers and because they express proportions better, we will use ems instead of pixels in all our discussions about sizing text.

Another interesting side effect of using ems is that nested elements with em measurement are compounded. Let me explain what I mean. Let's say you have the following bit of HTML.

```
<p style="font-size: 1.2em;">This is a paragraph</p>

<div style="font-size: 1.2em;">
  <p style="font-size: 1.2em;">This paragraph is nested.</p>
</div>
```

Is the first paragraph the same font size as the second paragraph? No. The first paragraph is about 19 pixels in size, the second is about 23 pixels in size. The second is larger because it also picks up the font size increase of its parent div. The first paragraph is 20 percent larger than the default font size, the font size for the second increased by 20 percent because of the parent div and then increased 20 percent again by its own font setting.

As you may guess, this can lead to problems if you don't pay close attention to how you nest and size your HTML. But it's also a very valuable tool. If you want to change the text size of a given page and make everything just a bit bigger, you could change the styling for every HTML tag on the page or you could add a style rule to change the font size of the body tag to 1.1 ems and bump up the size all tags in one easy change by 10 percent. This is a very powerful tool and something we will come back to momentarily.

Rem

The nesting capability of ems can be either a blessing or a curse, depending on how you structure your HTML and CSS. Even though ems are great for sizing text, the negative side effect I mention led to the development of the rem, which stands for "root em". If an element is sized with a rem instead of an em, the proportional size expressed in the em is sized in relation to the root of the document, the html tag. In other words, if we take our previous example and change the nested paragraph to use a rem, the size of the first paragraph and the second are now the same.

```
<p style="font-size: 1.2em;">This is a paragraph</p>

<div style="font-size: 1.2em;">
  <p style="font-size: 1.2rem;">This paragraph is nested.</p>
</div>
```

Using rems gives you the benefit of ems but makes it harder for you to accidentally change font sizes by nesting elements. Desktop browser support is good (IE 9+, Chrome, Firefox, Opera, Safari) but mobile browser support is ubiquitous in modern smartphones, so it can be safely used.

Line Height

Font size across mobile devices is remarkably consistent. Unfortunately line height (often called "leading", referring to the strips of lead between lines of text in printing presses) has no such uniformity. Just for a few examples, IE 10 on Windows 8 defaults to around 18.4 pixels, Android-based browsers (including Kindle browsers), Firefox OS and Opera around 19.2 pixels, Windows Phone 7 around 21.44 pixels, and iOS around 20.8 pixels.

It would be very reasonable to wonder why these (seemingly) strange decimal numbers were chosen. But if we convert the pixel sizes to ems, some of them seem less arbitrary. Android browsers have a default line height of 1.2 ems and iOS browsers have a default line height of 1.3 ems. Internet Explorer seems to work a bit differently though, with line heights of 1.15 ems for version 10 (desktop) and 1.34 for version 7 and 8 on the phone. We are left with the sizes in Table 5-2.

Table 5-2. *Default Line Heights for Mobile Browsers*

Browser	Pixels	Ems
Windows Phone 7, 8	21.44 px	1.34 em
iOS	20.8 px	1.3 em
Android, Firefox OS, Opera	19.2 px	1.2 em
Desktop IE 10 on Windows 8	18.4 px	1.15 em

Fortunately all of these browsers can be made consistent by a little CSS. Decide on the size you like, and set it with the CSS line-height property.

Responsive Text

Now that we have the core ideas in our mind, we can now think responsively and see how hard it is to style flexibly with text. Let's take a simple example, exemplified by Figure 5-2. The HTML for it is straightforward.

```
<h1>Lorem ipsum dolor sit amet</h1>
<p>Lorem ipsum dolor sit amet, consectetur adipiscing elit. Nullam vel justo eros...</p>
```

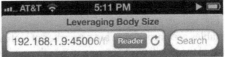

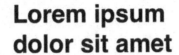

Figure 5-2. *Sizing text with media queries*

The CSS is as follows. The media query is missing from the first shot in Figure 5-2.

```
h1 {
  font-family: Helvetica, sans-serif;
  font-size: 2em;
}

p {
  font-family: Georgia, serif;
  font-size: 1.2em;
  line-height: 1.5em;
}

@media screen and (max-width: 400px) {
  body {
    font-size: 1.1em;
  }
}
```

Regardless of whether you would prefer the text to be smaller or larger on the phone, the technique is the same. Note that only the font size of the body was changed, but the heading and the paragraph both increased. The cascading effect of our em-based sizing makes it easy to change the size of all the text, larger or smaller, just by changing one element in a media query.

Flexible Tables

Flexible text is easy; flexible tables are hard. There are a number of techniques, all of which have their drawbacks. It may be the case that several of these will work for you, in which case you have multiple techniques you can use. Let's start with what already works well with tables and what doesn't and follow it up with some techniques to solve these problems.

Plain Tables

First of all, there is a level of flexibility built into HTML tables. Unless explicit widths are set on columns, tables will flex without any special treatment, at least up to a point. In order to accommodate smaller screens, tables will insert line breaks between words in table cells causing the text to wrap (just as browsers insert line breaks when a line of text in a paragraph gets too long), stretching the table vertically. Once line breaks can no longer be added to make a table narrower, the table will stop shrinking. If that is larger than the size of your flexible layout, the table will break it. For example, let's say you have a flexible layout that normally sizes just fine on an iPhone in portrait mode, which is 320 pixels wide. In this case the user can scroll vertically but not horizontally, because the width is 320 pixels and the browser knows that the user can't scroll horizontally because the content is the size of the device viewport. Now you add a table that is too large that (we will assume in our hypothetical case) will render at a minimum width of 500 pixels. Now your flexible layout that was 320 pixels is actually 500 pixels in width, and the user will have to scroll both horizontally and vertically to see all of the content. This is obviously not ideal. We need a better way.

Scrolling Table

A very simple way to make your table scroll within the width of the window is to wrap it in a div and set overflow: auto on the div. Though the data on the right side of the table might initially be hidden, this technique allows the user to scroll the table horizontally to see the whole thing. The simplicity of this technique is its strongpoint. This works great unless you want to support Android 2.x, which doesn't support scrolling an element in this way. You also have to be okay with the unsightly scrollbars that will appear on a desktop browser if the browser window is too small. Android 2.x is still quite popular at this time, so this technique really suffers. But perhaps in a few years this will no longer be the case.

De-table the Table

If the table is too large to fit on mobile devices, we can de-table the table by changing its layout. There are several techniques for doing this, although the result from all of them looks like Figure 5-3.

Page	Feb 1	Feb 2	Feb 3	Feb 4	Feb 5	Feb 6	Feb 7	Feb 8	Feb 9	Feb 10	Total	Max	Min	Avg
Serving static files from Node.js	101	68	61	111	122	131	104	84	55	70	907	131	55	90.7
Using the Selenium web driver	22	3	9	23	22	28	31	25	7	6	176	28	3	17.6
StructureMap and ASP.NET MVC - Getting Started	6	3	2	7	4	15	12	13	6	5	73	15	2	7.3

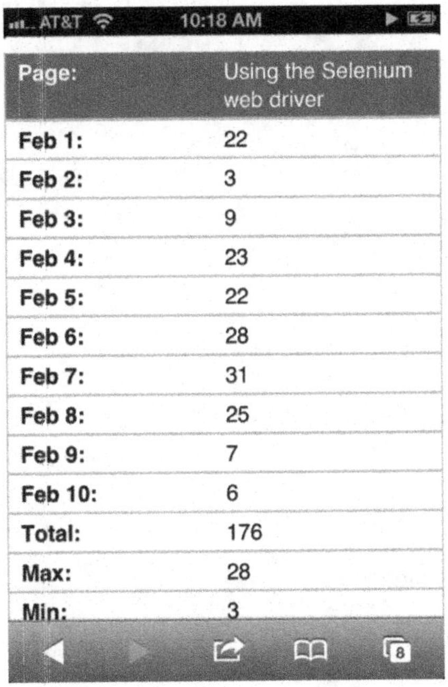

Figure 5-3. The same table, either in its default display or changed through media-query-based CSS

There are essentially two problems to solve here. First, the table elements have to have their default layout changed to something other than the default you get with HTML tables. Second, we want to get the column names from the header and put them to the left of the values as labels. Because I have three data rows and one row of header, this is going to be a difficult one to solve cleanly.

The first approach I tried is by Aaron Gustafson [http://blog.easy-designs.net/archives/2013/02/02/responsive-tables/]. To solve the first problem, he changes the tbody, tr, and td tags to display: block and hides the header. To solve the second problem, he repeats the header names in data attributes on the table cells and uses CSS to pull that out and display it when the media query kicks in. The table would look something like this:

```
<tbody>
  <tr>
    <td data-title="Page">Serving static files from Node.js</td>
    <td data-title="Feb 1">101</td>
    <td data-title="Feb 2">68</td>
    <td data-title="Feb 3">61</td>
    <td data-title="Feb 4">111</td>
    <td data-title="Feb 5">122</td>
    <td data-title="Feb 6">131</td>
    ...
```

The media query for de-tableing would look something like the following. I've highlighted the most important bits.

```
@media screen and (max-width: 960px) {
  thead {
    display: none;
  }

  tbody, tr, td {
    display: block;
  }

  td {
    padding-left: 50%;
  }

  td:first-child {
    background-color: #777;
    color: #FFF;
  }

  td:before {
    content: attr(data-title) ': ';
    display: inline-block;
    font-weight: bold;
    left: 10px;
    margin-right: 15px;
    position: absolute;
  }

  tr {
    margin-top: 15px;
  }
}
```

This is a very clever technique, though it has two flaws that we should mention. First, it doesn't work in Windows Phone 7.5. Traffic for this device is quite low, so this won't bother some people; however, it would be better to have a solution that worked for that device. Second, the extra data elements significantly expand the size of the table and repetition of content leads to maintenance annoyance though server or client-side templating can make this easier. This is a workable solution, but perhaps we can find an improvement.

A variation on this same display:block pattern can be found on CSS Tricks, a site run by Chris Coyier [http://css-tricks.com/examples/ResponsiveTables/responsive.php]. His approach put the labels for the data in the CSS. This is a selection from the CSS to implement this.

```
td:before {
  position: absolute;
  left: 0;
  padding-left: 10px;
}

td:nth-of-type(1):before { content: 'Page'; }
td:nth-of-type(2):before { content: 'Feb 1'; }
td:nth-of-type(3):before { content: 'Feb 2'; }
```

```
td:nth-of-type(4):before { content: 'Feb 3'; }
td:nth-of-type(5):before { content: 'Feb 4'; }
td:nth-of-type(6):before { content: 'Feb 5'; }
td:nth-of-type(7):before { content: 'Feb 6'; }
td:nth-of-type(8):before { content: 'Feb 7'; }
td:nth-of-type(9):before { content: 'Feb 8'; }
td:nth-of-type(10):before { content: 'Feb 9'; }
td:nth-of-type(11):before { content: 'Feb 10'; }
td:nth-of-type(12):before { content: 'Total'; }
td:nth-of-type(13):before { content: 'Max'; }
td:nth-of-type(14):before { content: 'Min'; }
td:nth-of-type(15):before { content: 'Avg'; }
```

One advantage that this approach has over the other is that it avoids messing up the DOM for this new display. It also cuts down on the duplication, so the label data is only duplicated once (the original data being in the header and the duplicated data in the CSS). However, now you have to keep your CSS in sync with your table data. Some may prefer this approach though I like it less. And it also doesn't work on Windows Phone 7.5.

Before we spend more time on the labels, let's solve the display issue with Internet Explorer. Moving everything to display: block did not work, so we will try something else. As it turns out, floating works great. As far as I can see, this works across all modern mobile browsers.

```
@media screen and (max-width: 960px) {

  td {
    float: left;
    padding: 8px 2% 8px 50%;
    position: relative;
    width: 48%;
  }
}
```

Space on the left is made for the labels, which we will come back to shortly. But as you can see, now that we learned how floats work (see Chapter 2 if you skipped it), this is a relatively straightforward approach.

Now back to the label problem. The issue here is that HTML and CSS don't really solve this problem, at least not elegantly. This is a new technique that the browsers are not ready for, and when this happens often the best approach is to use JavaScript. Our goal is to have a plain HTML table that would work responsively that has no duplicate label information. Here is the full implementation, starting with the HTML.

```
<table>
  <thead>
    <tr>
      <td>Page</td>
      <td>Feb 1</td>
      <td>Feb 2</td>
      <td>Feb 3</td>
      <td>Feb 4</td>
      <td>Feb 5</td>
      <td>Feb 6</td>
      <td>Feb 7</td>
      <td>Feb 8</td>
      <td>Feb 9</td>
```

```
          <td>Feb 10</td>
          <td>Total</td>
          <td>Max</td>
          <td>Min</td>
          <td>Avg</td>
        </tr>
    </thead>
    <tbody>
      <tr>
        <td>Serving static files from Node.js</td>
        <td>101</td>
        <td>68</td>
        <td>61</td>
        <td>111</td>
        ...
```

As you can see, the DOM is nice and clean. No extraneous attributes. Next comes the CSS.

```css
td {
  border: solid 1px #CCC;
  padding: 3px 8px;
}

thead td {
  background-color: #777;
  outline: solid 1px #000;
  color: #FFF;
}

@media screen and (max-width: 960px) {
  td:first-child {
    background-color: #777;
    color: #FFF;
  }

  tr:nth-of-type(odd) {
    background-color: #eee;
  }

  thead {
    display: none;
  }

  td {
    float: left;
    padding: 8px 2% 8px 50%;
    position: relative;
    width: 48%;
  }
```

```
  td:before {
    content: attr(data-title) ': ';
    font-weight: bold;
    position: absolute;
    left: 0;
    padding-left: 10px;
  }
}
```

This CSS is a mixture of Gustafson's and my own so that it will work in Windows Phone 7.5. The primary difference between my approach and those above that makes this work is that the previous approaches changed the CSS display attribute of the cells, which doesn't work on Windows Phone 7.5. However, floats work nicely, so we use those to change the layout of the table. We solve the duplicate data problem with a script script (which uses a little jQuery, as you can see) that will dynamically add the data attributes when the page is loaded.

```
<script>
  $(document).ready(function () {

    var headerCells = $('thead td');
    var dataCells = $('tbody td');

    var i, labelIteration = 0, labelIterationMaxLength = headerCells.length;
    for (i = 0; i < dataCells.length; i++) {
      $(dataCells[i]).attr('data-title', headerCells[labelIteration].innerText);

      labelIteration++;
      if (labelIteration == labelIterationMaxLength)
        labelIteration = 0;
    }

  });
</script>
```

Assuming there aren't any row or column spans, this seems to work pretty well. Of course there is a JavaScript dependency at this point, which some might not be comfortable with. This new approach gives you the same result on a small screen that we saw in Figure 5-3 above, though with the added bonus that it now works on Windows Phone 7.5.

FooTable

If you are okay with a JavaScript dependency, another choice to consider is using the FooTable library [http://themergency.com/footable/]. It also supports Windows Phone 7.5, which is a small bonus. This approach solves the problem by keeping the table format initially but collapsing the data, which you can drill down into. For example, here in Figure 5-4 is the same table we saw above using FooTable.

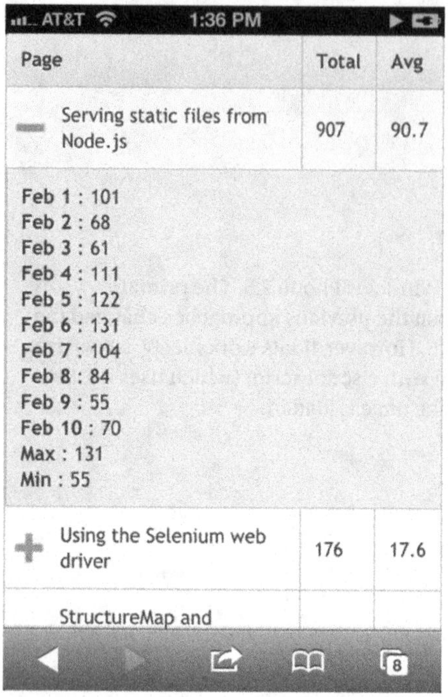

Figure 5-4. *Using FooTable to make my tables more flexible*

Frankly, there is no elegant way of solving this problem at this point. I have given you several options and there are more options/experiments out on the web for handling tables. As I said in the introduction, this is an area of web development that certainly needs to evolve and will over time.

Flexible Video

When I think of video on the web, I generally group usage into two categories: either you are embedding video directly into your site (like using the video tag) or you are including an iframe to a site like YouTube or Vimeo.

Because of the history of video on the web, it is important to note that if you want video to work on mobile, you can never use Flash or Silverlight as your only mechanism for delivering video. Support is either inconsistent or nonexistent, depending on the device. Your only cross-platform way to embed video across modern devices is to use HTML5 video. However, you can consider using Flash or Silverlight with an HTML5 video fallback. If that route makes sense for you, take a look at MediaElement.js [http://mediaelementjs.com/].

HTML5 Video

Let's start with the first case, that of using the HTML5 video element. I find that the HTML5 video is inconsistently flexible. I recorded a video and converted it to various video formats and the video was 568 pixels in width by default. To test this, I used the following.

```
<video controls src="/content/video/sample-video.webm">
  <source src="/content/video/sample-video.mp4" type="video/mp4" />
  <source src="/content/video/sample-video.ogg" type="video/ogg" />
</video>
```

Default Behavior

I applied no CSS to the element, so what I saw is default behavior. The results were inconsistent and unexpected. All iOS versions tested (5, 6, and 7) and Windows Phone 7 and 8 resized the element to fit snugly within my content area, even though I gave it no instructions to do so and went full-screen when the video started playing.

The new webkit-based Opera on Android 4.1 kept the video element at the expected size (568 pixels) when the page was loaded (it all did not fit on the screen) but switched to full-screen mode when playing.

Opera classic on Android 4.1 kept the video element at the expected size when the page was loaded and played it at that same size, with the rightmost portion of the video playing offscreen.

Firefox on Android 4.1 and Firefox OS both showed the video element as a rectangle with rounded edges and a play button. The size of this element was a fixed size taking up somewhere around 250 and 300 pixels. When the play button was hit, the video played without going full screen and played at the expected 568 pixels, so a good portion of the video was off the screen.

Chrome on Android 4.1 displayed the video element at around 80 percent of the width of the window. When the video was played, the element grew to 568 pixels.

The Android browser on Android 4.1 displayed the video element at around 150 pixels. When played, the page was zoomed out so the whole video could be seen on the screen. When finished, it did not zoom back to its original state.

The Android browser on my Android 2.3.5 LG P930 displayed the video element at around 150 pixels like the newer Android but switched into full-screen mode when running the video. When finished, the browser returned by the video element was rendered at the full 568 pixels.

Setting Max-width: 100 Percent

Instead of relying on the default behavior, I decided to use a little CSS and applied a max-width value of 100 percent to the video element on the page. The results were drastically different (and better). There was no change in behavior for Windows Phone or iOS, but their default behavior worked great, anyway.

The video element on the webkit-based Opera on Android 4.1 fit perfectly within the viewport and switched to fullscreen when viewing the video.

Opera classic on Android 4.1 fit perfectly within the viewport and played in the viewport.

Firefox on Android 4.1 and Firefox OS showed the same oddly sized rounded rectangle for the element but when played the video played snugly within the viewport.

The behavior on Chrome for Android 4.1 did not change.

The Android browser on Android 4.1 still displayed the video element at around 150 pixels; but when it played, the video fit snugly in the viewport, and there was no zooming.

The Android browser on my Android 2.3.5 LG P930 displayed the same behavior as before except when the video ended, the video element was fit snugly within the viewport.

Is It That Easy?

Apparently, yes, it is that easy. Setting a max-width of 100 percent on a video tag gets you relatively uniform behavior, at least in terms of the element sizing. There are still some differences, but they are relatively minor.

Embedding Video

The other case we need to handle is video embedding. YouTube will certainly be the most popular video type to embed, but Vimeo is common as well, so we will discuss both. Both of these use iframes for the content, so we need to discuss our options in getting these to be flexible for us.

The following is an example from YouTube followed by an example from Vimeo.

```
<iframe style="width: 420px; height:315px;"
  src="//www.youtube.com/embed/Hq2KXudEjkI"
  frameborder="0"
  allowfullscreen>
</iframe>

<iframe src=http://player.vimeo.com/video/69553622
  style="width: 500px; height: 281px;"
  frameborder="0"
  webkitAllowFullScreen
  mozallowfullscreen
  allowFullScreen>
</iframe>
```

As you can see, in both cases the iframes that the sites give you to embed have explicit height and width values in their styling. You could change that, but it would be nice to have a way of doing this universally. Here are a few options.

Setting Max-width: 100 Percent

The same trick we used with the video tag works surprisingly well on embedded video iframes. Vimeo did not work on all of my test devices (no support for Windows Phone 7.5) but YouTube did, so there is a problem with Vimeo's implementation. In all my test devices except the browser on Android 2 the max-width: 100 percent setting worked. In that case the iframe rendered at the size specified on the iframe rather than following the max-width rule. Another problem is that I changed the style on the iframe to do this, and you may not want to enforce that when videos are embedded in whatever site you are working on. Of course, you could set the max-width at 100 percent in an external style sheet, but that would target all iframes, which may not work for you.

Android 2 is still very common, so this approach may not be acceptable to everyone. Perhaps you should try something else.

Change the Dimensions with a Script

Another technique that works on all of my devices, including Android 2, is to resize the iframe with JavaScript. The sample code below was taken from CSS Tricks [http://css-tricks.com/NetMag/FluidWidthVideo/Article-FluidWidthVideo.php], so thanks to Chris Coyier for posting this. Here is the script, taken as-is from the site. Of course a sample of this is included in this book's sample code as well.

```
// Find all YouTube and Vimeo videos
var $allVideos = $("iframe[src^='http://www.youtube.com'],
  iframe[src^='http://player.vimeo.com']"),

  // The element that is fluid width
  $fluidEl = $("body");

// Figure out and save aspect ratio for each video
$allVideos.each(function () {

  $(this).data('aspectRatio', this.height / this.width)
```

```
        // and remove the hard coded width/height
        .removeAttr('height')
        .removeAttr('width');
});

// When the window is resized
$(window).resize(function () {

    var newWidth = $fluidEl.width();

    // Resize all videos according to their own aspect ratio
    $allVideos.each(function () {

        var $el = $(this);
        $el
          .width(newWidth)
          .height(newWidth * $el.data('aspectRatio'));

    });

    // Kick off one resize to fix all videos on page load
}).resize();
```

Though this requires JavaScript, it is the most consistent approach I have found to having nice responsive video embeds. Another nice option is the FitVids [http://fitvidsjs.com/] library (which Coyier also worked on) if you would rather embed a library that has multiple contributors and is probably kept up to date more than this script.

So flexible video has its challenges but overall is handled rather easily.

Flexible Images

We will end this chapter with a discussion of flexible images, a problem that is solved easily unless you want it solved *well*. First let's identify the problems and then start with the easy approaches since they will work fine in many cases.

The Problems

There are three major issues when it comes to responsive images. First, how do you size images when screen sizes can vary from mobile to desktop? Let's say you have a picture of a dog on your blog in portrait orientation that is 1,000 by 1,333 pixels in size. Everyone *obviously* wants to see this picture of your dog but your blog is responsive and the page might be 320 pixels wide or over 1,000. You could shrink the image to where it is less than 320 pixels wide so it fits well on mobile devices, but now it won't be as nice for your desktop users because they want to see as much detail about your dog as possible. Or you could keep it at its original size but your nice 320-pixel responsive width will be messed up because it will stretch to be the size of your largest piece of content, which in this case would be your loveable dog. What you need is a flexible way to resize that image so that both mobile devices and desktop browsers can view that image in a way that fits their context. In other words, size for different devices is the first problem.

The second problem is resolution. This is a problem for viewing devices of all types, but we will use the iPhone as our example here. The original iPhone was 320 by 480 pixels in resolution. So the screen was 320 hardware pixels wide and 480 hardware pixels high. In CSS, the screen was also 320 by 480 pixels. So if you loaded an image of your dog that was 200 pixels square, those pixels would fit very nicely. The iPhone 4 came out with a display was exactly twice that many pixels, 640 by 960 pixels. But, and this is the tricky part, the browser size in CSS remained 320 by 480 pixels. They maintained the same size in CSS to avoid breaking the browser but now everything needed to actually be increased in size so that the site would look basically the same on both devices, albeit with a better resolution. Things that are natively rendered by the browser, like text and borders, scale up without any issues. But images are problematic. What happens when you take an image that was 200 pixels square and have the browser increase that image to 400 hardware pixels square? You get artifacts and fuzzy images. And moving from a 200 pixel square to a 400 pixel square does not double the number of pixels but quadruples the number of pixels. So the browser has to scale that image up and in the process we get less than ideal images on the web, even though this is caused by the device screens getting better, not worse. So our second problem is getting images to work across different resolutions.

Our third problem is the issue of bandwidth. If you solve the resolution problem by always using higher resolution images and shrinking them down (we will talk about this technique below) in the browser, low-resolution devices are now downloading more data than they need. This obviously affects performance but also might cause problems for those who have to pay for their bandwidth. You may have uploaded a nice, high-resolution photo of your dog, but someone on his or her cheap Android device that has a low-resolution screen may now have to pay too much money to see your dog. So our third problem to solve is the bandwidth issue.

Solving for Image Size

The first issue is solved easily with CSS, though how you solve it will depend on how you are using the images. Let's say you have an image as a part of your content, something simple like this.

```
<img src="my-dog.jpg" alt="my awesome dog." />
```

This image is like that above, 1,000 by 1,333 pixels. If you want this to scale to fit its containing DOM element, you can give it the following CSS, and it will shrink when its container shrinks.

```
img {
  max-width: 100%;
}
```

If you are redoing the design of your blog and are making it responsive, this may be all you need to keep all your content images from messing up your nice responsive layout.

Background images, more often used in the design rather than the content, can be handled similarly.

```
.element-with-fancy-background {
  background-image: url(my-dog.jpg);
  -moz-background-size: 100%;
  -o-background-size: 100%;
  -webkit-background-size: 100%;
  background-size: 100%;
  background-repeat: no-repeat;
}
```

Because background size support is newer to many browsers, I would recommend using the vendor-prefixed version with the normal CSS property. But with the vendor prefixes, this is supported by all modern smartphone browsers. By using these two simple image-sizing techniques, we get easy control over our images and make them flexible.

Solving for Resolution and Bandwidth

Though the first problem is easy to solve, the second two are not. To move toward solving these issues, we need to know what we can know about the devices and will start there. Can we know the resolution of a device? Yes, most of the time, but with inconsistent methods. Let's take this one group of phones at a time.

The resolution of a browser running webkit can be determined by using the non-standard -webkit-min-device-pixel-ratio and -webkit-max-device-pixel-ratio media queries. For example, the iPhones with retina screens have a device pixel ratio of 2. The Galaxy SIII running Chrome or the default browser also reports a 2. The webkit-based version of Opera for Android also supports this media query.

```
@media screen and (-webkit-min-device-pixel-ratio: 2) {
  //whatever CSS you need for higher resolution devices
}
```

Firefox uses the more standards compliant resolution media query. My Geeksphone Keon running Firefox OS matches both of these two media queries.

```
@media (min-resolution: 159dpi) and (max-width: 160dpi) {
  //css
}

@media (min-resolution: 1dppx) and (max-resolution: 2dppx) {
  //css
}
```

■ **Note** Device/pixel ratio refers to the number of actual physical device pixels that make up each CSS pixel. In other words, a retina iPhone device is 640 actual pixels in width but the browser treats the screen as if it is 320 pixels in width, so it has a device/pixel ratio of 2. Non-retina devices are both 320 device pixels across in size and 320 pixels in width in CSS, so they have a device/pixel ratio of 1.

DPI, or dots-per-inch, refers to the number of pixels within the space of an inch on the screen. Going back to our iPhones, a device with a retina screen has 326 pixels per inch, so is 326 DPI. Non-retina iPhones are 163 DPI.

The first media query measures in terms of dots per inch, the second in terms of device pixel ratio. In terms of resolution, we can say that this device is not a high-resolution device. However, Firefox on the Galaxy SIII reports 320dpi and a 3dpr, so it is high-resolution. Note that this is a higher than what Chrome and the default browser report on the same device. Older versions of Opera on Android supported both of these versions of the resolution media query though the newer versions that are webkit-based only support the device pixel ratio media query above.

Windows Phone 7.5 and 8 only support the resolution media query for dpi but both are broken. They always display 96 dpi, though most (all?) newer Windows Phone 8 devices have higher-resolution screens.

All this means that we *can* know through media queries if the devices our users are using have high-resolution screens, unless they are using Windows Phone. But unless things change radically for Windows Phone, chances are that your users are not using those devices. You will just need to just make a choice and serve either low- or high-resolution images to these devices. As for the others, even though we may have to use two media queries to know the resolution, but we can know it.

So how do we use this information? Here's an example of how we would use this for background images. Let's say we have a div like this one.

```
<div class="my-dog-page">
</div>
```

The following CSS could be used to set the background image for that div appropriately.

```
.my-dog-page {
  background-image: url(dog-background-low-res.jpg);
  background-repeat: no-repeat;
  min-height: 264px;
  min-width: 200px;
}

@media (min-resolution: 2dppx) {
  .my-dog-page {
    background-image: url(dog-background.jpg);
  }
}

@media (-webkit-min-device-pixel-ratio: 2) {
  .my-dog-page {
    background-image: url(dog-background.jpg);
  }
}
```

Because background images are only downloaded when a CSS rule is applied, devices with low device/pixel ratios or don't support these media queries will only download the low-resolution image. That is the good news. Unfortunately devices that do apply the media queries will download both the low-resolution and the high-resolution images because both rules applied.

Of course you might be wondering what to do for something that is supposed to be responsive and work across a variety of screen sizes. To do that you can just add in another media query, perhaps like this one.

```
@media (min-width: 450px) {
  .my-dog-page {
    background-image: url(dog-background-medium.jpg);
    min-height: 594px;
    min-width: 450px;
  }
}
```

You can also mix media queries and combine page width with resolution to get even finer-grained control over your sizes and resolutions and perhaps even solve the problem of downloading both low and high resolution images completely.

I have taken this approach to certain types of images and it has worked well. This kind of approach works best for images that are used in the design of a page. Perhaps you have images for the menu options or use image backgrounds for sections of the page. What this doesn't work as well for is what I would call "content images." These are usually image tags in a page, perhaps in an article or as a piece of messaging. Though you could use this approach for image tags in a page to hide/show the appropriate image tag, this would be a bad idea. If the browser sees multiple image tags it will download them all, even if it shows only one of them based on your media queries. This would be very detrimental for the performance of your page and is not very bandwidth friendly. This is where the proposed picture element and PictureFill can be of use.

The Picture Element and Picturefill

There is a working draft of a proposed picture element being considered by the W3C [http://www.w3.org/TR/html-picture-element/] that would be very helpful in solving the content image problem. There is another addition in draft status for supplying a source set attribute for images [http://www.w3.org/html/wg/drafts/srcset/w3c-srcset/] that can be used with it (though it can be used separately as well) to give you even more flexibility. Here is some sample markup taken from the W3C page on the picture element that combines these proposed features.

```
<picture width="500" height="500">
  <source media="(min-width: 45em)" srcset="large-1.jpg 1x, large-2.jpg 2x">
  <source media="(min-width: 18em)" srcset="med-1.jpg 1x, med-2.jpg 2x">
  <source srcset="small-1.jpg 1x, small-2.jpg 2x">
  <img src="small-1.jpg" alt="">
  <p>Accessible text</p>
</picture>
```

This should remind you of the video element, where multiple possible sources are specified, because it is the same idea. But it has a twist in that media query syntax can be used to drive which source is to be used. It also allows you to specify lower- versus higher-resolution images images with the 1x and 2x markers, the idea being that the browser can determine the best size and resolution to use and download only that image. Unfortunately, this is yet to be supported on any mobile browsers.

Fortunately, a polyfill exists that allows you to have the capabilities of the picture element today. It is called Picturefill [https://github.com/scottjehl/picturefill]. Here's how you would use it. First, download the library and reference it in the page like this.

```
<script src="/scripts/picturefill.js"></script>
```

Then setup the element that will serve as your picture element stand-in.

```
<span data-picture data-alt="Me as a horse">
  <span data-src="/content/picturefill/horseman-small-low-res.jpg"></span>
  <span data-src="/content/picturefill/horseman-small.jpg"
    data-media="(min-width: 320px) and (min-resolution: 2dppx)"></span>
  <span data-src="/content/picturefill/horseman-small.jpg"
    data-media="(min-width: 320px) and (-webkit-min-device-pixel-ratio: 2)"></span>
  <span data-src="/content/picturefill/horseman-medium.jpg"
    data-media="(min-width: 400px)"></span>
  <span data-src="/content/picturefill/horseman-full.jpg"
    data-media="(min-width: 800px)"></span>

  <noscript>
    <img src="/content/picturefill/horseman-small.jpg" alt="Me as a horse">
  </noscript>
</span>
```

Figure 5-5 is what this looks like on my iPhone and in Chrome.

Using Picturefill

Picturefill is a polyfill library that gives you the capabilities of the proposed picture element. You can download picturefill from Github.

Figure 5-5. *Using Picturefill to control which image is rendered to a page. I can neither confirm nor deny if that's me with a horse's head*

The iPhone is using the small, high-resolution photo. Chrome is using the large photo. But if I view this on and iPhone 3G or a Windows Phone, I will see the small low-resolution photo because none of the other media queries apply and upgrade the image.

Another option that you have for this is to provide cropped images for smaller devices. In this example I could have supplied a cropped photo for the small image to focus more on the horse head. In cases where the shrinking the image obscures the content, this can be valuable.

How Practical Is All This?

One of the things that I like about responsive web design is that it is very practical. Though it adds some difficulties, it ends up solving more problems than it creates. But I think we have to ask how practical flexible images are for an application. If it wasn't obvious before, the sample for using resolution-based media queries with background images required three separate images and the Picturefill implementation above required four. This requires work and we need to ask if it is worth the effort.

In general, I tend to think the first is generally worth the effort and the second is only sometimes. In the case of images used for design elements on a page, it often makes sense to do this extra work because designs don't usually change that often, so a one-time cost of duplicating images and taking the time to write the extra media queries makes sense. This will save your users bandwidth and speed up the initial download of your website, both of which are important.

As far as Picturefill is concerned, there are a few things to consider. First, how often does the content change so that you would have to keep generating new images? If we are talking about a copy image on a web page that won't change often, then the Picturefill option makes sense. But what if I am writing a blog post? Should I create multiple copies of every image and write and test the queries to make sure it all works? I am quite busy and have no patience for this, notwithstanding the fact that not that many people read my blog anyway. The cost/benefit ratio seems more balanced toward cost. But if I were a newspaper website, for example, I think this would be different. If they have a responsive site, they may get a great deal of benefit out of doing the work and may have the staff to handle doing the extra work. So I think it's a matter of context and purpose. But if you have time and need the capability, you can create flexible images today.

Summary

Along with flexible layouts and navigation, flexible content is possible today. Responsive web design is a practical way to make your content work across multiple devices and desktop computers. Flexible text is easy to accomplish, but we need to start thinking in terms of ems instead of pixels. Flexible tables are still problematic but possible, and I showed you several options. Expect more options to come out of the web community; but what you see here should get you started. Flexible video is also quite possible, whether you are using video directly or embedding from other sites. Flexible images are easy to do but difficult to do well, yet browsers today support most of what you need to either make this work yourself, or you can use libraries like Picturefill to make it easier.

But what if you run into a problem? What if you have to support older browsers or you discover browser bugs that you find difficult to get around? That's what the next chapter is about. You can use display modes, view engines, and HTML helpers to give you the ability to adapt what you render to the devices and give you further control.

CHAPTER 6

■ ■ ■

Display Modes, View Engines, and Html Helpers

Ideally, a mobile site can have a single collection of HTML, CSS, and JavaScript files—we will refer to the three as client-side assets to keep things a little shorter—since this keeps things easier to manage and maintain. This is one of the appealing aspects of responsive web design. But sometimes this is not possible, either because the intended experience does not make sense to implement in a responsive manner, or because the targeted devices do not support the techniques. This is going to be particularly common when the goal is to support both a nice HTML 5 site with all the bells and whistles and a site for older devices that does not support modern browser features.

There are other times when splitting the client side makes sense as well, like if you want iPhone and Android to have different experiences or need to provide a special set of assets to a particularly buggy set of phones (at Match.com we have a few overrides specifically for buggy HTC Android devices). The same techniques I will show you below can help you handle all these scenarios.

As I mentioned, we use this technique in our mobile site at Match.com for doing a few overrides. More importantly, we use this technique to create a site for modern browsers and a site for less capable ones. A couple screenshots, here in Figure 6-1 should help to illustrate.

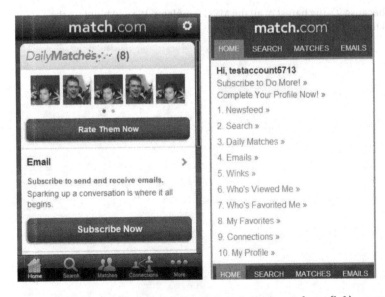

Figure 6-1. *The Match.com mobile website using a smartphone (left) versus an older device (right). Note that our app normally doesn't just include pictures of me in it. This screenshot has been slightly modified*

As you can see, there is quite a difference. The site on the left uses JavaScript, CSS gradients, and touch gestures but will only work on more advanced mobile browsers. The site on the right uses no JavaScript, basic CSS, and basic HTML but will run on a wide number of browsers because of its lowest-common-denominator approach to browser support. Both are running in the same ASP.NET site. This way we can support a wide range of customers but can supply a better experience for those that have a better browser and all that from a single site.

There are four primary techniques for accomplishing this in ASP.NET MVC.

- The default ASP.NET MVC Display Modes

- Custom Display Modes

- Custom View Engines

- HtmlHelpers

The first technique is not very flexible but it requires no work at all to implement if you are using ASP.NET MVC 4 or later. By default, mobile views can be specified with a simple file-naming convention. The second technique, using custom DisplayModes, is easy to use but is less powerful than our third option and only available in ASP.NET MVC 4 and later versions. The third, creating a custom view engine, works in all versions of ASP.NET MVC and is more complicated but provides you with the best way to get complete flexibility in your implementation. The fourth technique, using custom HtmlHelpers, is good for implementing this on a small scale, like for a single widget on a page.

Mobile Views

By default, ASP.NET MVC 4 and later allows you to create mobile-specific views through a naming convention. Let's create a simple site and see how this works. Because this feature was released with MVC 4 and is unchanged for MVC 5, we will use the MVC 4 templates. This simple site will also serve as the basis for exploring both DisplayModes and custom view engines.

Step 1: Create an Empty ASP.NET MVC 4 or 5 Site

We start with an empty site (see Figure 6-2) because it's the barest of all the MVC templates. We will build up the basics of what we need to have separate desktop and mobile views for a page.

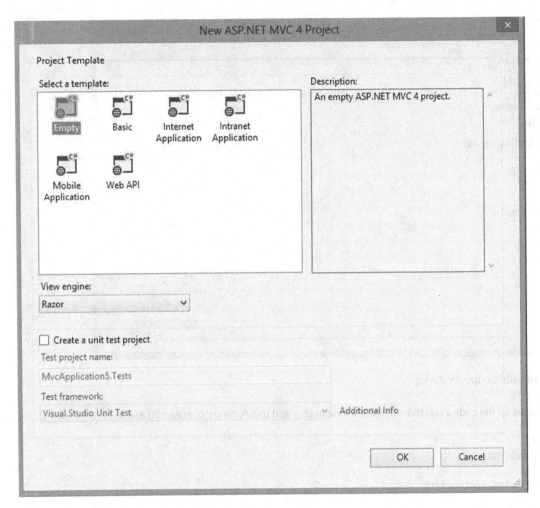

Figure 6-2. *The new ASP.NET MVC project dialog. Though the dialog is a bit different for ASP.NET MVC 5, you can still use the empty template*

Step 2: Create the HomeController

Next we need to start getting a page ready, so we need a controller. For those with less experience with ASP.NET MVC, the routing expects a default controller named "Home" and there is no reason to change that for our experiment. Creating the controller is particularly easy if we use the Add Controller dialog (Figure 6-3).

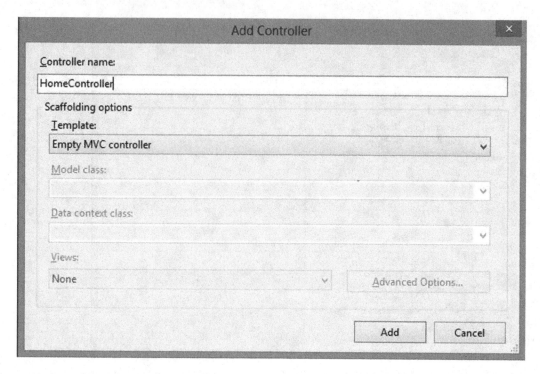

Figure 6-3. *The Add Controller dialog*

We will clean up the code a bit (remove some namespaces and unnecessary comments) and get the following:

```
using System;
using System.Web.Mvc;

namespace MobileApp.Controllers
{
  public class HomeController : Controller
  {
    public ActionResult Index()
    {
      return View();
    }
  }
}
```

Step 3: Create the View

Next we need a view. If we right-click in the action, we get the option for using the Add View dialog, which is what we want. It looks like this (see Figure 6-4).

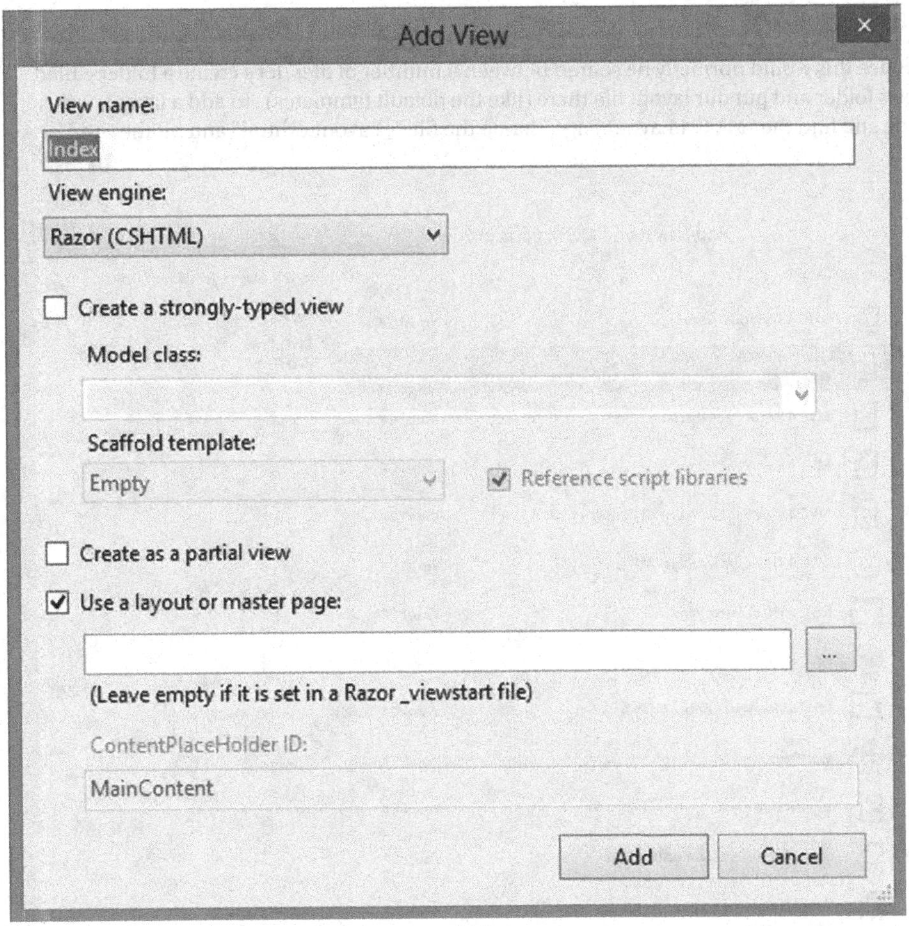

Figure 6-4. *The Add View dialog*

We want to create a view that will use a layout page, so the above will be fine. We will take this markup and make a few changes, to get the following:

```
@{
    Layout = @"~\Views\Shared\_Layout.cshtml";
    ViewBag.Title = "Default HTML";
}

<h2>Default HTML</h2>
<p id="output"></p>
<p>Lorem ipsum dolor sit amet, consectetur adipiscing elit.</p>
```

There are a few things to note at this point. First, we have specified a layout file that we have not yet created. We will do that next. Second, the <h2> says this is the "Default HTML". In a few steps, we'll be creating our "Mobile HTML", which will override this HTML when viewing the page on a mobile device. Third, there is a <p> tag that you will use via JavaScript. This is something you'll use later to show that you can have default and mobile JavaScript that differ with this technique.

Step 4: Create a Layout

Next we need a layout file. Since this would normally be shared between a number of files, let's create a folder called "Shared" in the existing Views folder and put our layout file there (like the default templates). To add a layout, we use the generic "Add Item" dialog and find the "MVC 4 Layout Page," name the file "_Layout.cshtml" and hit the "Add" button (Figure 6-5).

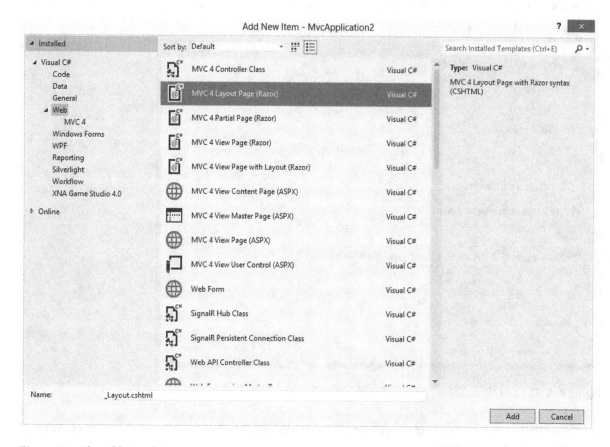

Figure 6-5. *The Add Item dialog*

We will keep the layout as is with the exception of two lines, which we will add to import some CSS and JavaScript. We will create these files next.

```
<!DOCTYPE html>

<html>
<head>
  <meta name="viewport" content="width=device-width" />
  <title>@ViewBag.Title</title>
  <link type="text/css" href="/content/style.css" rel="stylesheet" />
  <script type="text/javascript" src="/content/script.js"></script>
</head>
```

```
<body>
  <div>
    @RenderBody()
  </div>
</body>
</html>
```

Step 5: Create the CSS and JavaScript

We need to create the CSS and JavaScript file from the last step, so we create a directory called "Content" to store them in (like the default in the other MVC project types) and create the two files. This is the CSS that we put in the style.css file:

```
h2:after {
  content: 'Default CSS';
  display: block;
  font-size: .8em;
  font-weight: normal;
}
```

In order to show that one type of CSS is being shown rather than another (default now, mobile later), we are using the CSS content property. For those who aren't familiar, it is a way to insert text into a page through CSS. This is only occasionally a good idea since CSS is for presentation and HTML is for content, but in this case it makes it easy to demonstrate the technique.

This is the JavaScript that we put in the script.js file:

```
window.onload = function () {
  var output = document.getElementById('output');
  output.innerText = 'Default JavaScript';
}
```

Run what you have, and you should see Figure 6-6.

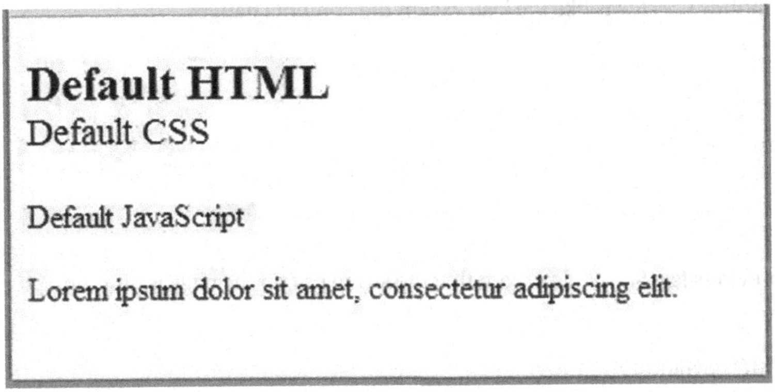

Figure 6-6. *The default view of the page*

111

Step 6: Create our Mobile Overrides

Now that we have our default view rendering for desktop browsers, let's create mobile versions of our assets. We will name our view "Index.mobile.cshtml". Here is the view markup:

```
@{
    Layout = @"~\Views\Shared\_Layout.cshtml";
    ViewBag.Title = "Mobile HTML";
}

<h2>Mobile HTML</h2>
<p id="output"></p>
<p>Lorem ipsum dolor sit amet, consectetur adipiscing elit. Mobile!</p>
```

And this is the layout, which we will name "_Layout.mobile.cshtml."

```
<!DOCTYPE html>

<html>
<head>
    <meta name="viewport" content="width=device-width" />
    <title>@ViewBag.Title</title>
    <link type="text/css" href="/content/style.mobile.css" rel="stylesheet" />
    <script type="text/javascript" src="/content/script.mobile.js"></script>
</head>
<body>
    <div>
        @RenderBody()
    </div>
</body>
</html>
```

The view makes a couple minor text changes so we can see the change in view. The layout page now references different CSS and JavaScript files. Our new mobile CSS file is like the last, except the content changes.

```
h2:after {
    content: 'Mobile CSS';
    display: block;
    font-size: .8em;
    font-weight: normal;
}
```

Our JavaScript file works just like the previous JavaScript file except that the string put on the page is different.

```
window.onload = function () {
    var output = document.getElementById('output');
    output.innerText = 'Mobile JavaScript';
}
```

If you change your user agent to that of an iPhone and revisit the page, you see the mobile version. In our case it would look like Figure 6-7.

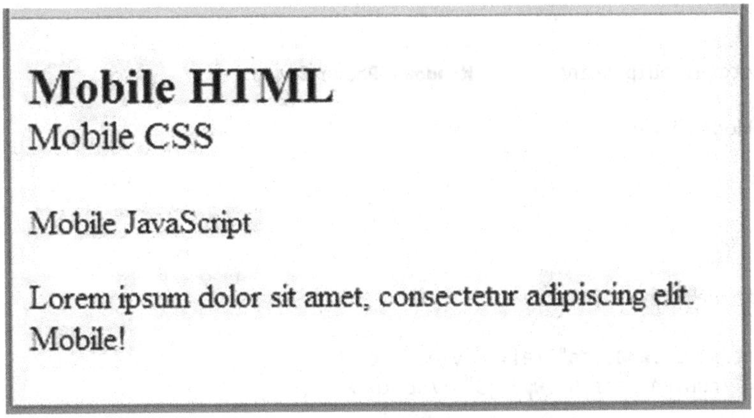

Mobile HTML
Mobile CSS

Mobile JavaScript

Lorem ipsum dolor sit amet, consectetur adipiscing elit.
Mobile!

Figure 6-7. The mobile view of the page

■ **Note**   If you do mobile web development you will find yourself changing your user agent string quite often to test different scenarios. Chrome users can go to Developer Tools, hit the settings gear in the bottom right-hand corner, choose the overrides menu, and override their user agent there. There are also a number of useful Chrome extensions for doing this as well. I often use one called "User-Agent Switcher for Chrome." Internet Explorer 10 users can open the F12 developer tools, look in the tools menu and find a menu option for changing the user agent. Firefox users will find the process for doing this requires more effort, so I would recommend using one of the many Add Ons that allow you to change it easily.

So ASP.NET MVC 4 gives you the ability to create mobile pages simply by creating alternate versions of view and layout pages that follow a simple naming convention, including "mobile" between the name of the view and the extension of the filename. **No controller changes were needed**. This approach requires no coding other than what I showed you above. This convention-based approach allows you to easily have different codes of all your client-side assets, HTML, CSS and JavaScript.

This handy built-in feature uses the ASP.NET's built-in code for determining mobile devices. If this built-in functionality gets you the desktop/mobile device split that you need for your project, you do not need the other approaches. But in many cases you will need more flexibility, such as when you need to have different views for different types of mobile devices. Using the DisplayMode feature of ASP.NET gives you more.

DisplayModes

Creating custom DisplayModes gives you another level of flexibility on top of the default capabilities we saw in the last section. DisplayModes can also be used along with the previous feature so we will simply build off of the site we just created. Let's say we wanted to show an alternate view for the Windows Phone 8. We can create overrides for all the same files we did before, except use the "filename.wp8.extension" format for all our files to stick with the naming convention. So our view (Index.wp8.cshtml) looks like this:

```
@{
    Layout = @"~\Views\Shared\_Layout.cshtml";
    ViewBag.Title = "WP8 HTML";
}
```

```
<h2>WP8 HTML</h2>
<p id="output"></p>
<p>Lorem ipsum dolor sit amet, consectetur adipiscing elit. Windows Phone 8!</p>
```

Our layout page (_Layout.wp8.cshtml) looks like this:

```
<!DOCTYPE html>

<html>
<head>
  <meta name="viewport" content="width=device-width" />
  <title>@ViewBag.Title</title>
  <link type="text/css" href="/content/style.wp8.css" rel="stylesheet" />
  <script type="text/javascript" src="/content/script.wp8.js"></script>
</head>
<body>
  <div>
    @RenderBody()
  </div>
</body>
</html>
```

Our JavaScript file (script.wp8.js) looks like this:

```
window.onload = function () {
  var output = document.getElementById('output');
  output.innerText = 'WP8 JavaScript';
}
```

And finally, our CSS (style.wp8.css) looks like this:

```
h2:after {
  content: 'WP8 CSS';
  display: block;
  font-size: .8em;
  font-weight: normal;
}
```

Setting Up a Windows Phone 8 DisplayMode

Now that you have made the override files, you can use a DisplayMode to show them for the appropriate phones. The best time to set this up is when the application starts. Here is our global.asax.cs, with the DisplayMode setup.

```
public class MvcApplication : System.Web.HttpApplication
{
  protected void Application_Start()
  {
    AreaRegistration.RegisterAllAreas();

    WebApiConfig.Register(GlobalConfiguration.Configuration);
    FilterConfig.RegisterGlobalFilters(GlobalFilters.Filters);
    RouteConfig.RegisterRoutes(RouteTable.Routes);
```

```
    //The condition that specifies if the DisplayMode should be used for a given request
    Func<HttpContextBase, bool> condition = (context) => {
      return context.GetOverriddenUserAgent()
        .IndexOf("MSIE 10.0; Windows Phone 8.0", StringComparison.OrdinalIgnoreCase) >= 0;
    };

    var wp8DisplayMode = new DefaultDisplayMode("wp8");
    wp8DisplayMode.ContextCondition = condition;

    //We want this DisplayMode to evaluate first, so it is inserted at the beginning of the list.
    DisplayModeProvider.Instance.Modes.Insert(0, wp8DisplayMode);
  }
}
```

The first thing to notice is that a condition needs to be specified, which is done by creating a Func<HttpContextBase, bool> that returns a Boolean value based on something in HttpContext regarding whether or not the a particular Display Mode should be used. In our case we are going to make a simple user agent check. If the user agent contains "MSIE 10.0; Windows Phone 8.0", a value of true will be returned. Otherwise, the function will return false. This check is not very robust, since an increment of either the browser version or device OS version would invalidate the code here. Our next chapter will deal in depth with parsing user agent strings and have a much better alternative, though this will do for now.

Since we have our Func, we can create our Display Mode instance, assign the condition and insert the condition into the first position of the modes used by the site. By default, an ASP.NET MVC 4 website already has two DisplayModes in the collection, the first for "mobile" (the default "mobile" feature we referenced earlier in the chapter is implemented as a Display Mode) and the second for the default view lookup. When deciding which view to render, the framework will iterate through the collection of modes in order and use the first that has a ContextCondition that returns true, so if we want our new Display Mode to ever be hit, we need to put it in the first position in the collection. Now if we render the page using a Windows Phone 8 device or spoof the user agent string, we get what you see in Figure 6-8.

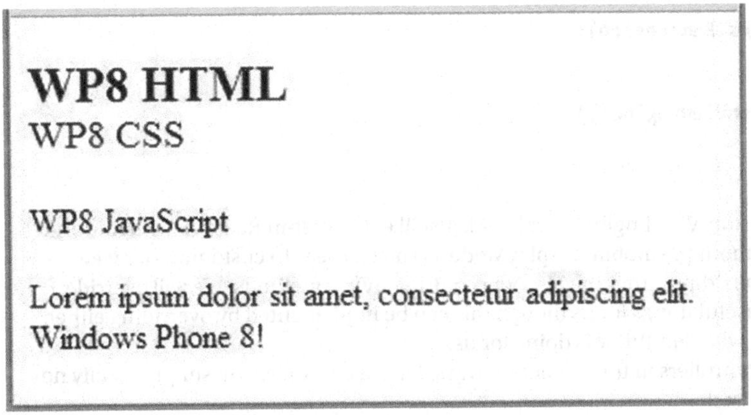

WP8 HTML
WP8 CSS

WP8 JavaScript

Lorem ipsum dolor sit amet, consectetur adipiscing elit.
Windows Phone 8!

Figure 6-8. *Our view customized for Windows Phone 8*

So by using DisplayModes, either by using the built-in set that gives you the "filename.mobile.extension" view choice or by creating your own custom Display Mode, you can customize the markup rendered by your ASP.NET MVC site for particular devices. And when you customize the markup rendered, you can also customize the CSS and JavaScript. For many this capability will be sufficient. But if you need more control, or are not using ASP.NET MVC 4 yet, perhaps a custom view engine is a good idea.

Custom View Engine

Custom view engines can be used to get complete control over how views are selected for rendering. We will implement the same features seen above as a custom view engine but then add another feature to allow A/B testing (more on this in a bit) of views on top of the mobile capabilities that we add. We will use the same site as before so we don't have to re-create all of those views and CSS files.

The easiest way to create our custom view engine is to inherit from the existing RazorViewEngine, like so:

```
using System;
using System.Web.Mvc;

namespace OurSite
{
  public class CustomViewEngine: RazorViewEngine
  {
  }
}
```

We can clear out the default view engines and use only our new view engine by changing the global.asax.cs application start method and remove the mobile DisplayMode that is created by default since we won't be needing it.

```
public class MvcApplication : System.Web.HttpApplication
{
  protected void Application_Start()
  {
    AreaRegistration.RegisterAllAreas();

    WebApiConfig.Register(GlobalConfiguration.Configuration);
    FilterConfig.RegisterGlobalFilters(GlobalFilters.Filters);
    RouteConfig.RegisterRoutes(RouteTable.Routes);

    DisplayModeProvider.Instance.Modes.RemoveAt(0);

    ViewEngines.Engines.Clear();
    ViewEngines.Engines.Add(new CustomViewEngine());
  }
}
```

Since we have not yet changed our CustomViewEngine, it will work just like the built-in RazorViewEngine and our site keeps working as it was, though without the mobile DisplayMode as you can see. To customize our view engine and how it finds files, we start by overriding either the FindView or CreateView methods. We will override CreateView because FindView does a few useful things for us though this can be implemented by overriding either. Since we will override CreateView, let's see what FindView is doing for us.

By default, views can be specified in controllers in three different ways. First, a controller can simply specify no name and the name of the method will be used.

```
public class HomeController : Controller
{
  public ActionResult Index()
  {
    return View();
  }
}
```

In this case the FindView method (which the RazorViewEngine inherits from BuildManagerViewEngine, which inherits the method from VirtualPathProviderViewEngine) will look for a view named "Index" based on the name of the method. Based on the controller name, the default location for this view would be "~/Views/Home/Index.cshtml."

```
public class HomeController : Controller
{
  public ActionResult Index()
  {
    return View("Foo");
  }
}
```

If a name for the view is specified as it is above, it will use this as the name of the file but continue to use the controller name for the path. The generated path for this would be "~/Views/Home/Foo.cshtml". If the default path lookup is insufficient, you can also specify the full path to the desired view like this:

```
public class HomeController : Controller
{
  public ActionResult Index()
  {
    return View("~/Views/Custom/Foo.cshtml");
  }
}
```

The FindView method of the view engine takes care of this process of path building and even uses the default DisplayModes to build the path. To avoid this work, it can be easier to override the CreateView method instead. That is what we will do in this case to keep things simple.

```
public class CustomViewEngine: RazorViewEngine
{
  protected override IView CreateView(ControllerContext controllerContext, string viewPath,
string masterPath)
  {
    return base.CreateView(controllerContext, viewPath, masterPath);
  }
}
```

The viewPath parameter passed into the CreateView method is the fully built path. We can interrogate and modify that and get our flexible view lookup. Assuming we go back to the plain controller with no name or path specified, viewPath will equal "~/Views/Home/Index.cshtml". We can start replicating the mobile file lookup functionality by making the following change to our new view engine.

```
public class CustomViewEngine: RazorViewEngine
{
  protected override IView CreateView(ControllerContext controllerContext, string viewPath,
string masterPath)
  {
    if (controllerContext.HttpContext.GetOverriddenBrowser().IsMobileDevice)
      viewPath = viewPath.Replace(".cshtml", ".mobile.cshtml");

    return base.CreateView(controllerContext, viewPath, masterPath);
  }
}
```

Unfortunately, this only handles the view naming. The layout path still needs to be modified. Layout paths specified by _ViewStart pages and in view files have not yet been read so the masterPath parameter will be blank unless it is specified in the Controller, which is not something we would want to have to do in every action method. The easiest thing to do is default it here, though this removes the value of setting the Layout property in either the View or the _ViewStart file.

```
public class CustomViewEngine: RazorViewEngine
{
  protected override IView CreateView(ControllerContext controllerContext, string viewPath,
string masterPath)
  {
    if (String.IsNullOrWhiteSpace(masterPath))
      masterPath = @"~/Views/Shared/_Layout.cshtml";

    if (controllerContext.HttpContext.GetOverriddenBrowser().IsMobileDevice)
    {
      viewPath = viewPath.Replace(".cshtml", ".mobile.cshtml");
      masterPath = masterPath.Replace(".cshtml", ".mobile.cshtml");
    }

    return base.CreateView(controllerContext, viewPath, masterPath);
  }
}
```

Now mobile view files will be picked up for mobile browsers. Let's add the ability to find views for Windows Phones. The change is relatively simple.

```
public class CustomViewEngine: RazorViewEngine
{
  protected override IView CreateView(ControllerContext controllerContext, string viewPath,
string masterPath)
  {
    if (String.IsNullOrWhiteSpace(masterPath))
      masterPath = @"~/Views/Shared/_Layout.cshtml";

    if (controllerContext.HttpContext.GetOverriddenUserAgent().IndexOf("MSIE 10.0;
Windows Phone 8.0", StringComparison.OrdinalIgnoreCase) >= 0)
    {
      viewPath = viewPath.Replace(".cshtml", ".wp8.cshtml");
      masterPath = masterPath.Replace(".cshtml", ".wp8.cshtml");
    }
    else if (controllerContext.HttpContext.GetOverriddenBrowser().IsMobileDevice)
    {
      viewPath = viewPath.Replace(".cshtml", ".mobile.cshtml");
      masterPath = masterPath.Replace(".cshtml", ".mobile.cshtml");
    }

    return base.CreateView(controllerContext, viewPath, masterPath);
  }
}
```

Though functional, this has a robustness flaw. If a Windows Phone 8 user visits a page that doesn't have a "wp8" override file, we get a 404 because the view was not found. The "mobile" override has the same problem. We should do some basic file existence checks to make sure a file exists before we try to reference it. This makes the code a bit messier but gives you much more flexibility.

```
public class CustomViewEngine: RazorViewEngine
{
  protected override IView CreateView(ControllerContext controllerContext, string viewPath,
string masterPath)
  {
    if (String.IsNullOrWhiteSpace(masterPath))
      masterPath = @"~/Views/Shared/_Layout.cshtml";

    string altViewPath = String.Empty;
    string altMasterPath = String.Empty;

    if (controllerContext.HttpContext.GetOverriddenUserAgent().IndexOf("MSIE 10.0;
Windows Phone 8.0", StringComparison.OrdinalIgnoreCase) >= 0)
    {
      CheckView(viewPath, ref altViewPath, "wp8", controllerContext);
      CheckView(masterPath, ref altMasterPath, "wp8", controllerContext);
    }

    if (controllerContext.HttpContext.GetOverriddenBrowser().IsMobileDevice)
    {
      if (String.IsNullOrWhiteSpace(altViewPath))
        CheckView(viewPath, ref altViewPath, "mobile", controllerContext);
      if (String.IsNullOrWhiteSpace(altMasterPath))
        CheckView(masterPath, ref altMasterPath, "mobile", controllerContext);
    }

    if (!String.IsNullOrWhiteSpace(altViewPath))
      viewPath = altViewPath;
    if (!String.IsNullOrWhiteSpace(altMasterPath))
      masterPath = altMasterPath;

    return base.CreateView(controllerContext, viewPath, masterPath);
  }

  private void CheckView(string viewPath, ref string altPath, string skinType, ControllerContext context)
  {
    string temp = viewPath.Replace(".cshtml", String.Format(".{0}.cshtml", skinType));
    if (FileExists(context, temp))
      altPath = temp;
  }
}
```

Adding A/B Testing

As I said before, if we just need basic mobile skin support, creating a custom view engine to do this is overkill and no better than using the default behavior or creating custom display modes. But if we need other custom lookup logic, it can end up being easier with a custom view engine. For example, you might want to have language-specific skins as well. Or perhaps you want A/B testing too. The following example shows you how you can implement the latter.

A/B testing is the practice of showing alternative pages/flows/designs, et al. to users for research. Perhaps you want to test two landing pages to see which one gets more people to buy your product. Maybe you want to show a certain feature to small set of users to guard against risk. Implementing this kind of feature for views is relatively easy to do with a custom view engine or custom DisplayModes. Because both are pretty flexible, it's often a toss-up to decide which to use. My general approach is to use DisplayModes when the conditional logic is simple and a custom view engine when the logic is more complex. Because A/B testing can get very complex, I will implement this with a custom view engine.

Essential to creating an A/B testing-capable view engine is the ability to determine if a view is in a test or not and if it is, what version should be used. Since this kind of question is very context-specific (how would I know what you would find useful for testing?), I will create a simple set of criteria. When a given view path comes in, it will check for a value in a test cookie called "testcookie". If the value is "a", the first version of the test skin will be shown. If the value is "b", the second version will be shown. If there is no cookie, the user is not in a test, and it will pick up the default file. Here is one way to write that function.

```
private string GetTestVersion(ControllerContext controllerContext, string viewPath)
{
  if (viewPath == "~/Views/Home/Index.cshtml") //The only path being tested
  {
    var testCookie = controllerContext.HttpContext.Request.Cookies["testcookie"];
    if (testCookie == null)
      return String.Empty;

    if (testCookie.Value == "a")
      return "v1";
    else
      return "v2";
  }
  else
  {
    return String.Empty;
  }
}
```

Next we would modify our CheckView function to also look for a test version of a file.

```
private void CheckView(string viewPath, ref string altPath, string skinType, string testVersion,
ControllerContext context)
{
  string temp = viewPath.Replace(".cshtml", String.Format(".{0}.{1}.cshtml", skinType, testVersion));
  if (FileExists(context, temp))
  {
    altPath = temp;
    return;
  }
```

```
    temp = viewPath.Replace(".cshtml", String.Format(".{0}.cshtml", skinType));
    if (FileExists(context, temp))
      altPath = temp;
}
```

Our CreateView function now needs some minor changes.

```
protected override IView CreateView(ControllerContext controllerContext, string viewPath,
string masterPath)
{
  if (String.IsNullOrWhiteSpace(masterPath))
    masterPath = @"~/Views/Shared/_Layout.cshtml";

  string altViewPath = String.Empty;
  string altMasterPath = String.Empty;

  string testVersion = GetTestVersion(controllerContext, viewPath);

  if (controllerContext.HttpContext.GetOverriddenUserAgent().IndexOf("MSIE 10.0; Windows Phone 8.0",
StringComparison.OrdinalIgnoreCase) >= 0)
  {
    CheckView(viewPath, ref altViewPath, "wp8", testVersion, controllerContext);
    CheckView(masterPath, ref altMasterPath, "wp8", String.Empty, controllerContext);
  }

  if (controllerContext.HttpContext.GetOverriddenBrowser().IsMobileDevice)
  {
    if (String.IsNullOrWhiteSpace(altViewPath))
      CheckView(viewPath, ref altViewPath, "mobile", testVersion, controllerContext);
    if (String.IsNullOrWhiteSpace(altMasterPath))
      CheckView(masterPath, ref altMasterPath, "mobile", String.Empty, controllerContext);
  }

  if (!String.IsNullOrWhiteSpace(altViewPath))
    viewPath = altViewPath;
  if (!String.IsNullOrWhiteSpace(altMasterPath))
    masterPath = altMasterPath;

  return base.CreateView(controllerContext, viewPath, masterPath);
}
```

We now have a custom view engine that supports multiple types of view lookups, both for devices and for A/B testing. The device detection still leaves a lot to be desired, but that discussion will have to wait till the next chapter.

HtmlHelpers

HtmlHelpers have been a part of ASP.NET MVC from the beginning and are useful for creating reusable bits of user interface. We are going to stick with our theme and build an HtmlHelper that will conditionally render some markup depending on the user agent of the browser.

The example here comes from something we made for Match.com's mobile website. We needed to display a map to users and wanted to use Google maps but were supporting devices that Google does not support. So we used the Google maps static image API to generate an image for all devices but for supported devices wrapped the image in a link to Google Maps. We built this using an HtmlHelper so we could use it anywhere easily. Here is a very simple HtmlHelper implementation to create this map.

```
public static class MapHelper
{
  private static string _imageMarkup = "<img src=\"http://maps.googleapis.com/maps/api/staticmap?
center={0}&zoom=13&size=400x300&sensor=false\" />";
  private static string _jsApiMarkup = "<a href=\"https://maps.google.com/?q={0}\">{1}</a>";

  public static MvcHtmlString Map(this HtmlHelper helper, string address)
  {
    string image = String.Format(_imageMarkup, address);

    string userAgent = helper.ViewContext.HttpContext.Request.UserAgent;
    if (userAgent.IndexOf("RIM OS", StringComparison.OrdinalIgnoreCase) >= 0)
      return MvcHtmlString.Create(image);
    else
      return MvcHtmlString.Create(String.Format(_jsApiMarkup, address, image));
  }
}
```

Once again, we have our rather unfortunate manual user agent string checking that we will remedy in the next chapter, but the basic idea should be straightforward. For users with "RIM OS" in their user agent string (BlackBerry devices), we just use the static image. Otherwise we still use the image but wrap it in a link to Google Maps.

Summary

In this chapter we have seen four techniques for controlling the HTML output of our site. Three techniques help us control this for full pages, one for small nuggets of markup. If we are going to control our markup and behavior in this way, we should have a robust way of interrogating browsers, and doing user agent checking as we did in the chapter is very problematic. In the next chapter we will discuss this problem and solutions for solving this on both the client and the server.

CHAPTER 7

■ ■ ■

Device and Feature Detection

In an ideal world we could always return the same HTML, CSS and JavaScript for any given page on our website. In the real world differences in capabilities and browser bugs will often necessitate some sort of client-side asset split. For example, JavaScript for doing photo uploads in the browser makes sense for recent iPhones and Android devices because they support the feature but not for older devices. Or perhaps you wish to use a feature of CSS for some devices and not others because of buggy support. In the last chapter we discussed how to do this. We saw that we could use custom View Engines, Display Modes, and HtmlHelpers to generate HTML for specific devices. And if you control the HTML, you control what CSS and JavaScript gets included. In this chapter you will learn how to do this *intelligently*, including learning techniques related to device and feature detection and discussions on where each one is useful.

Device Detection

When web browsers make requests, one of the HTTP headers passed to the web server is the "User-Agent" header, which is a string to identify to the server what kind of device is making that particular request. As an example of what you might see for a user agent, here is a very common one (at least for now), that of an iPhone running iOS 6.1.3.

Mozilla/5.0 (iPhone; CPU iPhone OS 6_1_3 like Mac OS X) AppleWebKit/536.26 (KHTML, like Gecko) Version/6.0 Mobile/10B329 Safari/8536.25.

In most mobile device detection, usually only a small portion of the user agent string is actually important. In this case, we would likely only need "iPhone OS 6_1_3" since it tells us that it is an iOS phone (as opposed to an iOS tablet) and the exact version of the operating system. This might seem like it would be a relatively straightforward process but this hope is completely misplaced because the variety of possible user agents is astounding. For example, every week Match.com's mobile websites (this does not take into account desktop browser user agents) get visited by thousands of distinct user agents. This includes new devices, as well as devices that have been around for years. If we take into account only the devices that hit our most advanced mobile site (which means iOS 4+ and Android 2.2+), we still get several thousand distinct user agents.

That being said, at this point certain user agents clearly dominate the pack. Sixty-two percent of our users fall into the top ten user agents (six iOS 6.x user agents, one iOS 5.1.1 and three Android 4.1.2 variants). The top thirty user agents make up 73 percent of our traffic, followed by a long tail of differing user agents. About 1,600 of the user agents were unique. Here are a few more samples.

- **Droid Razr** - *Mozilla/5.0 (Linux; U; Android 4.1.2; en-us; DROID RAZR Build/9.8.2O-72_VZW-16) AppleWebKit/534.30 (KHTML, like Gecko) Version/4.0 Mobile Safari/534.30*

- **Galaxy SIII** - *Mozilla/5.0 (Linux; U; Android 4.1.2; en-us; SCH-I535 Build/JZO54K) AppleWebKit/534.30 (KHTML, like Gecko) Version/4.0 Mobile Safari/534.30*

- **HTC Droid Incredible 2** - *Mozilla/5.0 (Linux; U; Android 2.3.4; en-us; pcdadr6350 Build/GRJ22) AppleWebKit/533.1 (KHTML, like Gecko) Version/4.0 Mobile Safari/533.1*

- **BlackBerry Bold Touch** - *Mozilla/5.0 (BlackBerry; U; BlackBerry 9930; en-US) AppleWebKit/534.11+ (KHTML, like Gecko) Version/7.1.0.755 Mobile Safari/534.11+*

- **Nokia Windows Phone 7** - *Mozilla/5.0 (compatible; MSIE 9.0; Windows Phone OS 7.5; Trident/5.0; IEMobile/9.0; NOKIA; Lumia 900)*

- **Nokia Windows Phone 8** - *Mozilla/5.0 (compatible; MSIE 10.0; Windows Phone 8.0; Trident/6.0; IEMobile/10.0; ARM; Touch; NOKIA; Lumia 920)*

- **Samsung Convoy 2** - *Opera/9.80 (BREW; Opera Mini/6.0.3/27.2314; U; en) Presto/2.8.119 320X240 Samsung SCH-U485*

Given the plethora of user agents and the difficulty of not only parsing the user agents in a consistent way but also of gleaning useful device information from them, perhaps leveraging someone else's work to do this would be wise.

Parsing User Agent Strings with WURFL

Fortunately a number of projects exist that make parsing user agents and gleaning device information a more reasonable task than doing it by hand. There are several useful options, including Device Atlas (https://deviceatlas.com/) and the device detection solution by 51degrees (http://51degrees.mobi/), but I have used the WURFL project extensively and will explain how it works here.

WURFL stands for "Wireless Universal Resource File" and has both library and data components that make it easy to look up information about devices and their capabilities from user agent strings. WURFL has both an open-source and commercial component and is owned by scientiamobile (http://www.scientiamobile.com/). The open-source resources are available on Sourceforge (http://wurfl.sourceforge.net/) and include both data and libraries/code for using WURFL with .NET (available via Nuget), PHP, or Java. There is also a commercially licensed library for C++. The freely downloadable data is often several months behind but those who buy a commercial license can get weekly updates to the database.

As of right now the database has 621 different fields for each device. Few developers will need anything more than just a few fields and some are relevant for newer phones only, and others only for older phones. For example, the fields about capabilities include "canvas_support," "css_gradient," "cookie_support," "gif_animated," and "https_support". You will also get other fields about the device, such as "resolution_height," "resolution_width," "device_os," "device_os_version," "mobile_browser" and "model_name."

To show you how easy it is to use WURFL, let's create a simple site and use WURFL for parsing our user agent strings. First I create a new ASP.NET MVC 4 project, call it WURFLSample and use the "Internet Application" template to help us get started quickly (see Figure 7-1).

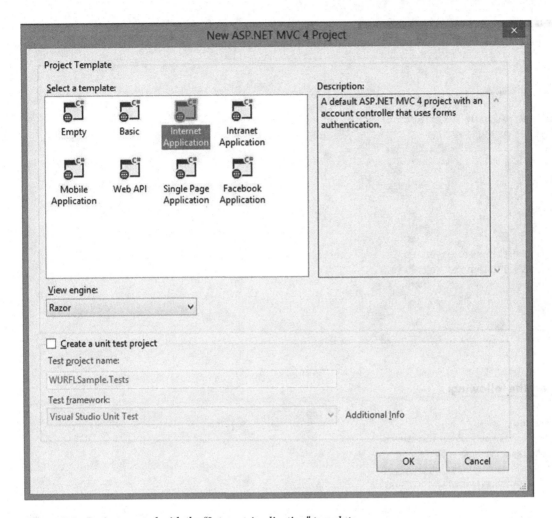

Figure 7-1. *Project created with the "Internet Application" template*

The Internet Application template is responsive (see Figure 1-5), so we can shrink our browser window to a small size like we would see on a mobile device and it sizes itself appropriately (see Figure 7-2).

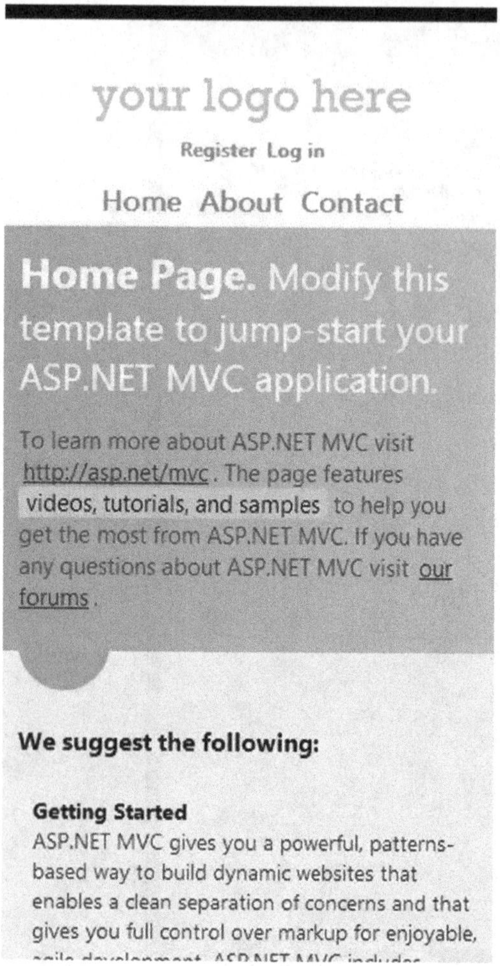

your logo here

Register Log in

Home About Contact

Home Page. Modify this template to jump-start your ASP.NET MVC application.

To learn more about ASP.NET MVC visit http://asp.net/mvc . The page features videos, tutorials, and samples to help you get the most from ASP.NET MVC. If you have any questions about ASP.NET MVC visit our forums .

We suggest the following:

Getting Started
ASP.NET MVC gives you a powerful, patterns-based way to build dynamic websites that enables a clean separation of concerns and that gives you full control over markup for enjoyable,

Figure 7-2. The Internet Application template viewed on a small screen

If you are using Visual Studio 2013, choose the MVC project template. You will have a similar setup. What we will do is create two alternative view files to the home page, one for older smartphones and one for newer smartphones. This means that we will want to know both the device OS and the version. You may recall from Chapter 6 that at Match.com we split devices into the large categories of more advanced devices and devices with more basic capabilities. We call these groups "super" (for "superphone") and "basic" respectively. The basic views are for devices that either have limited capabilities or are rare/old enough that keeping them on the super views is not worth the work. These views use very basic HTML and CSS and use no JavaScript. The super skins are where the vast majority of our mobile traffic goes, which includes Android 2.2+ and iOS 4+ (as of May 2013) and leverage a lot of browser features only available on new phones.

Implementing this feature without using something like WURFL would be tedious and error-prone. If we were just checking the operating system, a simple check for "Android" and "iPhone" in the user agent string would be simple enough and cover you for most users (the tiny variations in user agents strings can be maddening though). But we want to also pay attention to version, which WURFL already parses out for us. So we will start by creating our two new mobile views, which we will call "Index.basic.cshtml" and "Index.super.cshtml", based on the grouping mentioned above. To simplify things, we'll also clear out the content of the files and each will have one HTML tag, which will say "Default view!" for the default page, "Basic view!" for the basic view and "Super view!" for the super view. Now the homepage of the site will look like Figure 7-3.

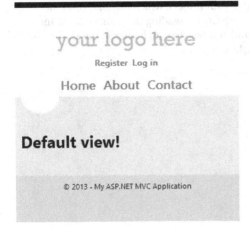

Figure 7-3. *The default view*

We will implement this feature using the DisplayMode feature of ASP.NET MVC 4. This DisplayMode feature allows you to easily return different HTML for different types of devices. All you need is a way to determine what to return and you supply a lambda expression for the context condition (see Chapter 6 for more information about this). We will use WURFL in the context condition of the DisplayMode because it makes parsing user agent strings easy. First let's get WURFL setup. Open solution explorer, right-click on "References" and choose "Manage Nuget Packages…" Find WURFL through an online search like you see in Figure 7-4.

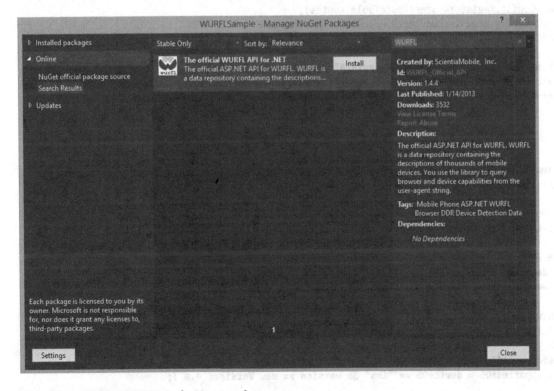

Figure 7-4. *Finding WURFL in the Nuget package manager*

Hit the "Install" button, accept the terms and WURFL will be added to your project, which includes both the data (now residing in a zip file in the site's App_Data folder) and the .NET library for reading the data. Because the data set is large and takes a while to load (several seconds on my machine), it is best to load it once at the start of the application and just reference a single instance. It could look something like this:

```
using System;
using System.Web.Http;
using System.Web.Mvc;
using System.Web.Optimization;
using System.Web.Routing;
using WURFL;
using WURFL.Config;

namespace WURFLSample
{
  public class MvcApplication : System.Web.HttpApplication
  {
    private static IWURFLManager _wurflManager;

    protected void Application_Start()
    {
      AreaRegistration.RegisterAllAreas();

      WebApiConfig.Register(GlobalConfiguration.Configuration);
      FilterConfig.RegisterGlobalFilters(GlobalFilters.Filters);
      RouteConfig.RegisterRoutes(RouteTable.Routes);
      BundleConfig.RegisterBundles(BundleTable.Bundles);
      AuthConfig.RegisterAuth();

      string wurflDataPath = Server.MapPath(@"~/App_Data/wurfl-latest.zip");
      var configurer = new InMemoryConfigurer().MainFile(wurflDataPath);
      _wurflManager = WURFLManagerBuilder.Build(configurer);
    }
  }
}
```

Now that WURFL is configured, we can setup our DisplayModes. This is how you could query WURFL and pick the supported devices.

```
var superMode = new DefaultDisplayMode("super");
superMode.ContextCondition = (context) =>
{
  IDevice device = _wurflManager.GetDeviceForRequest(context.Request.UserAgent);
  string deviceOS = device.GetCapability("device_os").ToLower();
  string versionString = device.GetCapability("device_os_version");

  Version version = new Version();
  Version.TryParse(versionString, out version);

  bool isSupportedAndroid = deviceOS == "android" && version >= new Version("2.2");
  bool isSupportediOS = deviceOS == "ios" && version >= new Version("4.0");
```

```
    if (isSupportedAndroid || isSupportediOS)
      return true;
    else
      return false;
};
```

The basic DisplayMode would be very similar. Only the name and conditions would change.

```
var basicMode = new DefaultDisplayMode("basic");
basicMode.ContextCondition = (context) =>
{
  IDevice device = _wurflManager.GetDeviceForRequest(context.GetOverriddenUserAgent());
  string deviceOS = device.GetCapability("device_os").ToLower();
  string versionString = device.GetCapability("device_os_version");

  Version version = new Version();
  Version.TryParse(versionString, out version);

  bool isSupportedAndroid = deviceOS == "android" && version < new Version("2.2");
  bool isSupportediOS = deviceOS == "ios" && version < new Version("4.0");

  if (isSupportedAndroid || isSupportediOS)
    return true;
  else
    return false;
};
```

Both would then be inserted into the DisplayModeProvider.

```
DisplayModeProvider.Instance.Modes.Insert(0, basicMode);
DisplayModeProvider.Instance.Modes.Insert(0, superMode);
```

At this point everything would be setup. So if you were browser with an iPhone using iOS6, you would see the screenshot on the left in Figure 7-5. If browsing with an iPhone using iOS 3, you would see the screenshot on the right.

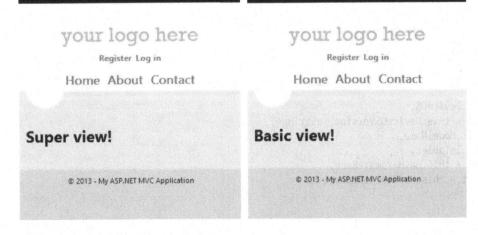

Figure 7-5. Super and basic views

Abstracting WURFL

When we used this at Match.com, we also found it helpful to gather this WURFL data into a class. There are a number of things about this that we found advantageous. First, this abstracts WURFL away from the rest of our code (just in case we want to change later). Second, this gives us a place to add other properties that we can infer from those retrieved from WURFL. For example, we have a property called "HasHardwareBack" that returns true for Android that we use to hide some back buttons in our app (since they aren't needed). When we start supporting Windows Phone on our super skins, we can add them in as well. Third, we put a ToJson() method on the object to convert it to JSON, which we embed in the page so that our client-side JavaScript has access to the same set of capabilities. Let's see how we can set all this up.

First we need our DeviceInfo object. Here is a fairly basic one. You would obviously replace the properties with the things from WURFL that you cared to use.

```
using System;
using System.Web.Script.Serialization;

namespace WURFLSample
{
  public class DeviceInfo
  {
    public string DeviceOS { get; set; }
    public Version DeviceOSVersion { get; set; }
    public string ModelName { get; set; }
    public string UserAgent { get; set; }
    public bool IsTablet { get; set; }
    public bool HasCookieSupport { get; set; }

    public bool HasHardwareBack
    {
      get
      {
        if (this.DeviceOS == "Android")
          return true;
        else
          return false;
      }
    }

    public string ToJson()
    {
      var data = new
      {
        deviceOS = this.DeviceOS,
        deviceOSVersion = this.DeviceOSVersion.ToString(),
        modelName = this.ModelName,
        isTablet = this.IsTablet,
        hasHardwareBack = this.HasHardwareBack,
        hasCookieSupport = this.HasCookieSupport
      };
```

```
        var serializer = new JavaScriptSerializer();
        var json = serializer.Serialize(data);
        return json;
    }
  }
}
```

Second, we need to gather that info on every request. On good way of doing that is to build up our DeviceInfo object on BeginRequest.

```
protected void Application_BeginRequest(object sender, EventArgs e)
{
  var context = new HttpContextWrapper(Context);
  IDevice device = _wurflManager.GetDeviceForRequest(context.GetOverriddenUserAgent());

  var deviceInfo = new DeviceInfo();
  deviceInfo.DeviceOS = device.GetCapability("device_os");
  deviceInfo.ModelName = device.GetCapability("model_name");
  deviceInfo.UserAgent = context.GetOverriddenUserAgent();

  //To avoid parsing failures for non-string types, we leverage TryParse
  bool hasCookieSupport = false;
  string strHasCookieSupport = device.GetCapability("cookie_support");
  Boolean.TryParse(strHasCookieSupport, out hasCookieSupport);
  deviceInfo.HasCookieSupport = hasCookieSupport;

  bool isTablet = false;
  string strIsTablet = device.GetCapability("is_tablet");
  Boolean.TryParse(strIsTablet, out isTablet);
  deviceInfo.IsTablet = isTablet;

  //Version class requires major.minor, so we make sure we get good info out of WURFL.
  string rawDeviceOSVersion = device.GetCapability("device_os_version");
  if (String.IsNullOrEmpty(rawDeviceOSVersion) == true) //default major
    rawDeviceOSVersion = "0";
  if (rawDeviceOSVersion.Contains(".") == false) //default minor
    rawDeviceOSVersion += ".0";
  deviceInfo.DeviceOSVersion = new Version(rawDeviceOSVersion);

  context.Items["DeviceInfo"] = deviceInfo;
}
```

So now any server-side logic has access to the device info. If we want to expose this to our view files, we can do so quite easily. I would do this by creating a custom Controller base class and have our site's controllers derive from this.

```
public class CustomBaseController : Controller
{
  protected override void OnActionExecuting(ActionExecutingContext filterContext)
  {
    ViewBag.DeviceInfo = filterContext.HttpContext.Items["DeviceInfo"];

    base.OnActionExecuting(filterContext);
  }
}
```

Note that the DeviceInfo object is now added to the ViewBag. This means that we can output this in our _Layout. cshtml file by changing the body tag like so:

```
<body data-device-info="@ViewBag.DeviceInfo.ToJson()">
```

Now we can grab that device info in JavaScript and use it if needed (we use a little jQuery here which is not necessary):

```
var data = $('body').data('deviceInfo');
console.log('mobile os', data.deviceOS);
```

All of that should get you started with device detection. It has its strengths and weaknesses, which we will discuss later in this chapter. For now, let's move on to another useful type of detection.

Feature Detection

Though device detection based on user agents will often make a lot of sense, there are a number of cases where feature detection is a better route. Feature detection involves using JavaScript in the browser to determine if the browser supports a feature; its primary benefit is that it is by design a forward-compatible approach. As new browsers come out, they generally just add new features instead of take away, so a site that uses feature detection can have functionality/visuals that get revealed gradually as people update their browsers. A simple script to do feature detection would be the following, which checks to see if the browser supports WebGL.

```
<script>
  window.onload = function () {
    if (!window.WebGLRenderingContext) {
      //WebGL is not supported :(
      //Hide the WebGL widget or perhaps show a message
    }
    else {
      //WebGL IS SUPPORTED! :)
      //Unleash the awesome
    }
  }
</script>
```

In most cases mobile browsers do not support WebGL, so at this point the negative case will be the normal on mobile devices. But as time goes on, WebGL support will likely grow and users on the supported browsers will get the experience your WebGL feature is coded for.

If you do a lot of feature detection, writing these scripts might get tedious. Fortunately there is a very popular open-source library that collects feature detection scripts called Modernizr (http://modernizr.com/) that can be very helpful. Modernizr supports a very large list of feature detections, and you can use the entire list on your site or, alternatively, you can pick and choose to generate a custom Modernizr build (see Figure 7-6).

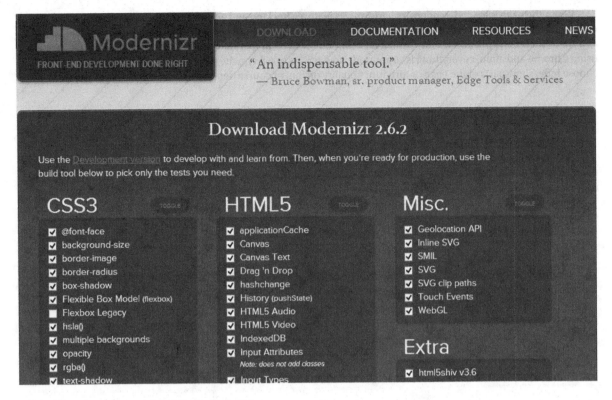

Figure 7-6. Creating a custom Modernizr build

When in use, Modernizr takes an interesting approach for specifying whether or not a feature is supported. The following is a screenshot (Figure 7-7) of a page on which I put a small Modernizr script.

```
<!DOCTYPE html>
▼<html lang="en" style class=" js flexbox flexboxlegacy canvas canvastext
webgl no-touch geolocation postmessage websqldatabase indexeddb hashchange
history draganddrop websockets rgba hsla multiplebgs backgroundsize
borderimage borderradius boxshadow textshadow opacity cssanimations
csscolumns cssgradients cssreflections csstransforms no-csstransforms3d
csstransitions fontface generatedcontent video audio localstorage
sessionstorage webworkers applicationcache svg inlinesvg smil svgclippaths">
  ▶ <head>…</head>
  ▶ <script type="text/javascript">…</script>
  ▼ <body>
    ▶ <header>…</header>
    ▼ <div id="body">
```

Figure 7-7. Modernizr in action on a page

133

When the page is loaded, Modernizr performs its feature checking and adds classes to the HTML tag specifying whether or not the feature in the Modernizr build is supported. If it is supported, the name of the feature will be listed as a class (such as "applicationcache") and if it is not, "no-" will be prepended (such as "no-touch"). In this case I am using Chrome and almost everything is supported. Now scripts or CSS on the page can look for these classes and choose hide/show parts of the page or turn functionality off/on, of course depending on the individual situation.

Practical Feature Detection

To keep this from being a bit nebulous, let's create a very simple scenario to show how this would work.

Let's say you need to perform an action where geolocation would be useful but you are not sure that every browser that hits your site will support the feature. For those that do, you will use the JavaScript geolocation api to request the user's location. For those that do not, you will show a field on the page that collects their postal code like this.

```
<div class="postal">
  <label>Postal Code: </label><input type="text" id="postal" />
</div>
```

Because you are using Modernizr, a class will be added to the HTML element of the page, either "geolocation" or "no-geolocation" depending on the browser. All you need to hide the field is a little CSS.

```
.geolocation .postal {
  display: none;
}
```

These same feature detections can be referenced in JavaScript as well like this:

```
if (Modernizr.geolocation) {
  console.log('hey, you have geolocation capabilities!');
}
```

There are numerous other ways this can be used. For example, let's say you create a site that can be used offline because of applicationcache. You might want to message the user telling them about this functionality but you might want to know if their browser supports it. By using feature detection you can tell those with modern browsers that they can open the site offline and those that do not that they could get this if they had a better browser/device.

Another good example would be to use feature detection to determine if the browser has touch capabilities. Touch can often be used to create a very distinctive form of interaction for the user, but you may need to have your webpage work one way for those who have touch-supporting browsers and another way for those who do not.

Those are just a few examples. For more discussion on doing feature detection, I would recommend both Dive Into HTML5's discussion [http://diveintohtml5.info/detect.html], which is general in scope and good, as well as MDN's article [http://diveintohtml5.info/detect.html], which focuses more on detecting DOM and CSS support.

Device Detection versus Feature Detection

Though I have heard some argue that you should always use feature detection and never device detection, this sets up a false dichotomy and is definitely a flawed assertion for several reasons.

First, feature detection relies on JavaScript to function, and this is not always going to be possible. Some people browse without JavaScript turned on (though I cannot imagine doing this, some people use the Web this way) but more importantly, many older mobile browsers do not support JavaScript at all.

Second, feature detection requires returning client-side assets to the browser before optimizing for capabilities, which means most bandwidth optimizations are ruled out. However, if you detect that the device visiting the site has no JavaScript support based on device capabilities, you can give them a lighter page, which is better for your bandwidth bill and will run faster on their device.

Third, not all feature set decisions on mobile can be made simply based on the existence of features. On the Match.com mobile website, we have a few features disabled for iOS 4.0 because the JavaScript engine in that OS was very slow. It had the features to do what we want, but it lacked the power to do them well. Feature detection will not solve this for you.

Fourth, feature detection alone may not help you avoid some browser bugs. Mobile browser bugs (much more common than I expected) will often be uncatchable by feature detection. Though the feature may exist, it may be broken.

But on the other hand, doing device detection based on user agents will put you in a constant battle to keep up-to-date. This is regrettable but sometimes necessary given the situation. Ultimately the answer to the question of device detection versus feature detection ends up with the most common but unsatisfying answer of all: it depends. In reality, device detection versus feature detection is a false dichotomy. Both techniques can be used beneficially.

Device detection also runs the risk of being wrong. Let's say you are using device detection to determine if a user has canvas support for his browser. As long as your database is always up-to-date and the parsing capabilities of your user-agent parsing library are never wrong, you can use device detection with confidence. But keeping the libraries up to date is a constant effort and you can never be sure that the library you are using is correct 100 percent of the time. Because of these reasons, in this case client-side feature detection is often the better choice.

Summary

Device and feature detection is a very important part of the world of mobile web development. Device detection involves interrogating user agents and making server-side decisions about what assets are returned with the web request. Feature detection involves using JavaScript on the client to determine if a feature is supported. This is a powerful technique as long as the user has JavaScript running on their web browser. But both can be used to customize the experience for the users of your website.

CHAPTER 8

■ ■ ■

Mobile Performance

The use of broadband-speed Internet gets most of us accustomed to a relatively instant Internet. But then we access it on our phones, at which point the Internet can get downright sluggish. This is mainly because mobile connection speeds are quite a bit slower than high-speed Internet. High-speed Internet unfortunately makes it easy to forget about performance because the high throughput covers over our sloppy development practices. I have frequently been guilty of this as well.

Not only do we need to start testing on our phones, we need to test with *Wi-Fi off*. The same page that takes several seconds to load on 3G will sometimes take less than a second with Wi-Fi turned on, so be sure to test for the disconnected user. And not only that, you should test in different locations with various levels of signal strength. Testing your mobile website on a slow connection can be a very humbling experience for the performance-conscious developer. For more information on how 3G and 4G connections affect performance and how to optimize for mobile bandwidth, I recommend a video by Ilya Grigorik called "Breaking the 1000ms Time to Glass Mobile Barrier [https://www.youtube.com/watch?v=Il4swGfTOSM].

The good news is that the most important techniques for a fast desktop website apply equally to mobile. This is particularly great news if you are developing a responsive website as we discussed in the first several chapters of this book. You optimize for one, and you optimize for both.

Web performance can be (and sometimes is) a book-length subject by itself, but we need to limit ourselves. The first thing I will do in this chapter is talk about some basic tools for measuring performance. I will then cover the most important performance tips for most sites. After looking at the list of performance techniques, you may notice that all are network related, in that they are about optimizing what happens between the server and the device. This is intentional, and the reason should be obvious: for mobile the biggest constraint is network bandwidth, and we need to optimize for that as much as possible.

Tools

Tools can be hugely helpful when performance tuning our websites. Two of these tools are useful for helping us see what is going on when we hit our website. One actually gives you advice on things you can improve. The first we will discuss is the Chrome Developer tools, the second is Fiddler.

The Chrome Developer Tools

The Chrome Developer Tools have a couple of functions that I find very useful for analyzing performance. The first is the Network tool. It looks like what you see in Figure 8-1.

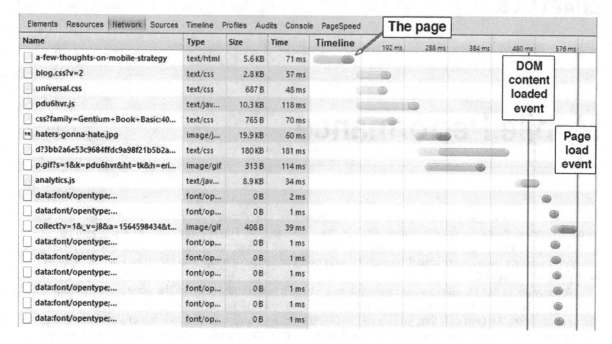

Figure 8-1. *The Network tab of the Chrome developer tools. This is a screenshot taken while browsing one of my unoptimized websites*

The network tab supplies you with nice graphical representation of how the various client-side assets were retrieved and how long it took. The first entry is the actual page and is delivered in 71 milliseconds (quite speedy), but this is rarely the measure of performance success as we will discuss below. Every other file will be requested after the initial page is delivered; and in this case, the browser didn't load all assets until 589 milliseconds had passed. As you can see, the browser is good at making requests in parallel, but if you have a script (pdu6hvr.js, the script file for Typekit) that loads a CSS file (line 7) that loads other assets (in this case, the fonts, lines 10–11, 13–18), those assets can only be downloaded after the calling script is finished. This slows everything down even more.

Another interesting piece of the Chrome developer tools is the Audits tab, seen here in Figure 8-2.

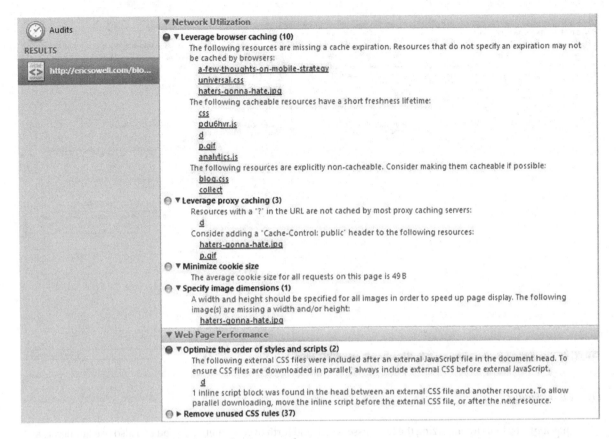

Figure 8-2. The Audits tab of the Chrome developer tools

The Audits tool applies some well-known performance rules to the page you are viewing. Recommendations are broken up between network and browser performance issues and includes color coding to help you see the more serious issues. The first suggestion contains a number of recommendations around caching, even breaking the caching issues into groups. This is a very handy way of finding easy things to improve your webpage performance. These caching issues as well as others will be discussed below.

Fiddler

Fiddler is a very useful web debugging proxy that is very useful for watching what's going on over the network. Its purpose is much more broad than website performance debugging, but I find it very useful for that as well. Here in Figure 8-3 is the same request from above as seen in Fiddler.

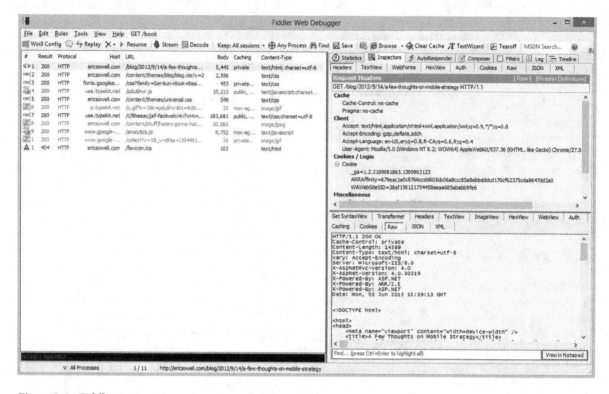

Figure 8-3. *Fiddler*

It has fantastic tools for analyzing the bits passed back and forth over the network. You can also use Fiddler as a proxy server. I have frequently found it helpful for debugging to proxy my phone through Fiddler to analyze the traffic. See the documentation for your phone and for Fiddler for setting this up (here is the documentation for setting this up for an iPhone: http://fiddler2.com/documentation/Configure-Fiddler/Tasks/ConfigureForiOS).

These are our basic tools for the chapter. There are many other tools out there that have their own strengths but these at least will get you most of what you need to know for tweaking network performance.

Performance Techniques

Now that you have seen the tools it is time to cover the principles. Rules that start with "Always" are always applicable. Those that begin with "Consider" are techniques that I have used that work great but will not be necessary in all cases.

Always Reduce the Number of HTTP Requests as Much as Possible

Reducing the number of HTTP requests before the page loads is the most important thing you can do to increase mobile performance. Additional requests require the browser to talk to the carrier, which will then fetch the resources and return them, all of which will take precious milliseconds away from your user and drain their battery. If you take a look at Figure 8-1, everything after the first three requests are from third-party plugins (Google Analytics and Typekit) and are out of my control (unless I chose to remove them). The first three requests are from my actual server and the second and third (both CSS files) can actually be combined to improve my network usage. So some of these things can be fixed.

In this particular case the savings may not be all that obvious to the users of my site but in many cases this is very important. The Match mobile website has 43 CSS files and 131 JavaScript files because we keep our client-side assets in nice maintainable chunks. But instead of including them all in the page separately and making 174 HTTP requests on every page load, we make only two because we combine our files. Another similar technique is to use CSS sprites (see "Consider Using CSS Sprites" below) to save on network requests for images. Whenever you can, *reduce the number of HTTP requests as much as possible*.

Always Use Gzip Compression

Gzip is a commonly used compression/decompression tool for web traffic. It is well supported on both browsers and servers and is something that should always be enabled. We will discuss how a browser requests it, how we can see that in our tools and how we can enable it in IIS.

The raw HTTP request from my browser to a server to fetch a page will look something like the following (this is an actual HTTP capture from Fiddler):

```
GET http://ericsowell.com/blog/2012/9/14/a-few-thoughts-on-mobile-strategy HTTP/1.1
Host: ericsowell.com
Connection: keep-alive
Cache-Control: no-cache
Accept: text/html,application/xhtml+xml,application/xml;q=0.9,*/*;q=0.8
Pragma: no-cache
User-Agent: Mozilla/5.0 (Windows NT 6.2; WOW64) AppleWebKit/537.36 (KHTML, like Gecko)
Chrome/27.0.1453.94 Safari/537.36
Accept-Encoding: gzip,deflate,sdch
Accept-Language: en-US,en;q=0.8,fr-CA;q=0.6,fr;q=0.4
```

The first line of the request describes the HTTP verb as well as the URL targeted by the request. The following lines are the HTTP headers passed in the request. These are bits of information for the server and proxies along the way that describe the client and how the client wants the request to be treated. The header related to this particular discussion is the "Accept-Encoding" header. My browser (Chrome 27) supports Gzip, deflate, and sdch. Gzip compression is the one we care about because it is more reliable than deflate (browser inconsistencies) and sdch is particular to Google Chrome and some of Google's servers. So the browser, when it makes the request, is telling the server that it supports Gzip. The server is not required to use any form of compression but should almost always do so because of the network bandwidth savings involved (it's not uncommon to see the final result to be 60–80 percent compressed).

But the client is just one part of the part of the equation. The server must be setup to handle the Gzip encoding request. If you have a site running on Azure, it is already setup for Gzip (which is a good thing). If you have your own server it may not be and it is not setup by default in IIS on Windows 8 so you may need to set it up. When requesting the page locally (without Gzip enabled), this is the raw HTTP response:

```
HTTP/1.1 200 OK
Cache-Control: private
Content-Type: text/html; charset=utf-8
Server: Microsoft-IIS/8.0
X-AspNetMvc-Version: 4.0
X-AspNet-Version: 4.0.30319
X-Powered-By: ASP.NET
Date: Mon, 03 Jun 2013 16:39:00 GMT
Content-Length: 14389

<!DOCTYPE html>
...followed by the rest of the page...
```

If the content was Gzipped, there would be another header that specified this, namely, "Content-Encoding: gzip". To fix this for the site, open up IIS Manager and choose the site you want to configure. There should be a "Compression" option (see Figure 8-4).

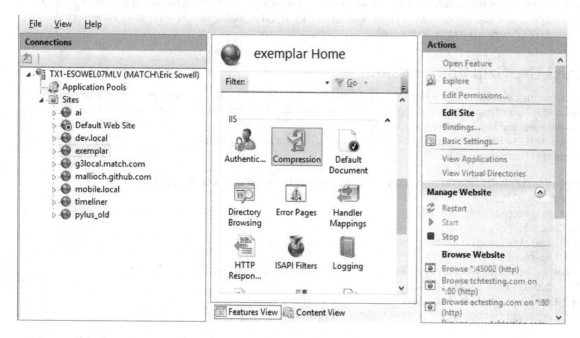

Figure 8-4. *IIS Manager*

Click on the compression option, and if the feature you need is not turned on (and it will not be by default), you should see the following in Figure 8-5.

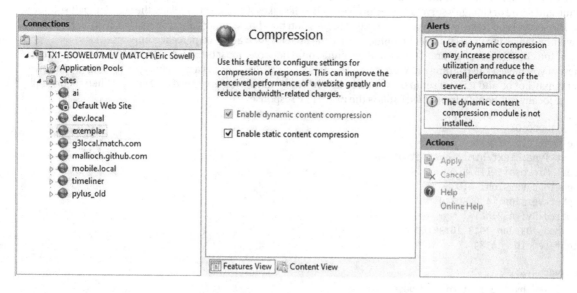

Figure 8-5. *IIS Manager compression page with dynamic compression off*

As you can see on the right, the dynamic content compression module is not installed. IIS will still do Gzip compression for static assets (like JavaScript and CSS files), but if I want my ASP.NET MVC views to be compressed, I will need to get dynamic content compression working. To install this, we find the "Turn Windows features on or off" for our computer, drill down into Internet Information Services ➤ World Wide Web Services ➤ Performance Features, select "Dynamic Content Compression" and hit "OK". Now if we look back in IIS Manager we see that it is installed, as you can see in Figure 8-6.

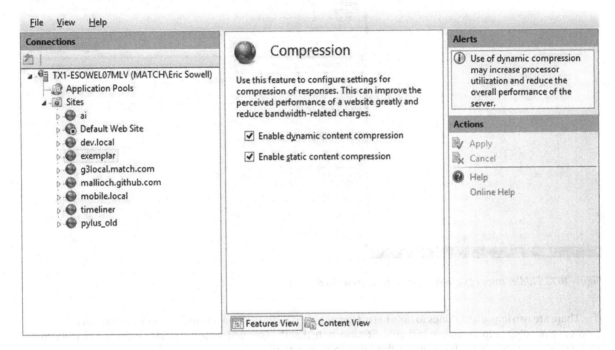

Figure 8-6. *IIS Manager compression page with dynamic compression installed and turned on*

At this point our MVC view will be compressed. Take a look at Figure 8-7. It has three requests to the same page. The first is a request locally without Gzip enabled. The second is a request to the site running on Azure with Gzip enabled. The third is a request to the site locally, now with Gzip enabled.

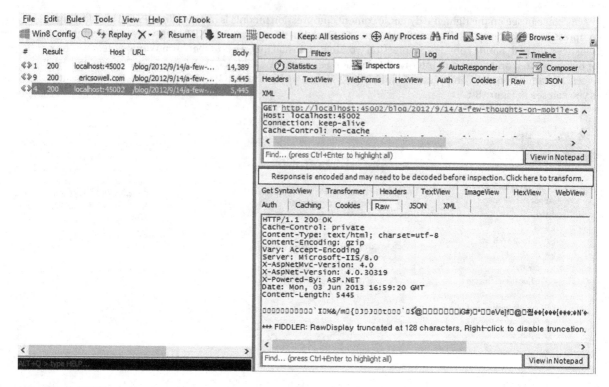

Figure 8-7. *Fiddler trace of Gzip request with Gzip enabled*

There are two important things to note here. First, the Gzip response (the one in focus in Figure 8-7) has a "Content-Encoding: gzip" header as it should. Second, note that the Gzipped response is 5445 bytes in size while the unzipped size is 14,389 bytes. It is almost a third the size after Gzipping.

Throughput on mobile is very important. Make sure your HTML, CSS, and JavaScript are all properly Gzipped.

Always Combine and Minify CSS and JavaScript

As discussed above, one of the most important rules of mobile web optimization is to reduce the number of HTTP requests for any given page. One of the best ways to do this is to both combine and minify your JavaScript and CSS.

Most sites have non-trivial amounts of both CSS and JavaScript and in most cases the developers have all this separated into multiple files since large files can be unwieldy. One or two large files are better from a performance perspective than many smaller files for a browser, so we need to combine these before we send them. Though this is good, it is also a good idea to minify the files as well as to limit the total bytes that have to travel over the network. Fortunately the ASP.NET has created a library to do both of these tasks easily.

Let's start with a simple layout page that contains references to three CSS files and three JavaScript files. It could look like this:

```
<!DOCTYPE html>

<html>
<head>
  <meta name="viewport" content="width=device-width" />
  <title>@ViewBag.Title</title>
  <link href="/content/cssfile1.css" type="text/css" rel="stylesheet" />
```

```
<link href="/content/cssfile2.css" type="text/css" rel="stylesheet" />
<link href="/content/cssfile3.css" type="text/css" rel="stylesheet" />
</head>
<body>
  <div>
    @RenderBody()
  </div>
  <script src="/content/jsfile1.js"></script>
  <script src="/content/jsfile2.js"></script>
  <script src="/content/jsfile3.js"></script>
</body>
</html>
```

Running this in Chrome, the Network tab of the developer tools (Figure 8-8) tells me the unhappy news that the simple page built on this layout page requires six HTTP requests.

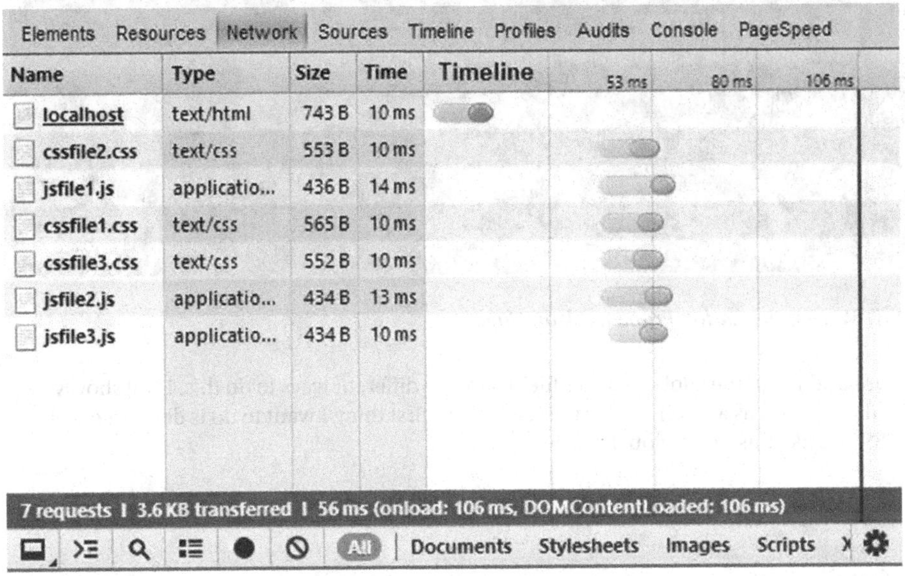

Figure 8-8. *The Network tab of Chrome showing seven requests for a single web page*

We can do better than this! To add Microsoft's bundling and minification package, right-click on the web project and choose "Manage Nuget Packages..." Search for the Microsoft ASP.NET Web Optimization Framework and install it (Figure 8-9 shows you what to look for).

Figure 8-9. *Microsoft ASP.NET Web Optimization Framework on Nuget*

Next we need to setup our bundling in the Global.asax.cs file. There are different ways to do this. I will show you one way and will leave the further options as an exercise for the reader. The first thing I want to do is define a bundle for both the JavaScript and CSS files like this in my global.asax:

```
using System;
using System.Web.Http;
using System.Web.Mvc;
using System.Web.Optimization;
using System.Web.Routing;

namespace MinifyThings
{
  public class MvcApplication : System.Web.HttpApplication
  {
    protected void Application_Start()
    {
      AreaRegistration.RegisterAllAreas();

      WebApiConfig.Register(GlobalConfiguration.Configuration);
      FilterConfig.RegisterGlobalFilters(GlobalFilters.Filters);
      RouteConfig.RegisterRoutes(RouteTable.Routes);
```

```
    var css = new Bundle("~/content/allcss", new CssMinify());

    var js = new Bundle("~/content/alljs", new JsMinify());

    BundleTable.Bundles.Add(css);
    BundleTable.Bundles.Add(js);
  }
}
```

This creates bundle objects and designates a URL for those bundles, specifies what kind of asset the bundle is for (CSS and JavaScript bundles work differently due to their different syntax), and adds those bundles to a global bundles collection for the application. Now we add the files for each.

```
using System;
using System.Web.Http;
using System.Web.Mvc;
using System.Web.Optimization;
using System.Web.Routing;

namespace MinifyThings
{
  public class MvcApplication : System.Web.HttpApplication
  {
    protected void Application_Start()
    {
      AreaRegistration.RegisterAllAreas();

      WebApiConfig.Register(GlobalConfiguration.Configuration);
      FilterConfig.RegisterGlobalFilters(GlobalFilters.Filters);
      RouteConfig.RegisterRoutes(RouteTable.Routes);

      var css = new Bundle("~/content/allcss", new CssMinify());
      css.Include("~/content/cssfile1.css",
        "~/content/cssfile2.css",
        "~/content/cssfile3.css");

      var js = new Bundle("~/content/alljs", new JsMinify());
      js.Include("~/content/jsfile1.js",
        "~/content/jsfile2.js",
        "~/content/jsfile3.js");

      BundleTable.Bundles.Add(css);
      BundleTable.Bundles.Add(js);
    }
  }
}
```

The configuration of the assets is done. We need only add the bundles to the layout page, which would look like this:

```
<!DOCTYPE html>

<html>
<head>
  <meta name="viewport" content="width=device-width" />
  <title>@ViewBag.Title</title>

  @System.Web.Optimization.Styles.Render("~/content/allcss")
</head>
<body>
  <div>
    @RenderBody()
  </div>

  @System.Web.Optimization.Scripts.Render("~/content/alljs")
</body>
</html>
```

There are two very interesting things about how this works that makes working with these combined assets quite pleasant. First of all, the assets are only combined if the web.config compilation debug value is false. This is great because combined and minified JavaScript assets are terribly hard to use when there are errors, since the combined JavaScript will now look like something like this:

```
(function(){console&&console.log("file1")})(),function(){console&&console.log("file2")}(),function()
{console&&console.log("file3")}()
```

. . . when before it looked more like this (three times over).

```
(function () {
  if (console)
    console.log('file 1');
})();
```

Without those line breaks, the line numbers we are used to in our JavaScript error messages are useless. We can avoid this in development because we will normally have debug set to "true," and we will get unminified JavaScript. But when we deploy, it all gets combined and minified for fast delivery.

Let's look at another network capture of our sample site in Figure 8-10, this time with debug set to "false" in our web.config.

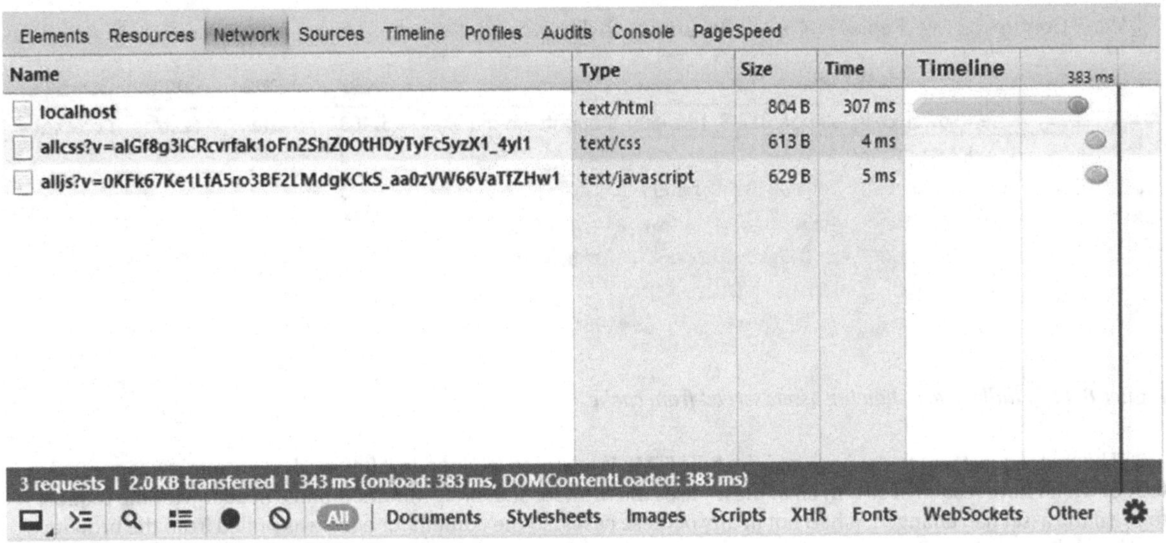

Name	Type	Size	Time	Timeline
localhost	text/html	804 B	307 ms	383 ms
allcss?v=alGf8g3ICRcvrfak1oFn2ShZ0OtHDyTyFc5yzX1_4yl1	text/css	613 B	4 ms	
alljs?v=0KFk67Ke1LfA5ro3BF2LMdgKCkS_aa0zVW66VaTfZHw1	text/javascript	629 B	5 ms	

3 requests | 2.0 KB transferred | 343 ms (onload: 383 ms, DOMContentLoaded: 383 ms)

Figure 8-10. *Our assets have been combined and minified*

Not only have our assets been combined so that we now have only three HTTP requests on the page instead of seven, but also a hash has been calculated for the content and appended onto the URL for the resource. This hash will get recalculated anytime we change our assets, which will allow us to cache that asset for a very long time without having to worry about stale assets. If any of the files change, the hash change will augment the URL, and browsers will re-request this file because the URL has changed, regardless of the client-side cache configuration set for a previous version of the file. For more on caching, see the next section "Always Cache Client-side When Possible."

Always Cache Client-Side When Possible

The fastest asset is the one you don't have to download at all. This is what client-side caching is all about. The first time assets from a site are requested by a browser, all the assets need to be retrieved either from the server or by some caching proxy in between the browser and the server. However, our focus here is on all the following requests. If the asset requested can be cached, then the browser either doesn't need to always retrieve the full payload or perhaps does not need to request it at all. There are several HTTP headers that we should understand that help control this.

If-Modified-Since

This header will sometimes be sent by the browser and indicates that the browser has a copy of the resource in cache but is checking with the server to see if a newer copy is available. If not, it will return a status of 304 with no content, which informs the browser to use what's in the cache. If new content is available, the content will be returned. This still requires a round trip to the server but can still save quite a bit of bandwidth. The following Fiddler trace (Figure 8-11) is from my blog.

#	Result	Host	URL	Body	Caching	Content-Type
1	200	ericsowell.com	/blog/2012/9/14/a-few-thoughts-on-mo...	5,468	private	text/html; charset=u
2	304	ericsowell.com	/content/blogcss?v=35rD9g0V41301Ixe...	0	private	
3	304	ericsowell.com	/content/stuff/haters-gonna-hate.jpg	0		
4	304	use.typekit.net	/c/9beeac/jaf-facitweb:i4:i7:n4:n7,jubila...	0	public, ...	
5	200	p.typekit.net	/p.gif?s=1&k=pdu6hvr&ht=tk&h=ericso...	35	max-ag...	image/gif
6	304	www.google-...	/analytics.js	0	Expires...	
7	200	www.google-...	/collect?v=1&_v=j8&a=1985750574&t=...	35	private...	image/gif

Figure 8-11. Fiddler trace showing assets served from cache

The first request was to the page and the full HTML is returned (Gzipped). Afterwards six assets are requested, four of which have results of 304. In all of these cases the browser sent an If-Modified-Since header with the request to see if the asset had changed. It had not in any of these cases, so the content for each was pulled from the browser cache, leading to a faster browsing experience.

Expires

The If-Modified-Since header is useful because it cuts down the total amount of bytes traversing the network before a page is rendered; but it would be even better if the request had not been necessary at all. This is where the Expires header is useful. The Expires header can be set on a page easily with just a little bit of code. For example, for the root of my blog I set the Expires header with this:

```
Response.Cache.SetExpires(DateTime.Now.AddMinutes(2));
```

This returns an Expires header two minutes in the future of the current request. This means the page will be cached by the browser for two minutes and if the page is requested again, it will pull from cache without checking across the network to see if it was updated. This particular use case is useful for someone browsing my blog. If they click around the blog much they will likely hit the root of the blog several times. If they do so quickly, the experience will be nice and snappy. But if the content on this page changed constantly, this would keep the data stale by two minutes and that might not be acceptable. How far you can set an Expires header into the future for a page will be dependent on each use case.

We should take a look at the example from our last performance tip and see what the HTTP response for the bundled assets is.

```
HTTP/1.1 200 OK
Cache-Control: public
Content-Type: text/css; charset=utf-8
Content-Encoding: gzip
Expires: Wed, 04 Jun 2014 02:57:22 GMT
Last-Modified: Tue, 04 Jun 2013 02:57:22 GMT
Vary: Accept-Encoding
Server: Microsoft-IIS/8.0
X-AspNet-Version: 4.0.30319
X-SourceFiles: =?UTF-8?B?YzpcZGV2XHRyYXNoXE1pbmlmeVRoaW5nc1xuaW5ppZnlUaGluЗ3NcY29udGVudFxhbGxjc3M=?=
X-Powered-By: ASP.NET
Date: Tue, 04 Jun 2013 02:57:22 GMT
Content-Length: 161
```

Fortunately, these are already given an Expires header of a year out from their creation (which is specified by the Date header), so as the user browses the site, the CSS and JavaScript will be served straight out of the cache. Expires headers can also be set in the web.config and IIS, which we will not cover here.

Cache-Control

The Cache-Control header is useful in conjunction with the Expires header. Potentially any number of intermediate proxies between the server and the browser can cache a resource. ISPs will frequently cache as will large corporations at times. Setting this header to "public" indicates that this resource can be cached by any cache, including but not limited to the cache of the browser. Setting this header to "private" indicates that the response is not to be cached by any shared cache (like that of your ISP) but only by the browser cache. Taking a look again at the HTTP response from one of the bundled assets, we can see that the Cache-Control header is in use.

```
HTTP/1.1 200 OK
Cache-Control: public
Content-Type: text/css; charset=utf-8
Content-Encoding: gzip
Expires: Wed, 04 Jun 2014 02:57:22 GMT
Last-Modified: Tue, 04 Jun 2013 02:57:22 GMT
Vary: Accept-Encoding
Server: Microsoft-IIS/8.0
X-AspNet-Version: 4.0.30319
X-SourceFiles: =?UTF-8?B?YzpcZGV2XHRyYXNoXE1pbmlmeVRoaW5nc1xNaW5pZnlUaGluЗ3NcY29udGVudFxhbGxGxjc3M=?=
X-Powered-By: ASP.NET
Date: Tue, 04 Jun 2013 02:57:22 GMT
Content-Length: 161
```

In this case, this indicates that the asset should be cached by everyone who can cache it, and it should be cached for a full year in accordance with the Expires header. For assets like this, caching for a long time makes sense.

If you want to set this in code for a page, you can do so as simply. It looks like the following:

```
Response.Cache.SetCacheability(HttpCacheability.Public);
```

Alternatively, you can set a max age on the Cache-Control header. To set the max age, do the following:

```
Response.Cache.SetMaxAge(new TimeSpan(DateTime.Now.AddMinutes(2).Ticks));
```

The max-age setting was something introduced in HTTP 1.1 to get around problems with clock synchronization inherent in the Expires header. The Cache-Control header now looks like the following:

```
Cache-Control: private, max-age=31536000
```

This sets a max age (good) but has now made the cache control private, which may not be good. You can solve this by adding yet another bit of code before the SetCacheability and SetMaxAge calls, which will now cause both settings to be taken into account. This new bit, with our other C# code can be seen in the following:

```
Response.Cache.SetExpires(DateTime.Now.AddMinutes(2));
Response.Cache.SetSlidingExpiration(true);
Response.Cache.SetCacheability(HttpCacheability.Public);
Response.Cache.SetMaxAge(new TimeSpan(0, 2, 0));
```

Another unexpected behavior you get when you set max age is that the SetMaxAge call overrides the time specified in the Expires header. As a general rule this should not be a problem; but you should be aware if you are going to use it.

In summary, cache your assets client-side when you can. This can significantly speed up your user's experience when browsing your website. For more information on caching, I recommend MDN's FAQ on caching [https://developer.mozilla.org/en-US/docs/HTTP_Caching_FAQ] and an article on caching from Google's developer site [https://developers.google.com/speed/articles/caching].

Always Optimize where CSS and Scripts are Included in the Page

Where a CSS or JavaScript file is placed in a page affects the performance (perceived or actual) of a page, sometimes dramatically. Those new to web development may not be aware of this principle, but it has been standard advice for a number of years. The rule is this: load CSS files in the head of the page and load JavaScript in the footer of the page.

If we go back to our bundling example above, you can see what this looks like.

```
<!DOCTYPE html>
<html>
<head>
  <meta name="viewport" content="width=device-width" />
  <title>@ViewBag.Title</title>

  @System.Web.Optimization.Styles.Render("~/content/allcss")
</head>
<body>
  <div>
    @RenderBody()
  </div>

  @System.Web.Optimization.Scripts.Render("~/content/alljs")
</body>
</html>
```

Why should CSS be included in the head of the page? If there are multiple CSS files, they can be downloaded in parallel but (depending on the browser) rendering will be blocked while the CSS is downloaded and parsed. Otherwise the browser would begin rendering and then have to re-render as the styling was applied. By including the CSS in the top of the page, we can avoid a flash of unstyled content where the page partially renders before CSS gets applied.

JavaScript assets behave differently than CSS assets. JavaScript files are not downloaded in parallel and will block the rendering as well as any other downloading that might occur. Because of this, it is generally recommended to put the JavaScript files at the end of the page. This allows the page to fully render (it has all markup and CSS) before the scripts are loaded.

Ultimately this rule is more about perceived performance than actual. We want the user to see the page rendered as soon as we can, but we want it to be rendered in its final form, so we include CSS at the top. The functionality added by the JavaScript can come shortly after.

There are two new attributes for the script tag, async and defer, that have decent mobile support (Android 3+, iOS 5+, BlackBerry 7+ and IE 10+). You will have to look at your traffic to determine how many of your users these new features would affect.

If a script tag has the async attribute (and the browser supports it), the JavaScript file will be downloaded without blocking other downloads, which is different from normal behavior. When the script is fully downloaded, however, rendering will be blocked as the JavaScript executes.

If a script tag has the defer attribute (and the browser supports it), the JavaScript file will be downloaded without blocking other downloads (like async) but its execution will be deferred till the page has finished parsing, at which time it will block any rendering but rendering should be done by that time anyway.

Unfortunately, using these attributes is risky. Browsers that do not support the behavior will block as the files are downloaded. Check your visitor stats before making your choice.

Consider Using CSS Sprites

The use of CSS sprites is a technique that attempts to follow rule #1: always reduce the number of HTTP requests as much as possible. Let me explain how this works. Let's say you have two elements on a page that both use an image for their visual (see Figure 8-12).

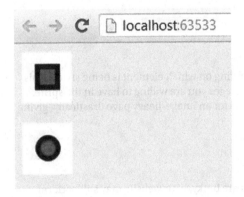

Figure 8-12. *Using a CSS sprite for the visuals for more than one element*

How are you going to implement this? The most straightforward way would be to include two image tags in the page and use them for the visuals. Functionally this is fine, but it is not very performance friendly because every image tag will require a new HTTP request. Even though two requests may be perfectly acceptable, if a wide variety of images were needed (perhaps for a menu with a number of options or for a wide variety of buttons) the multiple HTTP requests can be a real problem.

Alternatively you can use CSS sprites to achieve the same visual effect while limiting the number of HTTP requests. The screenshot in Figure 8.12 was created using a sprite. The following was the markup used for the two elements.

```
<div class="object1"></div>
<div class="object2"></div>
```

This simple markup was styled with the following CSS:

```
<style>
  .object1 {
    background-image: url('/content/sample-sprite.jpg');
    height: 50px;
    width: 50px;
  }
```

```
.object2 {
  background-image: url('/content/sample-sprite.jpg');
  height: 50px;
  width: 50px;
  background-position-x: -50px;
}
</style>
```

Though the image is referenced twice in the CSS, it is only downloaded once. Each div is 50x50 pixels square. The image is 100 pixels in width and 50 pixels in height and looks like Figure 8-13.

Figure 8-13. *Our image sprite*

The CSS uses the same background image but shifts it around depending on which element is being styled. This works with any number of images. The only constraint is the number of images you are willing to have in the sprite. And by using these sprites you can cut down the number of HTTP requests for an image-heavy page drastically, giving a better performance.

Always Optimize Your Images

Your HTML, CSS and JavaScript may be nice and lean, but if your images are bulky, your website may still perform poorly. Always optimize your images to give your users a better browsing experience. I have three recommendations around image optimization.

First, you have three commonly used images formats on the Web to choose from: GIF, PNG, and JPG. When you need an image, test to see which makes sense. Each has their strengths, and sometimes it's best to try all three on a given image to see which one gives you the best compression/quality/capability combination. GIF and PNG are both lossless compression formats that support transparency, something commonly needed in web design. JPG is a lossy compression format that does not support transparency. As a lossy compression format, JPG works great for photographs but not as well for images that include text or geometric shapes because of the tendency to blur things due to the compression. For things that need to be smaller but cannot be blurred, GIF, or PNG are usually better. PNG is the generally preferred image format for the web unless, of course, you are using an animated GIF. If you are unsure of the best image format in a given situation, try them all and see what works the best.

Second, image files often have extra data embedded in them that is not needed. Removing that data can reduce download sizes without a loss of quality. This is an easy win for mobile performance. I use the free "Image Optimizer" extension for Visual Studio 2012 by Mads Kristensen to do this optimization for me within Visual Studio. It uses both Yahoo's Smush.it (http://www.smushit.com/ysmush.it/) and punypng (http://punypng.com/) to compress images and you can see the results in the Visual Studio output window (Figure 8-14). Even if the savings are not huge, you get the savings without any negative side effects.

```
C:\dev\Exemplar\Exemplar\content\post-images\iacona-george-reader-1.jpg - using http://smushit.com
Before: 56345 bytes
After: 52579 bytes
Savings: 6.68%

C:\dev\Exemplar\Exemplar\content\post-images\nuget-packages-in-mvc-4-preview.png - using http://smushit.com
Before: 134259 bytes
After: 101656 bytes
Savings: 24.28%

C:\dev\Exemplar\Exemplar\content\post-images\ephesians-1-sinaiticus.jpg - using http://smushit.com
Before: 26647 bytes
After: 25288 bytes
Savings: 5.1%

C:\dev\Exemplar\Exemplar\content\post-images\jact-reader-2.jpg - using http://smushit.com
Before: 70012 bytes
After: 66360 bytes
Savings: 5.22%
```

Figure 8-14. *Savings gained by removing unnecessary data from images*

Third, only serve "retina-quality" images for devices that can benefit from them. Transferring these images to lower-quality displays uses extra bandwidth, slowing down your website for users that cannot benefit. See the section on responsive images in Chapter 5 for ideas on how to solve this problem.

Consider Using a Content Delivery Network

One of the most common performance recommendations is to use Content Delivery Networks (CDNs) as much as you possibly can. CDNs are in common use these days, but for those who aren't familiar with them, a CDN is a service that specializes in distributing content like images, CSS files, JavaScript, and videos on a broader geographical scale than the single location that a site might normally reside. In other words, if your website is on a server that physically resides in the United States, you can get a great deal of benefit by using a CDN that will make a copy of some of your assets and serve those assets from servers that are geographically dispersed.

This geographical proximity increases performance. Let's say you live in the United States and you visit a site that is hosted in Australia. Because of the sheer distance, the network latency will be greater. It may not matter if their site is highly optimized and replies in less than 100ms, if the distance is large, the content of the site may still take a while. And as you know, once the HTML arrives, it now has to fetch all the client-side assets that the page uses. And what if those assets request more assets? Given a long distance, this can seriously impact performance.

Enter the CDN. Let's say this Australian website kept their site where it was (creating a distributed server-side environment can be a lot of work). But they also started hosting all of their client-side assets on a CDN that had locations all over the world. Now when you request the site, the initial page request will still be just as slow, but the requests for client-side assets can go to geographically closer hosting, (potentially) increasing the response time dramatically.

For a personal site or perhaps a startup, the cost and hassle of setting up a CDN may not be worth the resources required. Your mileage may vary. I do not use a CDN for my personal site. But for higher-traffic sites, CDNs can be very beneficial.

Summary

Performance is an especially important consideration when developing websites for mobile devices. In this chapter you learned about some tools and a number of important techniques for making our mobile websites faster. There are far too many tools and techniques to cover here. For further reading, I recommend Steve Souders's *High Performance Web Sites* (O'Reilly, 2007) and Richard Kiessig's *Ultra-Fast ASP.NET 4.5* (Apress, 2012). Do whatever you can because every tiny thing can help; and be sure to test on devices with Wi-Fi turned off to experience what your real users will see when they use your site.

CHAPTER 9

■ ■ ■

Native APIs, HTML5, and CSS3 on Mobile Today

Everyone is talking about HTML5 these days, and with good reason. But many web developers don't pay much attention to the new features because they have to support older desktop browsers. Though this is understandable, it is still regrettable since good progressive enhancement and polyfilling (sometimes you can add the features to a browser if it doesn't have the feature natively) techniques can allow you to build pages that work on newer browsers that support HTML5 and older browsers that do not. Chapters 6 and 7 give you a number of tools for implementing progressive enhancement practices: so if you are unfamiliar with the idea, go back and read those. You will see some examples of polyfills in this and the upcoming chapters.

The good news is that the modern mobile browser landscape as we defined in the introduction to this book has a surprisingly rich level of support for HTML5, especially when compared to what we usually need to support in desktop web development. So in this chapter I will give all those developers who have been ignoring HTML5 a very brief overview of what works well on mobile devices. This means we will be avoiding much of the HTML5 features that have little support; so if it appears in this chapter, you can assume it will work for most of your mobile users. And because this is an overview of a large portion of HTML5 and CSS3, every feature will be discussed very briefly. Our goal here is to be thorough in terms of support but brief in terms of explanation. Because keeping a print book updated is impossible when it comes to the constantly evolving browser landscape, I recommend using resources like caniuse.com and mobilehtml5.org when in doubt about the browser support for a particular feature.

Those who haven't been keeping up with recent advances might be surprised as the number of vendor prefixes required to get many of the features in this chapter to work in the various browsers. They might even be wary. But in my experience there is little to worry about (though I will mention the bugs that I have found). In most cases the vendor-prefixed versions work much or exactly like their finalized counterparts, and using them is a natural part of an approach to web development that embraces progressive enhancement. That being said, prefixes are falling out of favor with browser vendors, so going forward we will probably see less of them. But to support mobile today, prefixing will be required for many features.

The year 2013 saw the release of a new mobile operating system that adds a number of features around native device access, namely Firefox OS. But even though the following features will be tested on Firefox OS, we will not be exploring all the capabilities that come with this new mobile OS. Because all apps for the OS are written in JavaScript, HTML5, and CSS3, many new device capabilities are available for this OS than for the others. But we will not be exploring these because Firefox OS has yet to become popular, and these new features aren't supported on other mobile platforms, so affects too few users to be overly concerned about on a general level at this point. This will likely change in the future as Mozilla has submitted proposals for these new APIs and some appear to be gaining traction.

In many of these examples you will notice a theme related to overcoming old limitations. For years we have been working around limitations in HTML and CSS by using images to do things that shouldn't require them and by using plugins like Flash and Silverlight to give us capabilities that the browser did not. Though we still have to work around browser limitations, many of the old problems have been solved and the solutions are stable and usable in the mobile world.

This chapter is organized into three sections, native phone APIs, new capabilities and visual tools. The "Native Phone APIs" section is about interacting directly with the hardware of the device. The "New Capabilities" section is about new functional tools that you can use in your mobile websites. The visual tools section is about features that are visual in nature, including HTML5 canvas, CSS3 and SVG.

Examples of all of the following can be found in the downloadable and online source code.

Native Phone APIs

There are a limited but important number of APIs available for the web developer that accesses the phone hardware. These APIs are often particularly useful for mobile devices.

Geolocation

The geolocation API is used to get a user's latitude and longitude and potentially other location information like altitude or speed. Your ability to get their location is restricted first of all by their privacy settings. For example, if the device is running iOS and if Settings ➤ Privacy ➤ Location Services is turned off, an error will be thrown when their location is requested. Assuming privacy settings allow it, the user will still be prompted to see if they want to allow you to use their current location. If they respond negatively, an error is thrown. If they respond positively, an object containing their location will be passed to your success callback. You can see this below.

```
window.addEventListener('load', function () {

    var success = function (position) {
      alert('lat: ' + position.coords.latitude + ', long: ' + position.coords.longitude);
    };

    var error = function () {
      alert('It did not work. Do you have this capability turned off?');
    };

    navigator.geolocation.getCurrentPosition(success, error);
});
```

Because errors are the browser's normal way of knowing that the call to get a user's location is not allowed, you should plan on always supplying both a success and error callback. Note that the call to getCurrentPosition is an asynchronous call. Depending on the device and how it chooses to determine the user's location, the call to get location can take some time. In my experience the call can either return immediately or take as long as 30 seconds. Consider giving the user some feedback indicating that the call to get their location is pending.

Photo Upload

Older mobile browsers did not allow the user to upload photos directly from the camera or phone storage though this was something the native SDKs allowed. For photo upload other options were necessary like emailing photos or integrations with third-party sites like Facebook. Fortunately this has recently changed and has been implemented in Android 4+, iOS6+ and BlackBerry 10.

The client-side method for accessing photos is to use the old-school file input tag even though for mobile browsers the behavior is not quite what you would expect from a desktop browser. On iOS, clicking on the input button brings up an action sheet allowing the user to take a photo with the camera or choose an existing photo from what is already saved on the device. On Android devices you get the same options but will also show any applications on the device that are registered to create/retrieve photos. This feature is nice though; in my experience you can't assume applications will return photo data in the same format that the camera or gallery will return it, which can obviously cause issues. Other than testing on a device with as many of the common photo applications as possible, I know of no good way to handle this. You will have to be very defensive in your programming.

In terms of a basic implementation that involves a simple post with an ASP.NET MVC controller to handle it, the markup involves a normal HTML form.

```
<form action="/url/to/post/to" method="post" enctype="multipart/form-data">
  <input type="file" name="fileData" id="file-input" />
  <input type="submit" value="Post" />
</form>
```

The server side implementation could look something like this.

```
[HttpPost]
public ActionResult UploadPhoto()
{
  string path = Server.MapPath(@"~/uploadspot/");

  foreach (string file in this.HttpContext.Request.Files)
  {
    var path = Server.MapPath(@"~/uploadspot/") + "somefilenameofyourchoice.jpg";
    var hpf = Request.Files[file] as HttpPostedFileBase;
    hpf.SaveAs(path);
    return Redirect("/some/page");
  }
}
```

Almost inevitably, once someone finds out they can send images from the browser, they ask if a thumbnail can be shown. The answer to this is a qualified "yes." Assuming you have an image tag on the page with an ID of "thumbnail," you could implement this feature in this manner:

```
window.addEventListener('load', load);
var fileInput, thumbnail;

function load() {

  fileInput = document.getElementById('file-input');
  thumbnail = document.getElementById('thumbnail');

  fileInput.addEventListener('change', fileSelected);
}

function fileSelected(evt) {
  var file = evt.target.files[0];

  var reader = new FileReader();
  reader.onload = fileRead;
  reader.readAsDataURL(file);
}
```

```
function fileRead(evt) {
  imageDisplay.src = evt.target.result;
}
```

On the change event of the file input the file is selected and read. The relatively new to HTML5 FileReader object (for more information, I recommend this article on MDN on using files in web applications: https://developer.mozilla.org/en-US/docs/Using_files_from_web_applications) is used to read the file as a data URL, which uses the Data URI scheme, a standard format for a base64-encoded version of a file. As an example, here is a 1x1 transparent PNG encoded as a Data URI.

data:image/png;base64,iVBORw0KGgoAAAANSUhEUgAAAAEAAAABAQMAAAAl21bKAAAAA1BMVEUAAACnej3aAAAAAXRSTl MAQObYZgAAApJREFUCB1jYAAAAIAAc/INeUAAAAASUVORK5CYII=

This format seems to have universal support in modern mobile browsers and can be safely used in all mobile browsers that support photo uploads.

Now I need to mention a couple caveats. First of all, you can't use the standard addEventListener method on FileReader for listening to the load event. This is not supported in the default Android browser that ships with early Android 4.x devices, so you should assign a function for the onload function on the FileReader as seen above.

Second, the method above has worked on all devices I have tested on except Samsung Galaxy S3 and S4. If a photo is taken with the camera on these devices in portrait orientation, the photo as rendered in the image tag will appear at a -90 degree angle. This happens in both Chrome and the default browser, so it is a problem with the manufacturer, not either of the browsers. Perhaps the easiest way to deal with this is to hide the thumbnail for these devices. It is unfortunate that this bug occurs on what are the best-selling Android devices.

Network Info API

If you need to know if the device has a connection to a network, there is an API to check. You can check a property on the window navigator or you can listen to an event. It would look like this.

```
window.addEventListener('load', load);

function load() {

  if (navigator.onLine)
    showOnline();
  else
    showOffline();

  window.addEventListener('online', showOnline);
  window.addEventListener('offline', showOffline);
}

function showOnline() {
  //code if online
}

function showOffline() {
  //code if offline
}
```

In my device testing, checking the navigator worked consistently. The online and offline events were more problematic across various browsers and devices, so use with caution.

Phone Calls and E-mail

As the world goes more mobile, the browsers we use most often have the ability to make phone calls, so phone number links to trigger a phone call can be very handy.

```
<a href="tel:4561234567">phone number</a>
```

The old standard format for e-mail links continue to work in mobile browsers.

```
<a href="mailto:foo@example.com">email address</a>
```

These formats have been around quite a while and seem to have universal support. This is generally straightforward, though automatic phone number detection can be a problem. Among my test devices, no Android or Firefox OS device did automatic phone number detection though Windows Phone 7.5 and iOS both do. So, for example, the number in the following paragraph will be treated like a phone number link in both of these devices.

```
<p>Phone number (456) 123-4567 in the midst of text.</p>
```

Windows Phone 7.5 and iOS will also turn "456 123 4567" and "456-123-4567" into phone number links. iOS is even more aggressive and will apparently turn any 10-digit number into a phone number, so 4561234567 in the midst of a paragraph will be treated as a phone number. This is great for all those businesses on the Internet that don't know how to mark up their contact pages so people can call them. This is unfortunate when one of these auto-detect algorithms picks up a number that it shouldn't. Fortunately for us, we can turn off this automatic browser detection on iOS by adding a meta tag to the page.

```
<meta name="format-detection" content="telephone=no">
```

Unfortunately, I have found no way to turn off this detection on Windows Phone 7.5. Windows Phone 8 does not seem to exhibit the behavior. According to MSDN [http://msdn.microsoft.com/en-us/library/ie/dn265018(v=vs.85).aspx], Internet Explorer 11 allows you to use the same meta tag for Internet Explorer on the Windows Phone platform, but that hasn't launched yet and doesn't help with older phones. Just be aware that this is the case, and if you care that this is happening, format the number you are using differently if you can and fool the browser.

Accessing Maps

How you access maps depends on the device you are targeting. For iOS devices, assuming you want to trigger the built-in iOS maps application that comes in iOS 6, a query to maps.apple.com is what you will need to use, like this: http://maps.apple.com/?q=cupertino. This will open up the native iOS maps application on the device if the device has it installed. For older versions of iOS, Google Maps will be opened in Safari.

For Android devices, you can use the same URL as above. When clicked, Android will give you the choice to open up the maps application. You could also choose to use http://maps.google.com/?q=cupertino because that works just as well for Android, but this may not open the native Google Maps application on iOS (this may depend on iOS version and how settings are configured).

Windows Phone 7.5 will open up the native maps on the device with either of the following two types of links:

```
<a href="maps:Cupertino">map</a> <!--lat/long also supported -->
<a href="http://www.bing.com/maps/?where1=cupertino">map</a>
```

Unfortunately only the first seems to work for Windows Phone 8. If iOS and Android supported the maps value for anchor tags then we would have a nice cross-browser solution, but this isn't the case. To get native map linking across multiple devices, you will have to conditionally render links based on device OS. Chapter 6 explains several methods for conditional rendering, so check there for ideas on how to implement this.

New Capabilities

With newer browsers comes newer functionality. In this section we go over what we can do with HTML and JavaScript that we couldn't do just a few years ago.

Web Sockets

Web sockets allow the browser and server to create a two-way socket connection. Normally the web works on a request/response, disconnected model. With web sockets this model is changed. Using web sockets would look something like this:

```
var connection = new WebSocket('ws://yoursite.com/websocketendpoint');
connection.onopen = function () {
  connection.send('connection opened');
};

connection.onmessage = function (evt) {
  console.log('Message from server:', evt.data);
};
```

But most will not be using web sockets directly. Web sockets in the mobile space still have modest support so it's usually advisable to use web sockets and some other technique, such as long-polling (this involves leaving a connection open with the server, which it completes whenever a message needs to be sent). There is also a server-side component as well. To solve the need for downgrade support and server-side support, I would recommend using SignalR. SignalR gives you what you need in both cases and is very easy to use. Here is how you would create a simple page that uses SignalR.

First, install SignalR through Nuget. A search for "SignalR" should be sufficient or you can type the following into the Nuget Package Manager Console:

```
PM> Install-Package Microsoft.AspNet.SignalR
```

Second, create a page in the website that contains the following script references, in this order. The location of your files for the first two may vary for your site. The version of the files may also be different. Check and see what you got when you installed SignalR. The last script tag needs to be left as-is.

```
<script src="~/content/jquery-1-9-0.js"></script>
<script src="~/scripts/jquery.signalR-1.1.3.js"></script>
<script src="~/signalr/hubs"></script>
```

Third, create a SignalR endpoint. Here is a very minimal implementation.

```
using Microsoft.AspNet.SignalR;

namespace MobileMvcSamples.SignalR
{
  public class SampleSignalRConnection : PersistentConnection
  {
    protected override System.Threading.Tasks.Task OnConnected(IRequest request, string
connectionId)
    {
      Connection.Send(connectionId, "You are now connected.");
```

```
        return base.OnConnected(request, connectionId);
    }

    protected override System.Threading.Tasks.Task OnReceived(IRequest request, string
connectionId, string data)
    {
        Connection.Broadcast(data);
        return base.OnReceived(request, connectionId, data);
    }
  }
 }
}
```

Fourth, register the endpoint in your global.asax.cs file in Application_Start *before any of the MVC registration*. If you do not put it before, your SignalR endpoint will likely not work.

```
RouteTable.Routes.MapConnection<SampleSignalRConnection>("sample", "/signalr/connect");
RouteTable.Routes.MapHubs();
```

You are now able to use SignalR in your site. Here is a simple example that lets multiple people send messages to each other on the same page.

```
<input placeholder="Put a message here." id="message" />

<button id="send">send</button>

<p style="border-top: solid 1px #CCC; padding-top: 20px;">Messages sent/received:</p>

<ol id="messages">
</ol>

<script>
  $(document).ready(function () {

    var sendButton = $('#send');
    var input = $('#message');

    var connection = $.connection('/signalr/connect');
    connection.start();

    connection.received(function (response) {
      $('#messages').append('<li>' + response + '</li>');
    });

    $('#send').click(function () {
      connection.send(input.val());
      input.val('');
    });

  });
</script>
```

Let's discuss this sample just a bit. The first thing that a page needs to do before using web sockets with SignalR is to create a connection with the server. In this case we setup the connection endpoint URL as "/signalr/connect", so connecting looks like this.

```
var connection = $.connection('/signalr/connect');
connection.start();
```

After a connection is established, messages can be sent

```
connection.send('this is a message');
```

or received.

```
connection.received(function (response) {
  //do something with the response
});
```

In the case of our example above, we read the value out of the input tag on the page and send that to the server. All messages that the server sends back are appended to the ordered list element. The interesting thing about this approach is not that we are sending messages to the server but that the server is sending messages to the browser. So if two people were to visit this page and one was to send a message, the message would get sent from the server to both. This kind of two-way communication can be very useful and leveraged to update a client real-time as events happen on a server.

But this is just the proverbial tip of the iceberg for both web sockets and SignalR. For more information, I recommend finding a dedicated book on the subject.

As for device support, iOS 4.2+, Android 4+ in Chrome, BlackBerry 10, Kindle Fire HD, and Windows Phone 8 all support web sockets. But using a tool like SignalR to mimic the behavior on other devices can often mitigate any reasons for avoiding this feature of HTML5.

On a final note, to use web sockets with ASP.NET you will need IIS 8 or later, which starts with Windows 8 and Windows Server 2012. The web socket protocol is not supported on IIS versions below this.

Web Storage

The new web storage features of HTML5 are available on all our modern smartphone browsers. These features allow you to store state on the client. Unlike cookies, this state is not sent on requests to the server. This state is kept on the client at all times unless you pull the data out and explicitly send it to the server. The amount of data you are allowed to store in web storage differs between the browsers though the allowable space should be at least 2.5 megabytes.

Web storage comes in two types, local storage and session storage. Data saved in local storage is kept on the device until the data is erased, which happen if the user clears their browser's cookies and data or if you delete it through code. Session storage data is kept until the browser session expires. So for example, if you store something in session storage and they close their browser window and come back, that data will no longer be there.

Both storage options store strings, not objects. If you have an object to store, serialize it to a string and store it then deserialize it when you retrieve it. The APIs for both look like this.

```
localStorage.setItem('localStorageKey', 'foo'); //Add the value to storage
var itemInStorage = localStorage.getItem('localStorageKey') //Retrieve the value from storage
localStorage.removeItem('localStorageKey'); //Remove the value from storage

sessionStorage.setItem('sessionStorageKey', '42');
var itemInSessionStorage = sessionStorage.getItem('sessionStorageKey')
sessionStorage.removeItem('sessionStorageKey');
```

```
//Here is an example using an object.
var obj = { name: 'Bob' };
localStorage.setItem('objectkey', JSON.stringify(obj));
var retrievedObj = JSON.parse(localStorage.getItem('objectkey'));
localStorage.removeItem('objectkey');
```

As a final note, iOS users browsing with the private browsing setting on for Safari will not be able to store data in web storage. Attempts to store data will raise a "QUOTA_EXCEEDED_ERR", the same error that would be raised if you reached the maximum storage allowed on the device. Other than handling this error, I know of no way of knowing if a user has private browsing turned on. If your use of web storage is critical to the function of your web application, consider falling back to cookies or to holding data in memory if you can.

Offline Web Applications

The Offline Web Applications feature of HTML5 adds another level of caching for the browser. This level of caching lies between the browser and normal HTTP caching (see Chapter 8 for more details on HTTP caching). By using this feature, you can cache a page and all its image, JavaScript, CSS, web font and other client-side assets in the browser, and the user can continue to use the assets even when offline.

You trigger this offline cache by setting a manifest file for a page, which you specify in the HTML tag like this:

```
<html manifest="/content/cache.appcache">
```

The manifest file specified tells the browser what to cache. The page itself is always cached, but you can specify in the manifest file if the linked CSS, JavaScript and other static files are to be pulled from the cache or from the network. Here is a sample manifest file.

```
CACHE MANIFEST
#version 11

CACHE:
/content/appcache/test.css
/content/appcache/your.js

NETWORK:
/content/appcache/test2.css
```

The first thing to note is that the file must begin with the words "CACHE MANIFEST". The next line is a comment and is optional (more on that in a bit). The CACHE and NETWORK sections are optional sections (there are a few more) and specify what files are to be put in the cache and which are to be retrieved over the network respectively.

How all this works can be a bit tricky. Let's say we have the above manifest specified for a page. When the page is requested by a browser that supports the Offline Web Application feature, it creates a cache for the files and downloads the files specified in the CACHE section. The next time the page is requested, the browser will not request the page but will check to see if the manifest has changed. If the manifest has changed, the browser will display what it has in the cache but will begin downloading a new version of the page and all assets specified in the CACHE section of the manifest. The browser does not reload the page with the newly retrieved cache assets. It will show those *the next time* the page is reloaded. Of course it will always download test2.css because it is contained in the NETWORK section.

Here is where the comment can be very useful. Let's say you have deployed your offline web app and people are using it but you need to update your test.css file. You make the changes to the file and then find that nobody has the new copy of your CSS file. Why? Because *the browser will never download a new copy of the cached assets until it sees that the manifest itself has changed.* This is where the version comment comes in handy. Bump the version up a number, and the browsers will see that the manifest has changed and will download a new copy of the files.

Fortunately the browsers give you some control over how this works via JavaScript. There are events on the window.applicationCache object that you can attach to so you can see in code what is happening with the application cache, like when it is checking for a new manifest, when it doesn't find one, when it does, as each asset is downloaded and when the new cache is ready. At that point you can choose to refresh the page with the new assets, though you might want to consider asking the user before doing so just in case they were in the middle of using your offline page.

If any of the cached assets failed to download, the application cache for the page will remain unchanged and the user will be able to continue on their merry way. If you find that your page is not changing even after changing the manifest, look for errors in download. This feature can be a bit annoying for the developer but it makes a great deal of sense for the user. Assuming they downloaded a working offline app, this feature protects their working environment when there are download issues, keeping them productive.

The Chrome developer tools are very useful when debugging application cache issues. They can show you all of the cached assets and write to the console anytime an application cache event fires, so it gives you excellent visibility into the workings of the cache. You can also go to chrome://appcache-internals/ where it will list all application caches saved in the browser. I have found the remove button handy many times as I've debugged issues.

Here is one final gotcha when it comes to using manifest files with ASP.NET and IIS, which is that IIS does not yet know how to handle .appcache files by default. But this is easily solved. Open the web.config in the root of your ASP. NET MVC project and add these two nodes to the staticContent section of system.webServer. If staticContent isn't specified yet, do so.

```
<configuration>
  <system.webServer>
    <staticContent>
      <remove fileExtension=".appcache"/>
      <mimeMap fileExtension=".appcache" mimeType="text/cache-manifest"/>
    </staticContent>
  </system.webServer>
</configuration>
```

This should make application cache work locally. If you are deploying to Azure, you need to mark the build action on the .appcache as "Content", otherwise the file may not be pushed.

Mobile browsers have excellent support for this feature. In our device test set, all of our browsers except that of Windows Phone 7.5 support this feature. That is a very brief introduction to offline web applications. If this has made you curious, I recommend checking out the HTML5 rocks website on this subject [http://www.html5rocks.com/en/features/offline] to help you learn more about the features and difficulties that come with using this feature.

Web Workers

JavaScript in the browser is single-threaded, and in most cases this is OK. But in the cases when it isn't, this is where HTML5 web workers come in very handy as they give you the ability to run a task in the background. Web workers have to be in a separate file and a simple one would look like this.

```
self.onmessage = function(event) {
  this.times = 0;

  setInterval(function() {

      var text = 'Hi! I have said this ' + this.times + ' time(s) before.';
      this.times++;

      self.postMessage({ message: text });
  },
  500);
};
```

This is a complete web worker script. Web workers execute in a different global context than the window and are referenced with "self" as you can see in the sample above. Here is how a page might use this worker.

```
var worker = new Worker('/content/webworkers/webworker.js');
worker.postMessage(''); //no value is necessary but an argument is required for wp8 only
worker.addEventListener('message', function(event) {
  //do something with the message, which will be contained in event.data;
});
```

The worker is an instance of a Worker object, which requires a JavaScript file to specify what the worker is to be doing. The contents of that file are what you saw above. The page communicates to the worker by calling postMessage and at that point the worker will begin. As I've coded it above, the worker uses postMessage to send a message back to the calling window every 500 milliseconds. When the message is received on the window thread, it executes in that context.

Web workers are available for iOS 5+ and Android 4+, Windows Phone 8, Kindle Fire HD and BlackBerry 10.

History API

The browser history object has been around quite a while, but in the last few years it has gained some new capabilities. In the days of yore, those who wanted to manipulate the browser history probably did so through updating the hash. For example, if you do this on a page

```
window.location.hash = 'foo';
```

you now have #foo appended to your URL and a step has been added into the browser history, so if the user hits his back button, he will go back to the page without the #foo appended to the end of the URL. This is very handy, but wouldn't it be nice to just change the URL itself?

Yes it would, and the new improvements are here to do just that. You can choose to change the URL without adding a step in the browser history by using the history.replaceState API. It looks like this:

```
history.replaceState({}, null, '/this/is/the/new/url');
```

Related is the version of the API that changes the URL but adds a step in the browser history. It looks like this:

```
history.pushState({}, null, '/this/is/another/new/url');
```

Both methods have two parameters before the new URL is passed. The first is state you could pass, the second would be the title, but I find that neither work consistently. Support for this API is rather sketchy on mobile because Android dropped support during versions 3.0-4.1, even taking only the last parameter into account. This API is very useful if you need history within a single page, but be prepared to handle a lack of support or use a polyfill like history. js [https://github.com/browserstate/history.js/] to smooth over the browser incompatibilities.

Audio and Video

Native audio and video are important additions to HTML5 and have universal support in modern mobile browsers. We spent some time with the video element in Chapter 5, as you may recall. The primary issue when it comes to both audio and video is that of format. The HTML5 specification does not define the allowable formats, and browser makers have each gone their own way. As of yet, there is still no universally accepted video format so the content provider will have to deliver videos in various formats. Generally H.264, WebM, and Theora will work. There are more audio formats supported including Ogg Vorbis, MP3, WAV, and WebM as well. For a list of supported formats across various browsers, see MDN [https://developer.mozilla.org/en-US/docs/HTML/Supported_media_formats].

Both tags have an easy mechanism for supplying multiple formats. Here is an example of a video tag:

```
<video>
  <source src="foo.webm" type="video/webm">
  <source src="foo.mp4" type="video/mp4">
  <source src="foo.ogv" type="video/ogg">
  <p>Your browser does not support HTML5 video.</p>
</video>
```

An audio tag with multiple formats would look similar.

```
<audio>
  <source src="foo.wav" type="audio/wav">
  <source src="foo.mpg" type="audio/mpeg">
  <p>Your browser does not support HTML5 audio.</p>
</audio>
```

In both cases the browsers select from the available sources, from top-to-bottom and choose the first supported format. If the tag is not supported by the browser at all, it will show the other source nested within the tag. Otherwise it will be hidden.

Better Semantics

HTML5 specifies a number of new semantic tags, like article, aside, section, nav, header, and footer. These don't give you greater capabilities per se but do help you write more expressive, semantic markup. If you are worried about using supporting browsers that do not support these elements, you can use the HTML5 shim script to add support through JavaScript [https://code.google.com/p/html5shim/]. Modernizr also provides this same support. But this should not be required in any of our test browsers.

Visual Tools

Along with our new functional tools we have a new set of visual tools. Due to the visual nature of the selection, most of these tools are innovations in CSS.

Web Fonts

One long-standing limitation in web development has been the dearth of available typefaces on the web. HTML and CSS has always been limited to the fonts installed on the machine, not on the server. And since Windows, Mac, and Linux have always had a different set of default fonts, web developers have been very limited in what they could use. Of course workarounds were developed, chiefly the use of images to replace text on the web, which was a hassle and less SEO friendly than plain text. This is no longer necessary. You can now use web fonts.

Web fonts allow you in CSS to specify a font to download to the browser. You use the @font-face CSS at-rule to specify the font, like this.

```
@font-face {
  font-family: Gentium;
  src: url(   '/content/webfonts/web/GentiumPlus-R.woff') format('woff'),
    url('/content/webfonts/GentiumPlus-R.ttf') format('truetype');
}
```

After this point you can use the font family name specified in the @font-face rule in your CSS as you would any other font.

Alternatively, instead of using web fonts directly you can use online font providers. Two popular choices are Typekit (https://typekit.com/) and Google Fonts (http://www.google.com/fonts). I have used the former on a number of projects, and it has worked great. Before you can a font on the Web, you have to obtain the right to use the font or find a font with an open-use policy. These font providers can be useful for finding a variety of usable fonts if you have trouble finding one for yourself.

Web font capabilities also allow the use of icon fonts. By using fonts instead of images for icons, you get scaling without degradation and more control over styling. If you want to see a good example of using icon fonts, check out http://fontello.com/. They allow you to easily create your own custom font for use in your websites and even provide the CSS you need as a part of the download.

Web fonts are well supported on mobile. In our standard device test set, only Android 2.1 and Windows Phone 7.5 couldn't handle the fonts.

Transitions

Transitions are a new feature added to CSS3 that allows you to specify how a CSS property is to transition from one value to another over time. For example, people have been using the pseudo-class ":hover" to change the visual state of DOM elements for a while. If you had a button with the ID of "click-me", you could use it like this:

```
#click-me:hover {
  background-color: #000;
  color: #FFF;
}
```

This changes the background color of the button to black and the color of the text to white. But what if you didn't want the *transition* between the default state and the hover state to be immediate? Without CSS-based transitions, you would probably use a JavaScript timer to change the value over time to get you the effect that you want. CSS transitions make this much easier. For example, if you change the CSS just a bit, you get this effect without having to resort to JavaScript.

```
#click-me {
  -webkit-transition: all .3s ease-in-out;
  -moz-transition: all .3s ease-in-out;
  -o-transition: all .3s ease-in-out;
  transition: all .3s ease-in-out;
}

#click-me:hover {
  background-color: #000;
  color: #FFF;
}
```

Though I added four new CSS properties, only one is really going to be applied by a browser and the rest are just to cover our bases for browsers with prefixed implementations. If we take the standard property, "transition: all .3s ease-in-out" as our example, this line says that all the CSS properties are to be transitioned if another style rule is applied (like hover), the transition is to last .3 seconds and the browser is to ease the transition in and out, so that it would transition more slowly at the beginning and end and would change the fastest in the middle.

Note that the transition is specified as a default state. This allows multiple states to apply to an element and all share the same transition rule. A transition rule can be targeted at a single CSS property, simply by changing the rule to something like this: transition: **color** .3s ease-in-out. As you might expect, not all CSS properties can be transitioned. MDN has a nice list if you are curious about seeing which can be transitioned [https://developer.mozilla.org/en-US/docs/Web/CSS/CSS_animated_properties]. As a rule of thumb, if the property is numeric (including color properties, which are numeric even if they don't seem to be), it can probably be transitioned.

Animations

Animations are another feature added to CSS3 that gives you much greater control over transitioning CSS properties from one state to another. CSS animations use keyframes to specify how an element is to change over time. Here is an example:

```
@-webkit-keyframes changify {
  0% {
    margin-left: 0;
  }
  50% {
    margin-top: 150px;
  }
  100% {
    margin-left: 250px;
  }
}

@keyframes changify {
  0% {
    margin-left: 0;
  }
  50% {
    margin-top: 150px;
  }
  100% {
    margin-left: 250px;
  }
}

.custom-animation {
  border: solid 1px #000;
  padding: 10px;

  -webkit-animation-name: changify;
  -webkit-animation-duration: 1s;
  -webkit-animation-iteration-count: infinite;
  -webkit-animation-direction: alternate;

  animation-name: changify;
  animation-duration: 1s;
  animation-iteration-count: infinite;
  animation-direction: alternate;
}
```

The above animation moves the element down, back up and to the right over a period of one second, rewinds itself and starts over again. For this to work well, you will need to specify -webkit-, -moz- and -ms- prefixing for both the keyframes and the animation properties. I only specified the webkit prefixes above as an example.

You have to be careful when it comes to browser support. Android 2.x, iOS 4, and the original Kindle Fire all have buggy implementations, and the animation doesn't work at all on Windows Phone 7.5.

Transformations

Have you ever wanted to skew, rotate, or scale an element on a page? If you have, CSS transformations are here for you. The allow you to do all three easily through CSS. And if you use all the vendor prefixes (-o-, -ms-, -webkit- and -firefox-), they work across our entire device test suite. Here is some sample CSS without the prefixes. Given four divs

```
<div class="div1">
  This is a box.
</div>
<div class="div2">
  This is a box.
</div>
<div class="div3">
  This is a box.
</div>
<div class="div4">
  This is a box.
</div>
```

with some simple styling plus these transformations, you get what you see in Figure 9-1.

```
.div1 {
  transform: rotate(90deg);
}

.div2 {
  transform: skew(-25deg);
}

.div3 {
  transform: scale(0.5);
}

.div4 {
  transform: rotate(90deg) skew(-25deg) scale(1.2);
}
```

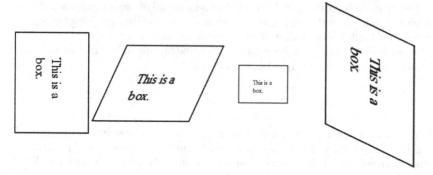

Figure 9-1. *Transformations, either singly or combined, applied to some divs*

With the appropriate vendor prefixes (-moz-, -webkit-, -o- and -ms- in this case), the CSS rules work against our entire test device set.

Gradients

Another visual tool you get with CSS3 is the ability to create gradients in CSS. This can be a huge timesaver. A few years ago we would have had to create images for this. Take, for example, these squares in Figure 9-2.

Figure 9-2. *The top gradient is a linear gradient, the bottom a radial gradient*

The CSS for both of these is as follows.

```
.linear {
  border: solid 1px #000;
  height: 150px;
  width: 150px;

  background: -moz-linear-gradient(top, rgba(30,87,153,1) 0%, rgba(125,185,232,1) 100%);
  background: -o-linear-gradient(top, rgba(30,87,153,1) 0%,rgba(125,185,232,1) 100%);
  background: -webkit-gradient(linear, left top, left bottom, color-stop(0%,rgba(30,87,153,1)),
    color-stop(100%,rgba(125,185,232,1)));
  background: -webkit-linear-gradient(top, rgba(30,87,153,1) 0%,rgba(125,185,232,1) 100%);
  background: linear-gradient(to bottom, rgba(30,87,153,1) 0%,rgba(125,185,232,1) 100%);
  filter: progid:DXImageTransform.Microsoft.gradient( startColorstr='#1e5799',
endColorstr='#7db9e8',
    GradientType=0 );
}

.radial {
  border: solid 1px #000;
  height: 150px;
  width: 150px;

  background: -moz-radial-gradient(center, ellipse cover,  rgba(21,61,107,1) 0%,
rgba(137,204,255,0.28) 100%);
  background: -webkit-gradient(radial, center center, 0px, center center, 100%, color-
stop(0%,rgba(21,61,107,1)),
    color-stop(100%,rgba(137,204,255,0.28)));
  background: -webkit-radial-gradient(center, ellipse cover,  rgba(21,61,107,1)
0%,rgba(137,204,255,0.28) 100%);
  background: -o-radial-gradient(center, ellipse cover,  rgba(21,61,107,1) 0%,rgba(137,204,255,0.28)
100%);
  background: radial-gradient(ellipse at center,  rgba(21,61,107,1) 0%,rgba(137,204,255,0.28) 100%);
  filter: progid:DXImageTransform.Microsoft.gradient( startColorstr='#153d6b',
    endColorstr='#4789ccff',GradientType=1 ); /* IE6-9 fallback on horizontal gradient */
}
```

An understandable first impression of this CSS would be that this is clearly too much CSS to generate a simple gradient. You can only consistently get cross-browser gradients if you use a gamut of browser-specific prefixes (the standards-compliant property is in bold). If you do so, you can reliably get linear gradients for all common desktop browsers and our standard device set. You can reliably get radial gradients for all but Internet Explorer 6-9 and early Android browsers.

If you look closely at the different variations you will also notice that the specification for each is different. Webkit even changed its format along the way so two different formats are required to get fullest support. Because life is too short and learning all of these variations is of little value, I recommend using a tool to generate them. I use "The Ultimate CSS Gradient Generator" from ColorZilla [http://www.colorzilla.com/gradient-editor/] because setting up a gradient is easy and the tool is free.

Shadows

Creating the effect of a shadow also used to be something we would accomplish with images instead of CSS. Fortunately this is now a solved problem for mobile. Shadows in CSS come in two forms, text shadows and box shadows. Apply the following CSS to some text, and you will see what is in Figure 9-3.

```
.text-shadowing {
  font-family: Helvetica, Verdana, sans-serif;
  font-size: 2em;
  text-shadow: 5px 20px 5px #000;
}
```

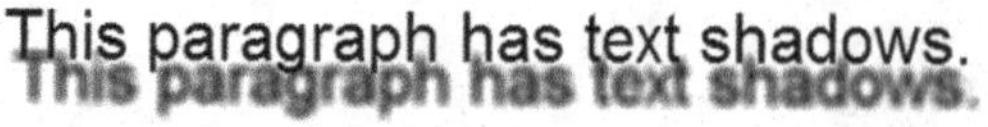

This paragraph has text shadows.

Figure 9-3. *Basic text shadows applied to a paragraph*

Shadows for DOM elements are just as easily applied, as you can see in Figure 9-4.

```
.box-shadowing {
  border: solid 1px #000;
  box-shadow: 2px 10px 15px rgba(150, 150, 150, 1);
  height: 100px;
  width: 100px;
}
```

Figure 9-4. *Basic box shadow applied to a div*

In the case of both types of shadows, the first pixel value sets the horizontal offset for the shadow, the second the vertical offset, the third the blur radius (0 produces a hard line at the edge, higher values increase the blur) and the fourth the color of the shadow. Box shadows support another parameter, that of inset, to apply the shadow inside the element.

I recommend including the -webkit- prefix for box shadows, otherwise older webkit-based browsers (iOS and Android) will not display the shadow. With that prefix box shadows are supported universally in our test device set with the exception of Windows Phone 7.5.

Border Radius

Another common reason to create images for website designs was to get rounded corners for DOM elements. You can achieve the same effect with the new CSS border radius property. If you apply the following CSS, you get the image in Figure 9-5.

```
.round-me {
  border: solid 1px #000;
  border-radius: 15px;
  height: 100px;
  width: 100px;
}
```

Figure 9-5. *An example of border radius*

The CSS border radius property is supported on all of our target test devices.

Opacity and RGBA

There are now two ways to manage opacity in plain CSS, the use of the opacity property and the use of RGBA. Though both can create a translucent element in a page, they do it very differently, so one will apply in some cases and not in the other. Let's start with some HTML.

```
<div class="container">
  <div class="other">
      behind
  </div>
  <div class="main-element">
      This is a box.
  </div>
</div>
```

Here I am going to use CSS to position one element behind another, and we will turn the element on top translucent. Here is the example using opacity.

```
.container {
  position: relative;
}

.other {
    background-color: #F00;
    border: solid 1px #000;
    padding: 15px;
    position: absolute;
    width: 200px;
    top: 30px;
    z-index: 1;
}

.main-element {
    background-color: #FFF;
    border: solid 1px #000;
    height: 100px;
    left: 35px;
```

```
  opacity: .4;
  position: absolute;
  top: 0;
  width: 100px;
  z-index: 10;
}
```

With this you see the image in Figure 9-6.

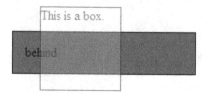

Figure 9-6. *The whole div is translucent because we are using the opacity property*

Opacity values range from 0 to 1, with 0 being completely transparent and 1 being completely opaque. The important thing to note that will contrast this with RGBA is that everything about the overlying element is translucent, background color, text, and border. If you remove the opacity and change the background color to the following, you see the image in Figure 9-7.

```
background-color: rgba(255, 255, 255, .5);
```

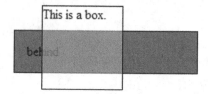

Figure 9-7. *Only the background is translucent because the color is only applied to the background*

RGBA uses a different notation for color than the usual hexadecimal notation, although it is the same color specification. The last value expresses the alpha value for the color and corresponds to the opacity property above in effect and in specifying the values. Note that in this case the text and border are completely opaque and only the background color is translucent because only the background color is translucent, not the whole element.

Both RGBA and Opacity are supported by all of our test devices.

Multiple Backgrounds

Sometimes it can be helpful to layer background images to achieve a certain design for a page. Fortunately, multiple background images can now be specified for an element. Here is an example:

```
.background-me {
  background-image: url('/content/svg/circle.svg'),
    url('/content/images/bacon_100.jpg'),
    url('/content/images/hogan_100.jpg');
```

```
background-position: top left, bottom right, bottom left;
background-repeat: no-repeat;

border: solid 1px #000;
height: 200px;
width: 200px;
}
```

Note that the background images are comma-delimited, as are the instructions on where these images are to appear. Though it is unlikely that you will need to create a background that is a combination of a red circle, a piece of bacon, and a recursively mustached Hulk Hogan, the point is that you can quite easily do so with the multiple-background feature of CSS. Figure 9-8 actually looks like the following in a browser:

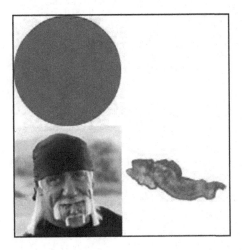

Figure 9-8. *An example of using multiple background images in a single div*

Browsers that support SVG (see below for more on what SVG is and what devices support it) can use SVG files alongside images for multiple backgrounds. This CSS background feature is supported by all of our test devices.

Canvas

The canvas element in HTML5 is an incredibly capable visual tool and my personal favorite addition to come with HTML5 and CSS3. Canvas is named perfectly, as it gives you canvas upon which you can paint anything you can think of, assuming you also have the JavaScript skills to implement it. It all starts with a simple HTML element.

```
<canvas id="the-canvas">
</canvas>
```

Canvas is painting is entirely done in JavaScript. Here is a sample script that draws a few shapes.

```
window.onload = function () {

  var canvas = document.getElementById('the-canvas');
  var context = canvas.getContext('2d');
```

```
//This draws a polygon
context.beginPath();
context.moveTo(10, 10);
context.lineTo(50, 10);
context.lineTo(60, 20);
context.lineTo(5, 80);
context.lineTo(30, 30);
context.closePath();

context.strokeStyle = '#000';
context.stroke();

context.fillStyle = '#F00';
context.fill();

//This draws a circle
context.beginPath();
context.arc(100, 100, 35, 0, Math.PI * 2);

context.fillStyle = '#00F';
context.fill();

//This draws a rectangle
context.beginPath();
context.fillStyle = '#0F0';
context.fillRect(200, 20, 50, 50);
}
```

This script draws what you see in Figure 9-9.

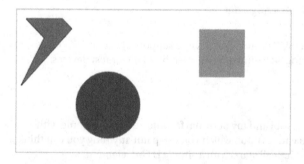

Figure 9-9. *Some sample HTML5 canvas drawing*

The canvas is an incredibly capable and sometimes complex feature of HTML5. There are several books dedicated to drawing on canvas and with good cause. If you want to see a more practical example of using canvas, you will see a useful example in Chapter 10 of this book.

The canvas element is supported by all of our test devices.

SVG

Unlike everything else in this chapter, SVG is neither HTML, CSS, nor JavaScript. SVG stands for "Scalable Vector Graphics" and is another standard altogether. SVG provides a lightweight, XML-based way of drawing vector shapes. Here is a sample of SVG that draws a red circle.

```
<svg xmlns="http://www.w3.org/2000/svg" height="100" width="100">
  <circle r="50" cx="50" cy="50" fill="#F00" />
</svg>
```

SVG can both the inlined into a page with HTML content or referenced in an external file, though support for external SVG is a bit better than inline. Vector images created in SVG can often be smaller than their raster jpg and png counterparts. As you might imagine, more complex shapes will make for much more complex SVG markup. If the devices you support also support SVG, consider using this often overlooked standard. Unfortunately Android 2.x does not support SVG, so this will be a problem for most mobile sites since Android 2.x devices are still common.

Summary

Our most common smartphone browsers are more capable than many would assume. The oldest mobile operating systems we tested on here, Android 2.1 and iOS 4, are surprisingly capable. In some cases a visual feature can be used even though it isn't necessary, and older browsers simply won't see the visual upgrade. This is often an appropriate approach. As for functionality, sometimes it will be best to turn off a feature for devices that don't support the technology. Native photo upload is a good example. For browsers that support it, the feature can really make our sites more usable. For those who don't, we can use techniques like what we saw in Chapter 6 to conditionally hide the newer features.

But as you can see from above, in many cases this will not be necessary. The mobile Web is more advanced than most think.

CHAPTER 10

■■■

Programming for Touch

One of the most exciting capabilities that our modern mobile device browser landscape gives us is the ability to program for touch. By leveraging these touch capabilities, we can create better and more natural experiences for our users. Unfortunately, programming for touch can be difficult, and there are a number of browser incompatibilities. In this chapter we will discuss the core concepts, the APIs available, which browsers they are supported in, and how to write code that works on all the most recent devices as well as on the desktop. We will finish the chapter off with a sample that is of very practical use and shows off touch well.

The Browser Touch APIs

Before we discuss how we can create rich touch experiences for our users, we have to determine what devices we can target. Even though the APIs are often quite different, you should be able to create good touch experiences for at least the following devices:

- iOS (2.0+, which include iPhones, iPod Touches and iPads),
- Android (2.1+),
- BlackBerry (7+ has support but in most cases version 10 is likely what you would want to target),
- Firefox OS,
- Windows Phone 8 and Windows 8 devices with touch screens (like the Microsoft Surface).

I feel I need to note the conspicuous absence of Windows Phone 7 from this list since those who develop on Microsoft technologies like ASP.NET MVC are more likely to own a Windows Phone 7 device than the general populace. Windows Phone 7 has only rudimentary touch support and you will not be able to do anything with touch on these devices other than the basic built-in mouse emulation (more on that below).

As you can see from this list, almost all modern smartphones support nice touch capabilities. This is very exciting. The only problem is that the browsers have different APIs. This is even more difficult if you want to build something that uses either touch or mouse. Touch browsers emulate certain mouse events, which means touch screens by default generally handle mouse events well (though not hover); but browsers by default do not do the reverse. If you only program for touch, a mouse user will likely not be able to interact with what you built. So we need to be able to handle all types of input.

Let's start by talking about the individual APIs and discuss which devices support which APIs before we think about how to use the various APIs in tandem.

Click Events

The mouse click event is supported across all the touch-input mobile device browsers listed above. If you think about it, the reason is obvious. If mobile browsers did not emulate this event, all existing websites that use the standard mouse click event would be broken on mobile phones. This would have broken most of the Internet's JavaScript. Even though this emulation keeps the web from breaking, most mobile browsers have a built-in 300ms time delay for this event to allow the browser time to determine if a touch event was intended instead. This lag can make a site feel sluggish, so it's often a good idea to also use touch events instead of just click events. But at least the browser manufacturers didn't break backward compatibility on the Web. Though the mouse emulation keeps the Web working, this is not an event that will be important for touch programming.

Mouse* Direction Events

Another set of mouse events that are emulated in mobile, mouseless browsers are the various mouse* direction events (the asterisk here and throughout the chapter marks a wildcard, so it is a shorthand for referring to several different events that all start with the word "mouse"), including mouseup, mousedown, mousemove universally but also mouseenter and mouseleave in Internet Explorer. Like the click event, on most mobile devices these mouse events also have the 300ms delay so are not ideal for creating a good touch experience on the Web. Even though desktop browsers may need these events, they will not be useful for touch programming.

Touch* Events

Apple added touch* events in iOS 2, and these events have become the standard event mechanism for all webkit browsers (mobile Safari, Android browser, Chrome for Android, BlackBerry 10 and the latest webkit-based Opera browsers) as well as Firefox. This means that for the vast majority of smartphone users, these are the core touch events we will use. There are four touch event types: touchstart (when the touch starts), touchmove (when the touch moves), touchend (when the touch has ended) and touchcancel (when the system cancels the touch, which it could do for any number of reasons that may differ between devices, like if a user drags the touch point off the device or the device interrupts the user to invoke another action). Unlike the emulated mouse events, these do not have the built-in 300ms delay, making them nice and responsive.

Event listeners for touch events are attached just like normal events. It would look something like this.

```
var element = document.getElementById('anElementId');

element.addEventListener('touchstart', function () {
  //do touch logic
});
```

The touch event object is different than the mouse event object and contains new touch-specific changes. Most importantly, touch events are multi-touch capable and the event contains an array of touch objects that represent all the touches to the device. Each touch is given a unique identifier which will remain unchanged during the lifetime of the touch, though the index of the touch in the array of touches could change due to other touches ending and being removed from the array.

The touch event also has rotation and scale information. The rotation's initial value is 0 and stays 0 if only one touch is active. Once a second touch is registered, rotation is measured in positive (clockwise) or negative (counter-clockwise) degrees from the start location of the event. Rotation would be useful for implementing a touch interface that rotates an element on the page.

The scale's initial value is 1 and stays 1 if only one touch is active. Once a second touch is registered, the scale either decreases if the two touches are moving closer to each other or increases if the touches are moving further away. This value is measured from the beginning of the touch event, and increases or decreases depending on the direction of the touches. Scale would be an appropriate value to use to implement pinch and zoom in a touch interface.

Since these events are the core events for all touch programming for webkit-based browsers and Firefox, these will be used extensively and explained in more depth below. They will also be used in a sample in the next chapter on Advanced Touch Programming.

Gesture* Events

Apple added gesture* events in iOS 2 along with touch* events but these have not been implemented in other browsers. The three gesture events are gesturestart, gesturechange, and gestureend. They are a higher-level encapsulation than the touch events and just give you rotation and scale values. Because they are unique to iOS and give you nothing that touch* events don't already give you, we will not be spending any more time on these events.

Pointer* Events

Microsoft added pointer* events in Internet Explorer 10 and are what you would use to develop touch interactions for Internet Explorer 10 on Windows 8 and Windows Phone 8. Pointer* events are conceptually very different from webkit touch* events because they are intended to encapsulate interaction by mouse, pen and touch. In Internet Explorer parlance each contact with these inputs is considered a pointer, so the events are called "pointer events." They are prefixed in Internet Explorer 10, so they will all include "MS" at the beginning but are still simply pointer events. In Internet Explorer 11 they have been unprefixed. Since Internet Explorer 11 is still relatively new and version 10 requires the prefixed version, we will use that throughout in our samples and discussion. Available events include:

- MSPointerDown (when the pointer interacts with the target with a virtual "button", which is either a mouse button, a pen touch or a finger touch)

- MSPointerUp (when the pointer stops interacting with its virtual "button")

- MSPointerEnter (when a pointing device enters the hit area of the target)

- MSPointerLeave (when the pointer has left the bounds of the target)

- MSPointerMove (when the pointer changes state within the target, such as position)

- MSPointerOut (when the pointer has left the bounds of the target, similar to MSPointerLeave)

- MSPointerOver (when a pointer has moved into the boundaries of a target but has not touched the target, like hovering)

- MSPointerCancel (when the system has determined to cancel the event)

As you can see, the available events are both more extensive and a bit more overwhelming. From a API standpoint, pointer* events are also different than webkit touch events in that each pointer raises a separate event instead of all touch points being in an array on the event object of a single event. But like webkit touch events, each pointer is given its own unique pointer ID, which it keeps throughout its lifetime and will be very helpful in some cases for distinguishing pointer events from each other.

Because this is the only way to do touch-based programming in Internet Explorer 10 and 11, we will be using these extensively, and these will be explained in more depth below when we get to the samples. I should also note that Google, Mozilla, and Opera are all considering supporting pointer events, so in the future these events may have much broader applicability.

MSGesture* Events

Microsoft added some built-in gesture events for Internet Explorer 10 that are extensions of and work with pointer* events. The gestures include MSGestureTap, MSGestureHold, MSGestureStart, MSGestureChange, MSGestureEnd, and MSIntertiaStart. Unfortunately, the setup takes a bit more code than all the previous events.

```
var domElement = document.getElementById('element');

var gesture = new MSGesture();
gesture.target = domElement;

domElement.addEventListener('MSGestureStart', function(evt) {
    if (evt.type == "MSPointerDown") {
      gesture.addPointer(evt.pointerId);
      return;
    }
});

domElement.addEventListener('MSGestureTap', function(evt) {
    //do gesture stuff, happens after the gesture object is registered to the event.
});
```

As you can see, these gestures require a separate MSGesture object. At the beginning of a user's gesture action a MSPointerDown event fires, at which point the gesture is hooked up with the event's pointerId. After this point other event listeners for the gesture events will fire when appropriate. As you can see, this is a bit more complicated than setting up gesture events for iOS. The main impediment to using them though is that they only work on Internet Explorer.

That being said, if you are going to be implementing gestures across devices, the only way to get rotation and scale values in Internet Explorer 10 is to use the MSGestureChange event. As the touch points rotate, the rotation value in on the MSGestureChange event object will have something other than its default value of 0, a negative decimal value if rotating left, a positive rotation value if rotating right. The rotation value is expressed in radians and is the amount of rotation since the last MSGestureChange event, not since the beginning of the gesture. As for scale, the distance between the touch points change, the scale value on the MSGestureChange event object will have something other than its default value of 1, a decimal value slightly less than 1 indicating the distance is decreasing or a decimal value slightly more to indicate that the distance is increasing. Like the rotation value, this is the change since the last change, not since the beginning of the gesture.

Gesture and Rotation Differences

It is important to call out at this point that not only are MSGesture * and touch* incompatible, but their rotation and scale values are incompatible as well. Both rotation and scale are measured from the beginning of the interaction in touch* events. For MSGestureChange events, these values are measured since the MSGestureChange event, not the first. Also, rotation is expressed in degrees for touch* events and radians for MSGesture* events. Though managing these differences is not difficult, it ought to be mentioned to avoid the confusion this might create later.

If you want to normalize the two models so that they act the same (important if you want to write something that works in all touchable browsers), you can do so like the following. Here is a minimal example of combining touchmove and MSGestureChange events to get consistent rotation and scale values.

```
var theElement, totalScale = 1, totalRotation = 0;

window.onload = function () {

  theElement = document.getElementById('theElement');

  theElement.addEventListener('MSPointerUp', function (evt) {
    totalScale = 1, totalRotation = 0; //Need to reset the counters
  });

  theElement.addEventListener('touchend', function (evt) {
    totalScale = 1, totalRotation = 0; //Need to reset the counters
  });

  theElement.addEventListener('touchmove', function (evt) {
    evt.preventDefault();
    var info = normalizeRotationAndScaleForTouch('touch', evt.rotation, evt.scale);
    //code that uses the info
  });

  //Note that we need to wrap this in a feature test so we don't have an error on platforms
  //  that don't support the MSGesture object.
  var gesture;

  if (window.MSGesture != undefined) {
    gesture = new MSGesture();
    gesture.target = theElement;
  }
  var eventListener = function (evt) {
    if (evt.type == "MSPointerDown")  // add pointer on MSPointerDown event
    {
      gesture.addPointer(evt.pointerId);
      return;
    }

    var info = normalizeRotationAndScaleForTouch('pointer', evt.rotation, evt.scale);
    //code that uses the info
  }

  theElement.addEventListener('MSGestureChange', eventListener, false);
  theElement.addEventListener('MSPointerDown', eventListener, false);
}

function normalizeRotationAndScaleForTouch(type, rotation, scale) {
  if (type === 'touch') {
    totalScale = scale;
    totalRotation = rotation;
  }
```

```
else {
  totalScale = totalScale * scale;
  //this multiplication converts radians to degrees
  totalRotation = totalRotation + (rotation * 57.2957795);
}

return {
  scale: totalScale,
  rotation: totalRotation
};
}
```

It is unfortunate that the browser implementations of rotation and scale are so different because it requires workarounds for things that could otherwise be rather straightforward. Unfortunately, we have several other differences to discuss.

Touch Location

Before we write some samples using the touch* and MSPointer* events above, we need to discuss cross-browser compatibility issues around knowing where you clicked. The target element is available through the target value on the event so that is easy to determine; but what if you want to know where *within the element* you clicked? This is more complicated than it should be.

Assuming we want to write something that works with mouse input as well as either touch* or MSPointer* events, the following x/y coordinate locations (or a subset depending on the browser/event type) are given in the event objects: x/y, clientX/clientY, layerX/layerY, offsetX/offsetY, pageX/pageY and screenX/screenY. In theory, these would be consistent across the browsers; in reality, this is not the case. When I noticed discrepancies, I ran a test. I placed an element about 2000 pixels down on a page and 20 pixels from the left of the screen and 20 pixels from the top. It has a 1 pixel border. On my iPhone, it looked like Figure 10-1.

Figure 10-1. Our sample touch element

For desktop browsers, I positioned the browser window about 300 pixels from the left of the screen. I then clicked/touched this element very close to the top left-hand corner of the element and gathered the following results in Table 10-1.

Table 10-1. *How Different Browsers Calculate x and y Positions*

	iOS Safari Touch	IE Pointer Event	IE Mouse Click	Android Default Browser	Android Chrome	Firefox Desktop	Firefox OS	Chrome Desktop
x/y	-	35/24	35/21	-	-	-	-	34/21
client x/y	34/22	35/24	35/21	33/31	28/30	32/19	31/20	34/21
layer x/y	-	35/24	35/21	-	-	32/2072	-	34/2053
offset x/y	-	14/6	4/4.6	-	-	-	-	4/2
page x/y	34/2071	35/2069	35/2066	33/2062	28/2058	32/2072	31/2092	34/2053
screen x/y	34/2071	35/79	35/76	33/31	57/70	317/114	31/20	320/103

Let's go through these results and see which would make the best candidate: x/y, layer x/y and offset x/y coordinates are missing in most cases, so clearly none of these will work.

Client x/y measures the distance from the left and top edges of the client, which in the case of mobile devices is the edge of the browser-rendering surface. This does not take into account the browser chrome, which varies in size from browser to browser and this accounts for some of the differences. This property seems to behave consistently across all devices and would be a good candidate if you want to know the distance from the edge of the rendering surface. The above might make you think that it gives us a good starting point for knowing where we clicked/touched in an element, but the values are only so close because the element happens to be a consistent distance from the top and the left. Scroll the page up a bit and touch, and the values are no longer helpful because it measures the distance from the edge of the client, not the edge of the target element.

Page x/y is the distance from the left and top edge of the page, which will generally be the same as the left edge of the screen but different from the top unless the element clicked/touched is at the top of the page and there has been no scrolling. But if the page is scrolled horizontally or vertically, page x/y will reflect the scrolled distance. In my sample page the DOM element was scrolled down around 2000 pixels, which is why the y values are around 2000.

Screen x/y values generally measure the distance from the element to the top of the physical screen. My desktop browser examples were both taken with the browser about 300 pixels from the left of the screen and 100 pixels from the top, so they also behave correctly even though they look higher. Unfortunately Safari on iOS miscalculates this value but in most cases the screen position is going to be irrelevant, so the bug is of little consequence.

If we want to know the x/y coordinate within the element, the offset x/y value that only a few of our browsers give us is what we want. In lieu of this event value, we can calculate the value we need. The target object for all of our events has an offsetLeft and offsetTop value, which represents the x and y distance of the element from the left and top respectively and this seems to work in all browsers. So we can take our page x/y value and subtract our target elements left/top values to get the actual x/y coordinate inside the element that we clicked. The function would look like this.

```
function getPositionFromTarget(evt, target) {

  return {
    y: evt.pageY - target.offsetTop,
    x: evt.pageX - target.offsetLeft
  };
}
```

In this case the variable evt is the mouse or touch event, in which both have the page x/y value, and the target is the target of the event. Like I said, it is more complicated than it should be, but at least the problem is solvable after a little investigation.

Touch Screens, Touch Events, and Default Behavior

Before we build something, I should explain a little more about the event model that touch devices use, how the touch* and MSPointer* models discussed above behave differently, and what effect that has on us when writing our touch code. As mentioned above, touch screens emulate mouse events so that they don't break the Web. The browser makers add the 300ms delay to allow multiple touches to happen (like in the case of a double-tab to zoom, a common browser action) before they fire the mouse click event. Because of this, touch events fire before mouse events so these touches can be captured. Let's see this in action. Let's attach the events we care about to an element and see what happens.

```
element = document.getElementById('anElement');

element.addEventListener('mousedown', function () { console.log('mousedown'); });
element.addEventListener('mousemove', function () { console.log('mousemove'); });
element.addEventListener('mouseup', function () { console.log('mouseup'); });
element.addEventListener('click', function () { console.log('click'); });
element.addEventListener('touchstart', function () { console.log('touchstart'); });
element.addEventListener('touchmove', function () { console.log('touchmove'); });
element.addEventListener('touchend', function () { console.log('touchend'); });
element.addEventListener('touchcancel', function () { console.log('touchcancel'); });
element.addEventListener('MSPointerDown', function () { console.log('MSPointerDown'); });
element.addEventListener('MSPointerUp', function () { console.log('MSPointerUp'); });
element.addEventListener('MSPointerEnter', function () { console.log('MSPointerEnter'); });
element.addEventListener('MSPointerCancel', function () { console.log('MSPointerCancel'); });
element.addEventListener('MSPointerLeave', function () { console.log('MSPointerLeave'); });
element.addEventListener('MSPointerMove', function () { console.log('MSPointerMove'); });
element.addEventListener('MSPointerOut', function () { console.log('MSPointerOut'); });
element.addEventListener('MSPointerLeave', function () { console.log('MSPointerLeave'); });
element.addEventListener('MSPointerOver', function () { console.log('MSPointerOver'); });
```

On my iPhone 4S running iOS 6, if I tap on the element I get the following events in this order:

```
touchstart
touchend
mousemove
mousedown
mouseup
click
```

Note that the touch events come first before the mouse and click events are emulated. If I attempt to scroll by swiping down on the element, I get something different.

```
touchstart
touchmove
touchmove
...
touchend
```

In this case the browser has prevented the mouse emulation because it detects that I want to scroll the screen, not "click" on the element. If you want to tap on an element and prevent the mouse emulation yourself, you can call the preventDefault method on the event object in the touchstart handler. If you have a click event handler and a touchstart handler attached to the element because you want to support both desktop and touch screen, calling preventDefault will keep the click event from firing. The approach taken with touch events is quite clever, because it allows you to attach behavior to both touch and click events so desktop and touch browsers can both function, but allows you to cancel the click action if the touch action executes. Canceling default behavior will also keep the mobile browser from its default behavior of scrolling the screen on a touch move, something we will need in our sample below.

The touch event model is very different in Internet Explorer 10. With the same event handlers, a tap produces the following:

```
mousemove
MSPointerOver
MSPointerDown
mousedown
MSPointerUp
mouseup
click
MSPointerOut
```

By looking at the pairings, you can see which older mouse events correspond to which pointer event. If I try to cancel the other events by calling preventDefault on the event object like above, I get interesting results.

```
mousemove
MSPointerOver
MSPointerDown
MSPointerUp
click
MSPointerOut
```

That the initial mousemove still fires is not surprising since it occurs before the pointer events can fire. But after the first preventDefault is called, the other mouse events are not fired. Also note that the click event is *not* cancelled, unlike the behavior we saw with touch events. Because we cannot cancel the older events, we should not let click and mouse events coexist with pointer events on any element so as to avoid duplicate behavior. This implementation detail of Internet Explorer 10 is unfortunate, as it will require more work.

Another bit of unfortunate behavior is that a CSS property needs to be applied to the element to cancel scrolling on pointer movement.

```
-ms-touch-action: none;
```

Since the pointer event model does not play well with the older emulated events, we need to have a way of determining if the click event is something we should avoid attaching. Fortunately, this is easy.

```
if (window.navigator.msPointerEnabled) {
  //attach pointer events
}
else {
  //attach click or mouse events
}
```

We will show all of this in the sample below.

Building a Simple Touch Sample

For the rest of this chapter, we are going to work on a couple very simple widgets to show you how we can make basic touch interaction work. We will include mouse interaction as well just in case you want to see how to target desktops as well as touch screens.

What we want to do is use an HTML5 Canvas element and draw a dot on the canvas wherever we click or touch. If you haven't used Canvas, don't worry, I will explain everything as we go.

Creating a Page

To get started, we create a page and add a canvas tag similar to the following.

```
<!DOCTYPE html>
<html>
  <head>
    <title>A Simple Touch Sample</title>
  </head>
  <body>
    <p>Touch it!</p>
    <canvas id="theCanvas" style="border: solid 1px #111;" height="250" width="250">
    </canvas>
  </body>
</html>
```

This will give us a small canvas with a border so we can see it. The page will look something like Figure 10-2.

Figure 10-2. A simple canvas

Another piece of setup that we will need for all of our interactions is to attach the event handlers. We will do this in the window onload event. This is the code to set this up. If you are following along, feel free to add all this JavaScript directly into the page or include it in a separate file.

```
function load() {
  //attach events here
}

window.addEventListener('load', load);
```

Now that we have our foundation ready, we can write the real code.

Drawing

Our goal is to draw a circle on the canvas wherever the user clicks or touches. Here is a very short introduction to drawing on HTML5 canvas.

To draw on a canvas, the first thing you need to do is get a reference to the canvas and get the 2d rendering context from that canvas element. We will do this in the load event.

```
var canvas, context;

function load() {
  canvas = document.getElementById('theCanvas');
  context = canvas.getContext('2d');

  //attach other events here
}

window.addEventListener('load', load);
```

The context object from the getContext method is of type CanvasRenderingContext2D. The way I like to think of the canvas and the context is to think of the canvas as the painter's canvas and the context as the brush. When programming for canvas, you don't issue drawing commands to the canvas. You are drawing *on* the canvas. You issue commands to the drawing instrument, the context, and the brush that will create whatever you tell it to create.

Let's write the method that will draw the circle on the canvas.

```
function draw(x, y) {
  context.fillStyle = '#F00';

  var radius = 6;
  var startRadian = 0;
  var endRadian = Math.PI * 2;

  context.beginPath();
  context.arc(x, y, radius, startRadian, endRadian);
  context.fill();
}
```

There are several things that need to be explained here, but this is all the canvas code we will need to draw our little circles. Circles in a canvas are drawn with a path. A path can include multiple lines straight lines and can also include arcs, which is what we will need to draw a circle. Paths in canvas can either be filled, stroked, or both. By calling the stroke command, the outline of the path is drawn. By calling the fill command, the path is filled. If both are called, both are executed. Both fill and stroke have styles, which is how you set the color. On the first line of our method, I set the fill style to the RGB value of red.

A little further down we begin our path. We immediately draw an arc to create our circle. There is no circle command for canvas, so if you want a circle, you have to draw one using an arc. The arc method takes x and y to specify the center of the circle, the radius of the circle (the distance from the center of the circle to the edge), the start radian and the end radian. For those unfamiliar with radians, they are an alternative to specifying sections along the circumference of the circle; in other words, it is another way of specifying what some might use degrees for. A circle has two Pi radians and the start point for an arc is on the right. So if the arc command was started at 0 and ended at one Pi and then filled, it would look like Figure 10-3.

Figure 10-3. *A half-filled circle*

But we want the circle filled all the way, so we use two Pi radians. After creating the arc, we call the fill method that fills in the path, and we are done! You can see the result in Figure 10-4. We have our drawing function.

Figure 10-4. *A circle*

Starting Implementation Using Mouse Events

Now let's hook up our first event, the mouse event. As you can see below, we also need our function from before to find our position within the target. In the case of mouse events, we pass in the event object itself and the target separately. You will see why I am separating these below.

```
function load() {
  canvas = document.getElementById('theCanvas');
  context = canvas.getContext('2d');

  canvas.addEventListener('click', function (evt) {
    var position = getPositionFromTarget(evt, evt.target);
    draw(position.x, position.y);
  });
}
```

```
function getPositionFromTarget(evt, target) {

  return {
    y: evt.pageY - target.offsetTop,
    x: evt.pageX - target.offsetLeft
  };
}
```

And what's our result? Here in Figure 10-5 is our canvas after a few clicks.

Touch it!

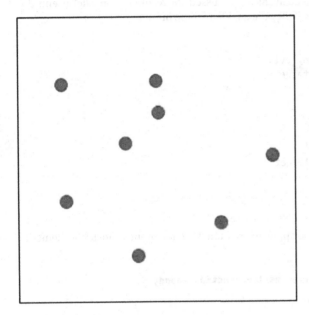

Figure 10-5. *Our Canvas after a few clicks*

Starting Implementation Using Touch Events

With that framework in place, hooking up a touch event is fairly simple. You may recall from our discussion on the touch event API above that the sum total of touches is in an array of touches on the event object. We will either need to retrieve the first and draw it, or draw all of them. Since making this multi-touch is simple, let's draw all of the touches.

```
canvas.addEventListener('touchstart', function (evt) {
  evt.preventDefault();
  var i, position;
  for (i = 0; i < evt.touches.length; i++) {
    position = getPositionFromTarget(evt.touches[i], evt.touches[i].target);
    draw(position.x, position.y);
  }
});
```

It is important in our case to remember to call preventDefault on the event object. As mentioned above, emulated mouse events will fire after touch events. If we are handling both, we need to call preventDefault on the event object to prevent the mouse events from firing if the touch events fire.

On the touch event object there are two other arrays of touches, changedTouches and targetTouches. The changedTouches value contains an array of all the touches that changed since the last event. The targetTouches array contains a list of all the touches that started on the target element and are still on the target element. We will be using neither now though later we will use the changedTouches array.

Starting Implementation Using Pointer Events

That was easy enough. Let's use pointer events. Unlike touch events, these do not come in an array and act more like the mouse event, except that multiple can happen simultaneously. As we discussed above, mouse and click events do not work well with pointer events, so we should check to see if they are enabled for the browser.

```
if (window.navigator.msPointerEnabled) {
  canvas.addEventListener('MSPointerDown', function (evt) {
    var position = getPositionFromTarget(evt, evt.target);
    draw(position.x, position.y);
  });
}
else {
  canvas.addEventListener('click', function (evt) {
    var position = getPositionFromTarget(evt, evt.target);
    draw(position.x, position.y);
  });
}
```

There is one more addition we need to make. We need to apply the -ms-touch-action: none value to the element to prevent any accidental scrolling or pinch and zoom.222.

```
<canvas id="theCanvas" style="border: solid 1px #111; -ms-touch-action: none;"
  height="250" width="250">
</canvas>
```

Improving Our Implementation

Before we change this sample app into something more useful, I want to refactor it a bit to improve the performance. In general, when using Canvas it is best to draw when the browser is ready to draw instead of drawing when a touch event happens. This can help performance (and is also a common practice in game frameworks) because drawing can potentially be an expensive operation. To do this, I create an array for the touches and the event handlers now add the position to that array. As an example, here is the updated click event handler.

```
canvas.addEventListener('click', function (evt) {
  var position = getPositionFromTarget(evt, evt.target);
  touches.push(position);
});
```

If we are not drawing when we record an event, we need to know when to draw. Modern browsers now support an API for this called requestAnimationFrame. This method is called by the browser whenever it is ready to paint the screen. Since this is a relatively new feature, it is best to get browser-prefixed versions or use a timeout if the unprefixed version is not available. A very simple implementation would look like this.

```
var requestAnimFrame = window.requestAnimationFrame ||
  window.mozRequestAnimationFrame ||
  window.webkitRequestAnimationFrame ||
  window.msRequestAnimationFrame ||
  function(callback){
    window.setTimeout(callback, 1000 / 60);
  };

function draw() {
  context.clearRect(0, 0, canvas.width, canvas.height);
  var i;
  for (i = 0; i < touches.length; i++) {
    var touch = touches[i];
    drawCircle(touch.x, touch.y);
  }

  requestAnimFrame(draw);
}

requestAnimFrame(function () {
  draw();
});
```

The requestAnimationFrame function is intended to be called recursively. In this case we get the proper function for the browser, define a draw function that loops through all the touches and draws them, and then we start the requestAnimationFrame recursive loop.

Another change you should notice is the new call to clearRect at the beginning of the draw loop. At the beginning of the drawing operation it clears the canvas before drawing all of the circles. Now that the circles are drawn repeatedly, over time the circles lose their shape because they are drawn on top of themselves over and over, and the muted colors in the anti-aliased edges of the circles pile up on each other, eventually leading to a blocky-shaped circle. To avoid this, we clear the circles each time before drawing. Now we have completed our simple touch demo.

Capturing Handwriting

Let's turn this from a simple demo into a useful tool. You may not have realized it, but we have just created the foundation for a signature capture element that works on desktops and touch devices. Now let's take it all the way. We will start by getting the mouse working; and to do that we need to make two big changes. First, we need to move away from the click event and use the mousedown, mousemove, and mouseup events to simulate putting down a pen, writing, and picking it up again. Second we need to stop drawing circles and switch to lines.

Mouse Events

Here are our new mouse events.

```
var isWriting = false;

canvas.addEventListener('mousedown', function (evt) {
  var position = getPositionFromTarget(evt, evt.target);
  touches.push([]);
  addTouch(position);
  isWriting = true;
});

canvas.addEventListener('mousemove', function (evt) {
  if (isWriting) {
    var position = getPositionFromTarget(evt, evt.target);
    addTouch(position);
  }
});

canvas.addEventListener('mouseup', function (evt) {
  var position = getPositionFromTarget(evt, evt.target);
  addTouch(position);
  isWriting = false;
});

function addTouch(position) {
  var touchArray = touches[touches.length - 1];
  touchArray.push(position);
}
```

Handwriting involves discreet units of lines and curves, which we will call "segments." For example, when someone signs their name, they will usually pick up the pen at least once during the process to separate the first and the last name, or to dot a letter. So we are going to store our positions in segments, which are arrays of individual points. When the touch/pointer/mouse starts, a new segment will be started. As movement occurs, those positions will be recorded. When the touch/pointer/mouse sequence ends, that segment will be finished. In the code above, on mousedown a new array to hold that segment of touches is added to the touches array. When touches are added they are added to this new array. If the cycle begins again, a new array is created. We also keep a variable called "isWriting" around to know if we should be writing or not in mousemove.

Now we need to change our draw logic. Our new draw loop looks like the following:

```
function draw() {
  context.clearRect(0, 0, canvas.width, canvas.height);

  var i;
  for (i = 0; i < touches.length; i++) {
    drawSegment(touches[i]);
  }

  requestAnimFrame(draw);
}
```

```
function drawSegment(segment) {
  var i, firstTouch = true;
  for (i = 0; i < segment.length; i++) {
    var touch = segment[i];

    if (firstTouch) {
      firstTouch = false;
      context.beginPath();
      context.moveTo(touch.x, touch.y);
      continue;
    }

    context.lineTo(touch.x, touch.y);
  }

  context.strokeStyle = '#000';
  context.stroke();
}
```

First we loop through the segments and draw each one. Each segment will constitute its own path, so the first touch of the segment begins the path and the context is moved to that location. Thereafter the context draws a new line to each location. When all the lines have been drawn, the line is stroked black so we can see it.

Touch Events

The touch and pointer APIs are multi-touch but a signature widget would not normally be, so we will constrain our code to only handle one touch at a time. Here is my implementation using touch events.

```
var currentTouchId;

canvas.addEventListener('touchstart', function (evt) {
  evt.preventDefault();
  currentTouchId = evt.touches[0].identifier;
  touches.push([]);

  position = getPositionFromTarget(evt.touches[0], evt.touches[0].target);
  addTouch(position);
});

canvas.addEventListener('touchmove', function (evt) {
  evt.preventDefault();

  var i, position;
  for (i = 0; i < evt.changedTouches.length; i++) {
    if (evt.changedTouches[i].identifier !== currentTouchId)
      continue;
    position = getPositionFromTarget(evt.changedTouches[i], evt.changedTouches[i].target);
    addTouch(position);
  }
});
```

We do not need the touchend event in this case. As long as the first touch stays in contact with the element, it will remain the first in the array. When all the touches are removed and a new touch is started, this new touch will reestablish the current touch ID and will be the new primary touch for writing.

Pointer Events

Next we need to implement pointer events. Pointer events are not stored in an array like touch events are, so we can't depend on that array like we did in our last implementation. Fortunately, the differences are minor. Here is the code.

```
canvas.addEventListener('MSPointerDown', function (evt) {
  if (currentTouchId)
    return; //there is already an active touch, don't start a new one

  currentTouchId = evt.pointerId;
  touches.push([]);
  var position = getPositionFromTarget(evt, evt.target);
  addTouch(position);
});

canvas.addEventListener('MSPointerMove', function (evt) {
  if (evt.pointerId !== currentTouchId)
    return;

  var position = getPositionFromTarget(evt, evt.target);
  addTouch(position);
});

canvas.addEventListener('MSPointerUp', function (evt) {
  //delete the touch id so we can start a new touch
  currentTouchId = undefined;
});
```

In this case we need the currentTouchId to be undefined when the first touch sequence is finished, so we handle the MSPointerUp event and delete it there.

Saving It to the Server

Now that we can take someone's signature, we need to save this to the server. Let's start with the client-side code to do this. We need to add a button and attach an event handler when someone clicks it.

```
var saveButton = document.getElementById('save');
saveButton.addEventListener('click', function () {
  saveCanvas();
});
```

The saveCanvas method can be implemented as follows:

```
function saveCanvas() {
  var imageData = canvas.toDataURL('image/jpeg', 1);

  var formData = new FormData();
  formData.append('fileData', imageData);

  var xhr = new XMLHttpRequest();

  xhr.addEventListener('load', function () { alert('uploaded!'); });

  xhr.open('POST', "/touch/upload", true);
  xhr.send(formData);
}
```

The raw data on the canvas can be retrieved as an array of bytes or as a base64 encoded string. I find it a bit easier to save to the server as a string, so I use the toDataURL method on the canvas object to get the string. I then send that string via Ajax to the server using the XMLHttpRequest object. The following is our server-side implementation.

```
[HttpPost]
public ActionResult Upload(string fileData)
{
  string dataWithoutJpegMarker = fileData.Replace("data:image/jpeg;base64,", String.Empty);
  byte[] filebytes = Convert.FromBase64String(dataWithoutJpegMarker);
  string writePath = Path.Combine(Server.MapPath("~/upload"), Guid.NewGuid().ToString() + ".jpg");
  using (FileStream fs = new FileStream(writePath,
                            FileMode.OpenOrCreate,
                            FileAccess.Write,
                            FileShare.None))
  {
      fs.Write(filebytes, 0, filebytes.Length);
  }

  return new EmptyResult();
}
```

When a canvas base64 encodes a file, it puts a marker at the beginning of the file identifying what type it is. When saved to disk, we don't need that marker. All we need is the raw base64 encoded string. So we take that string, remove the marker, convert it to bytes, and save it to disk.

The final result of all this looks something like what you see in Figure 10-6. I have written my initials, although you could use something like this to draw anything, from a signature to a smiley face.

Figure 10-6. *My initials, written in my browser on a canvas*

Summary

As you can see from the above, programming for touch can be complicated. Despite this, you should learn how the APIs work because touch is the primary means of interacting with our mobile devices today, and there is no reason to assume that will change. We have seen one working, practical example of using touch that will work across a wide range of modern devices. The next chapter will delve further into touch, and you will learn how to implement gestures and how to build more touch into your mobile websites.

CHAPTER 11

■ ■ ■

Advanced Touch Programming

In the last chapter we introduced touch events and discussed the basics of using them. In this chapter we will dive deeper with a few more complicated examples and techniques for managing the differences between the browser touch models. There are screenshots of what we are building in this chapter; but screenshots cannot express the activity in a touch-based sample very well, so I encourage you to try them on the live sample site discussed in the introduction.

Being able to handle the plain touch/mouse/pointer events is very handy, but soon most will want to be able to use gestures. Gestures are higher-level combinations of events and other factors like swiping, tapping, double-tapping, pinching, and zooming. Thinking and programming in these abstractions is a great way to express actions. But to do this really well, it would be nice to be able to create custom events so we can attach gestures as we do other events. Let's turn to that now.

Creating Custom Events

Ideally, when attaching a gesture to an element, it would be nice to use code like this:

```
var swipeable = document.getElementById('swipeable');

swipeable.addEventListener('swipeleft', left);
swipeable.addEventListener('swiperight', right);
```

Unfortunately you are not going to be able to do that. Elements don't know about "swipeleft" and "swiperight" gestures. However, I can show you how you can get something like this:

```
var swipeable = document.getElementById('swipeable');

var gesture = new CustomSwipeGesture(swipeable); //Custom functionality attached here
swipeable.addEventListener('swipeleft', left);
swipeable.addEventListener('swiperight', right);
```

In this case the CustomSwipe object encapsulates the logic around collecting touch/mouse/pointer events. Let's walk through how to create this.

Custom events are relatively easy to create in JavaScript. The problem is that different browsers do so in different ways. Let's start with the event model of Webkit-based browsers and Firefox. The syntax is fairly straightforward. Let's create a custom event and fire it when the touchend event fires on an element.

```
var element = document.getElementById('theThing');
var myCustomEvent = new CustomEvent('stoppedtouching');
```

```
element.addEventListener('mouseup', function (evt) {
  //Normally more will be involved here since we're just mimicking the mouseup event. That will come in a bit.
  evt.target.dispatchEvent(myCustomEvent, evt);
});
```

```
element.addEventListener('stoppedtouching', function (evt) {
  //Your new event is firing. Cool.
});
```

Now imagine if the "stoppedtouching" event became "tap", "swipeleft", or "pinch" and you get the idea. Unfortunately, this code doesn't work for Android 2.x or for IE 10, so if we want to support as many devices as we can, we should use something that works across them all. Fortunately for us, this functionality can be added to the browsers that don't have it. This is called a polyfilling. We are adding behavior to the browsers that they don't natively have so that we can code as if they did. Here is a polyfill that adds the level of custom event support that we need.

```
//This is based on the polyfill on MDN: https://developer.mozilla.org/en-US/docs/Web/API/CustomEvent
//  It was originally meant just for IE. This now covers older Androids.
(function () {

  //IE10 has the custom event object but it doesn't work like the other browsers :(
  var isIE = window.navigator.userAgent.indexOf('MSIE') > -1;
  if (window.CustomEvent && !isIE) {
    //Firefox for Android, Chrome for Android, Android 4.x default browser, Opera, Firefox OS, iOS
    return;
  }

  function CustomEvent(eventName, params) {
    params = params || { bubbles: false, cancelable: false, detail: undefined };

      var evt = document.createEvent('Event');
      evt.initEvent(eventName, true, true)
    return evt;
  };

  //Older Androids don't have the CustomEvent object, so we only want the prototype for IE.
  if (window.CustomEvent) {
    CustomEvent.prototype = window.CustomEvent.prototype;
  }

  window.CustomEvent = CustomEvent;
})();
```

With this in place we can now create our custom gesture using custom events.

Creating a Gesture

A gesture is usually going to be based on activity related to at least one event and have logic around screen positioning and time. In our example, we are going to implement a gesture for swiping left or right on an element. Doing this well requires taking into account multiple events, position on screen and time, so it's a good example.

We can consistently get the information from the browser across devices to infer gestures; but the gestures themselves do not come built into the browser, at least not in a cross-browser-friendly way. You may recall from our last chapter that touch events give us rotation and scale. We can also get rotation and scale from gesture events in Internet Explorer 10, but it also supplies tap, hold, and intertia start gestures, but these only work in IE 10 at the moment. So to get cross-platform gestures, we have to create them.

I will call this "LazySwipe" because it waits until after the swipe is complete to fire the event. I am going to create this as a function that I can instantiate that will take the element to add the custom gesture to. The shell of it all would look like this. You can see that I've already created my custom events.

```
window.LazySwipe = (function () {
  function swipe(element) {

    this.element = element; //This is the element all of the gestures will be attached to.
    this.swipeLeftEvent = new CustomEvent('swipeleft');
    this.swipeRightEvent = new CustomEvent('swiperight');
  };
  return swipe;
})();
```

The first thing I want to do is attach all the event handlers I want to pay attention to. Since we'll create this to work on desktop and mobile, we'll handle touch, mouse, and pointer events. Here is my new constructor.

```
function swipe(element) {

  this.element = element;
  var self = this;

  //These events for firefox and webkit-based browsers
  element.addEventListener('touchstart', function (evt) { self.start.call(self, evt); });
  element.addEventListener('touchmove', function (evt) { self.move.call(self, evt); });
  element.addEventListener('touchend', function (evt) { self.end.call(self, evt); });

  //If we want to support pointer events, we need to make sure mouse events are disabled. See
  // chapter 10 on why this is required.
  if (window.navigator.msPointerEnabled) {
    element.addEventListener('MSPointerDown', function (evt) { self.start.call(self, evt); });
    element.addEventListener('MSPointerMove', function (evt) { self.move.call(self, evt); });
    element.addEventListener('MSPointerUp', function (evt) { self.end.call(self, evt); });
  }
  else {
    //These events for all browsers that support mouse events
    element.addEventListener('mousedown', function (evt) { self.start.call(self, evt); });
    element.addEventListener('mousemove', function (evt) { self.move.call(self, evt); });
    element.addEventListener('mouseup', function (evt) { self.end.call(self, evt); });
  }

  this.swipeLeftEvent = new CustomEvent('swipeleft');
  this.swipeRightEvent = new CustomEvent('swiperight');
};
```

There are a few things to note about this. First, I'm mapping all of the various "start" events (touchstart, mousedown, and MSPointerDown) to a generic start method so I can treat them in a unified manner. I'm doing the same for both the move and end events as well. Second, because of context switching in JavaScript caused by event handlers, I'm forcing the context to always be that of the function instance by using the JavaScript call method on the functions to force the context. If you are used to using jQuery, this is something you would use the proxy method for. For more information about the call method and its kin, apply, see this excellent blog post by K. Scott Allen: http://odetocode.com/blogs/scott/archive/2007/07/05/function-apply-and-function-call-in-javascript.aspx. Next we need to create our start, move and end functions.

```
swipe.prototype.start = function (evt) {
  evt.preventDefault();
  //We need to know where we started from later to make decisions on the nature of the event.
  this.initialLocation = this.getPositionFromTarget(evt)
}

swipe.prototype.move = function (evt) {
  //Do nothing yet
}

swipe.prototype.end = function (evt) {
  var currentLocation = this.getPosition(evt, this.element);

  //If you end to the right of where you started, you swipe right.
  if (currentLocation.x > this.initialLocation.x) {
    this.element.dispatchEvent(this.swipeRightEvent, evt);
  } //If you end to the left of where you started, you swipe left.
  else if (currentLocation.x < this.initialLocation.x) {
    this.element.dispatchEvent(this.swipeLeftEvent, evt);
  }
}

swipe.prototype.getPosition = function(evt) {

  var pageX, pageY;
  if (evt.touches) { //If this is a touch event
    pageX = evt.changedTouches[0].pageX;
    pageY = evt.changedTouches[0].pageY;
  }
  else { //If this is a mouse or pointer event
    pageX = evt.pageX;
    pageY = evt.pageY;
  }

  return {
    y: pageY,
    x: pageX
  };
}
```

For a swipe gesture, we need to know where we started, because it's from that point that we'll determine if we are moving left or right, so we capture that when the start event occurs. At the end we need to check the final location to see if we've gone left or right. If we went left, we dispatch the swipeleft event. If we went right, we dispatch the swiperight event.

I also provided a function for determining location. How you determine location is different depending on whether it is a touch, mouse, or pointer event, so we abstract that into this getPosition method.

We now have a basic swipe gesture in less than 80 lines of JavaScript, but it's far from perfect. Let's fix a few of the flaws. Right now it would detect a swipe left if the user ended one pixel to the left of his or her start location. This is hardly a swipe. So we'll add a minimum required distance. Here is our new end method.

```javascript
swipe.prototype.end = function (evt) {
  evt.target.innerHTML = 'end';

  var currentLocation = this.getPosition(evt, this.element);
  var delta = Math.abs(currentLocation.x - this.initialLocation.x);
  if (delta < 80)
    return;

  //If you end to the right of where you started, you swipe right.
  if (currentLocation.x > this.initialLocation.x) {
    this.element.dispatchEvent(this.swipeRightEvent, evt);
  } //If you end to the left of where you started, you swipe left.
  else if (currentLocation.x < this.initialLocation.x) {
    this.element.dispatchEvent(this.swipeLeftEvent, evt);
  }
}
```

Now we only fire the event if the user moved their finger over 80 pixels. Of course the minimum delta could be tweaked. Another thing to watch is their vertical movement. A swipe would only be triggered if a minimal amount of vertical space was traversed. How would we do that? Here is one way.

```javascript
swipe.prototype.start = function (evt) {
  evt.preventDefault();
  //We need to know where we started from later to make decisions on the nature of the event.
  this.initialLocation = this.getPosition(evt)
  this.inProgress = true;
}

swipe.prototype.move = function (evt) {
  var currentLocation = this.getPosition(evt, this.element);
  var verticalDelta = Math.abs(currentLocation.y - this.initialLocation.y);
  if (verticalDelta > 50) {
    this.inProgress = false;
  }
}

swipe.prototype.end = function (evt) {
  if (!this.inProgress)
    return;

  //...the rest of the method
}
```

Before we mentioned that you will often have to handle multiple events (we are doing that already) as well as pay attention to position (we are also doing that). We are not paying any attention to time. Let's say we only want our swipe gesture to fire if the user is moving his or her finger quick enough. We could do this:

```
swipe.prototype.start = function (evt) {
  evt.preventDefault();
  //We need to know where we started from later to make decisions on the nature of the event.
  this.initialLocation = this.getPosition(evt)
  this.inProgress = true;
  this.startTime = new Date();
}

swipe.prototype.end = function (evt) {
  evt.target.innerHTML = 'end';

  var timeDelta = new Date() - this.startTime;
  if (timeDelta > 700) //milliseconds
    return;

  if (!this.inProgress)
    return;

  //...the rest of the method
}
```

We now have a pretty reasonable swipe gesture that we can attach like this.

```
<style>
#swipeable {
  -ms-touch-action: none;
}
</style>

<div id="swipeable">
  Swipe This
</div>

<script>
window.addEventListener('load', load);

var swipeable;

function load() {
  swipeable = document.getElementById('swipeable');

  new LazySwipe(swipeable);

  swipeable.addEventListener('swipeleft', left);
  swipeable.addEventListener('swiperight', right);
}
```

```
function left() {
  swipeable.innerHTML = 'left you have swiped';
}

function right() {
  swipeable.innerHTML = 'right you have swiped';
}
</script>
```

Now we need to put it to good use.

Making a Swipeable Image Widget

Let's make a swipeable image widget. We want it to look like Figure 11-1 left image when the page loads and the right image after the user swipes.

Figure 11-1. *An image widget that you can swipe!*

Let's say we start with this bit of markup:

```
<div id="carousel">
  <div id="image-container">
    <img class="carousel-item" src="/content/images/css_100.jpg" />
    <img class="carousel-item" src="/content/images/dice_100.jpg" />
    <img class="carousel-item" src="/content/images/bacon_100.jpg" />
    <img class="carousel-item" src="/content/images/ready_100.jpg" />
    <img class="carousel-item" src="/content/images/meat_100.jpg" />
    <img class="carousel-item" src="/content/images/dragonfruit_100.jpg" />
  </div>
</div>
```

The styling we need to get this right looks like the following:

```
/* This is the outer container of the widget. Note especially overflow and width values. */
#carousel {
  border: solid 1px #000;
  height: 100px;
  margin: 0 auto;
```

```
  overflow: hidden;
  width: 300px;
  -ms-touch-action: none;
}

/* This container is the full width of the images and moves left and right to give us the sliding affect.
   The images are each 100 pixels in width a piece for a total of 600 pixels. Note the transition
here. */
#image-container {
  width: 600px;

  -moz-transition: all .4s;
  -webkit-transition: all .4s;
  -o-transition: all .4s;
  transition: all .4s;
}

/* This makes the images stack up to the right of each other */
#carousel img {
  display: block;
  float: left;
}
```

To shift the images to the left when we swipe, all we need to do is apply the following CSS class to the image container. And since we have a transition set on the container, the browser will animate the movement.

```
.left {
  -moz-transform: translate3d(-300px, 0, 0);
  -ms-transform: translate3d(-300px, 0, 0);
  -o-transform: translate3d(-300px, 0, 0);
  -webkit-transform: translate3d(-300px, 0, 0);
  transform: translate3d(-300px, 0, 0);
}
```

Back in Chapter 9 ("Native APIs, HTML5 and CSS 3 on Mobile Today") I discussed a few CSS transformations, including the CSS transform: translate property. The transform: translate3d is the 3d version of this same CSS property, allowing you to translate an element along the z-axis along with the x and y axis. It may seem like an odd choice here but translate3d is definitely the right CSS to use in this case. Though you could use absolute positioning to move the image container or CSS transform: translateX to do so, neither are likely to use the GPU. But in most cases transform3d will involve the GPU and give you faster animations, even if you aren't using the z-axis.

Now comes the JavaScript. It looks almost exactly like the script we were using to test the initial swipe implementation. The differences are highlighted.

```
<script>
window.addEventListener('load', load);

var carousel, imageContainer;

function load() {
  carousel = document.getElementById('carousel');
  imageContainer = document.getElementById('image-container');

  var gesture = new LazySwipe(carousel);

  carousel.addEventListener('swipeleft', left);
  carousel.addEventListener('swiperight', right);
}

function left() {
  imageContainer.className = 'left';
}

function right() {
  imageContainer.className = '';
}
</script>
```

And that's all that's required to create a swipeable image widget. Once you abstract the swiping into a reusable bit of JavaScript, the implementation is fairly trivial. In a real-world scenario this might be a bit more complicated. Perhaps you want potentially unlimited groups of three pictures to show. In those cases you may find it easier to dynamically generate the CSS. But the difficult touch problems are solved.

Scaling, Rotating and Moving Things

The last sample of this chapter will show us how to do a number of things, including implementing scaling, rotation, and movement of an element on the page. For a visual, we're going to build what you see in Figure 11-2. The image on the left is the image unchanged, on the right the image has been moved, rotated and zoomed.

Figure 11-2. *A picture we can move, pinch, zoom or rotate*

The need to do these things is a very practical need for some applications; but just as important, this is going to require us to face some of the trickier issues in touch programming. First, we're going to have to normalize the various touch-event models. iOS's touch events mostly work like those in Firefox, Opera, and Chrome but with subtle but important differences. On top of that is the very different model of touch programming that Internet Explorer 10 gives us. Making these work together elegantly can be a challenge. Second, we are now dealing with multi-touch. Our examples so far have been single-touch only. This will use single-touch for moving a photo, but two touches will be required to scale or rotate. All this will be difficult; but if you break it down right and take it a piece at a time, you should have a better understanding of how to create more advanced touch experiences.

Because this requires multi-touch capabilities, the browsers you can target with this is more limited than before. First of all, all desktop browsers that aren't multi-touch capable and/or aren't being used on a touch-capable monitor are crippled and can't do any of the pinching, zooming, or rotating without making serious accommodations that won't be made here. Second, phones that only support single-touches in their browsers are also out. This means Android 2.x will not run this sample. As for what we *can* target, note the following: Android 4.x (default browser, Chrome, Firefox, Opera), iOS 4+, Firefox OS, Blackberry 10, Windows Phone 8 and Internet Explorer 10 on a Surface device, or similar touch-capable hardware.

Getting Started

Let's start by creating the basic shell. We will use a lot of the same patterns as we did in the last sample, so you will recognize some of this. We will call this function "Pincher".

```
window.Pincher = (function () {

  var pincher = function (element) {
    this.element = element;

    //This is where we will store info about all of the active touches
    this.touchInfo = {
      touchLookup: {},
      touchArray: []
    };

    this.mode = 'none'; //move, resize are other modes
    var self = this;

    this.element.addEventListener('touchstart', function (evt) { self.start.call(self, evt) });
    this.element.addEventListener('touchmove', function (evt) { self.change.call(self, evt) });
    this.element.addEventListener('touchend', function (evt) { self.end.call(self, evt) });

    this.element.addEventListener('MSPointerDown', function (evt) { self.start.call(self, evt) });
    this.element.addEventListener('MSPointerMove', function (evt) { self.change.call(self, evt) });
    this.element.addEventListener('MSPointerUp', function (evt) { self.end.call(self, evt) });
  }

  return pincher;
})();
```

Here we have a function that takes the element that we will attach the behavior to. We wire up our event listeners as well (though no mouse this time). This is very similar to the previous sample. The differences include the mode and the touchInfo object. The mode signifies the mode of action the code is in, which is either "none" (no touches are "active"), "move" (one finger is touching) or "resize" (more than one finger is touching, and encompasses rotate as well as resizing). The touchInfo object is explained in the next section.

The DOM for the page and for hooking this all up is fairly concise. Also, given how we are going to construct this, you can have multiple elements on the page that you can manipulate: all you have to do is instantiate new instances of Pincher.

```
<head>
  <meta name="viewport" content="width=device-width, initial-scale=1.0, maximum-scale=1.0,
user-scalable=0" />
  <title>Pinch</title>

  <style>
    #the-picture {
      height: 200px;
      margin: 20px 0 0 20px;
      width: 200px;
      position: absolute;
      -ms-touch-action: none;
    }
  </style>
</head>
<body>
  <img src="~/content/images/dragonfruit_500.jpg" id="the-picture" />

  <script src="/content/advancedtouchprogramming/pincher.js"></script>
  <script>
    window.addEventListener('load', load);

    function load() {
      var picture = document.getElementById('the-picture');

      var pincher = new window.Pincher(picture);
    }
  </script>
</body>
```

Normalizing the Touch Methods

The touchInfo object is for holding our touch information. Since we have different touch models working in the same code, we could either have code for handling the different models scattered throughout the file, as we had to handle the differences. Or we can normalize the behavior and have all the interesting code (that around scaling, moving, and rotating) all working off a single model. The latter approach makes it all so much easier, so that's what we'll do.

Our approach is to take that bit of code and create a custom model of the touches. Let's look at it again.

```
this.touchInfo = {
  touchLookup: {},
  touchArray: []
};
```

We will be managing either one or two touches but no more. In a sample where you are rotating or scaling an image, more than two touches makes no sense. To manage these touches, I'm putting them into both into an object for key-based lookups (all the touch implementations have identifiers for touches we can use) and into the array to remember the order the events happened (the first touch happened first, the second happened second).

We have three points at which we need to normalize the behavior, at the start of a touch, when the touch changes and when the touch ends. You saw above how we hooked up the code. Let's look at these methods in turn.

```
pincher.prototype.start = function (evt) {
  evt.preventDefault(); //prevent scrolling
  this.registerTouch(evt);
  this.setMode();
}
```

This is the method that fires on touchstart and MSPointerDown. We call preventDefault as we normally do to prevent page scrolling. We will examine the setMode function in the next section. The registerTouch method is very important at this point and looks like this.

```
pincher.prototype.registerTouch = function (evt) {
  //It is in this method that we normalize the touch model between the different implementations

  if (evt.touches) { //touch events
    //find all the touches in the touch array that haven't been registered and do so.
    for (var i = 0; i < evt.touches.length; i++) {
      var evtTouch = evt.touches[i];

      if (!this.touchInfo.touchLookup[evtTouch.identifier]) {
        //Instead of storing the actual touch object, we just store what we need. The actual object
        //  isn't persisted in non-iOS webkit so this normalizes more with that pattern.
        var touch = {
          identifier: evtTouch.identifier,
          pageX: evtTouch.pageX,
          pageY: evtTouch.pageY
        };

        this.addTouchToLookup(touch);        }
    }
  }
  else { //pointer events
    //pointer events are normally collected in a group but we need to do that so we know how
many touches
    //  there are.
    var touch = {
      pageX: evt.pageX,
      pageY: evt.pageY,
      identifier: evt.pointerId
    };
    this.addTouchToLookup(touch);  }
}

pincher.prototype.addTouchToLookup = function (touch) {
  this.touchInfo.touchArray.push(touch);
  this.touchInfo.touchLookup[touch.identifier] = touch;
  touch.indexInArray = this.touchInfo.touchArray.length - 1;
}
```

The first half of the method normalizes touch events into our custom touch model. As we discussed in the last chapter, touch objects are stored in arrays on the event object. The two arrays we'll use are the touches array and the changedTouches array. When a touch first appears it will be in the touches array, so we use that one in this method. The normalization process takes the touches out of the array; and if the touch doesn't yet exist, we create our custom object and add it to our touch model. In a multi-touch scenario, the first touch will fire and we'll add that to our touch model. When the second touch fires the touch start event, both touches will be in the array, and we need to find only the new one and create a custom touch model for that particular one. This is why we loop through the touches collection looking to see if any touches are not yet registered, which we do on line 8 of the sample above.

Before we move on to the next section, I should point out how you can avoid one other problem you could potentially run into when creating something like this. When a touch event fires, that touch object in the array is given an identifier, which implies that it's more than just a bundle of data. It's an object representing that touch. Question: once you move that touch and the move event fires, is the touch object you used in the touch start the same object? Answer: it depends. On iOS, it's the same object. So for iOS, we could have just put the touch object in our touchInfo object and used it later because it's properties (like pageX and pageY) would get changed as the touch moved. But on Android it isn't the same object. It's a new object with the same pointer ID as the object in the touch start event. So if you need to know where this point is as it moves, you need to handle this difference. We do that by looking up the custom touch event object and updating it. More on that just below.

The second half normalizes the pointer event model that Internet Explorer 10 uses. In that model each touch is entirely independent. So we will be gathering up the touches to coordinate them, normalizing the pointer event model more toward the touchevent model. Because the touch model for touch events doesn't distinguish in the event object which of the touches in the touches array is actually the one started with that event, it's actually easier to normalize the pointer event model to our new structure than the touch event model.

So that was normalizing at the point of touchstart and MSPointerDown. Now we normalize at the point of touchmove and MSPointerMove. This is the function called:

```
pincher.prototype.change = function (evt) {
  this.updateTouchEvent(evt);

  if (this.mode === 'move') {
    this.move(evt);
  }
  else if (this.mode === 'resize') {
    this.resize(evt);
  }
}
```

Right now all we are concerned with is the call to the updateTouchEvent method. The others we will deal with in the next section. The updateTouchEvent function finds the custom touch object we need and updates the position.

```
pincher.prototype.updateTouchEvent = function (evt) {
  var touch, i = 0;

  if (evt.touches) {
    for (i; i < evt.changedTouches.length; i++) {
      touch = evt.changedTouches[i];
      this.touchInfo.touchLookup[touch.identifier].pageX = touch.pageX;
      this.touchInfo.touchLookup[touch.identifier].pageY = touch.pageY;
    }
  }
}
```

```
  else {
    touch = this.touchInfo.touchLookup[evt.pointerId];
    touch.pageX = evt.pageX;
    touch.pageY = evt.pageY;
  }
}
```

Once again, you have to handle both event models. The identifier for pointer events is "pointerId", so you can use that to find the pointer event. The identifier for touch events is "identifier", so you use that one to look up the custom touch object needed. Because we are dealing only with changed touches, you can look in the changedTouches array for touch events and just update for those.

When a touch ends, we have to do our final normalization. The touch end function looks like so:

```
pincher.prototype.end = function (evt) {
  this.removeDeadTouches(evt);

  this.setMode();

  //If one of the two touches has ended, need to prep for the next time two touch and can resize
  and rotate.
    if (this.touchInfo.touchArray.length < 2) {
      this.originalDistanceBetweenTouchPoints = null;
      this.currentTransformValue = this.activeTransformValue;
    }
}
```

The bit we are most concerned with at this point is the call to removeDeadTouches, which is where we normalize these ended touches.

```
pincher.prototype.removeDeadTouches = function (evt) {

  if (evt.touches) { //touch events
    //for touch events it's hard to tell which touch ended, so we'll just remove ones from our
    state that
    //  are no longer in the touches array.
    var ids = '', i = 0;
    for (i; i < evt.touches.length; i++) {
      var touch = evt.touches[i];
      if (ids.length > 0)
        ids += '|';
      ids += touch.identifier;
    }

    for (var key in this.touchInfo.touchLookup) {
      if (ids.indexOf(key) === -1) { //need to remove the touch
        this.touchInfo.touchArray.splice(this.touchInfo.touchLookup[key].indexInArray);
        delete this.touchInfo.touchLookup[key];
      }
    }
  }
```

```
  else { //mouse and pointer events
    var touch = this.touchInfo.touchLookup[evt.pointerId];
    this.touchInfo.touchArray.splice(touch.indexInArray);
    delete this.touchInfo.touchLookup[touch.identifier];
  }
}
```

Once again, the function has two parts. The first part removes the completed touch event objects from the custom touch model. Since there is no obvious way to tell which touch actually ended with the firing of the event, we look through all of them and remove all that are no longer present.

The pointer events are a little easier to deal with yet once again. Because the touch that ended is passed with the event object, we can easily find the one to remove and do so.

At this point all the normalization logic is done. Now all touch work can be done in a browser-independent way. It wasn't simple but it will make the rest of the code much more straightforward.

Moving

Now to the actual business of manipulating the image. We will start with moving because it is the easiest action to understand. The DOM manipulation is always in one of two modes, move or resize. Move mode involves one touch point, resize involves two. The setMode method, which is called any time a touchstart/MSPointerDown event fires or a touchend/MSPointerUp event fires, sets the mode. The method looks at our normalized touch model to determine how many touches are active.

```
pincher.prototype.setMode = function () {
  // we need to reset this so on the the next move can have an starting offset.
  this.startingOffset = null;

  if (this.touchInfo.touchArray.length === 1)
    this.mode = 'move';
  else if (this.touchInfo.touchArray.length === 2)
    this.mode = 'resize';
  else
    this.mode = 'none';
}
```

When a change event (touchmove or MSPointerMove) fires, we look at the mode and decide what to do.

```
pincher.prototype.change = function (evt) {
  this.updateTouchEvent(evt);

  if (this.mode === 'move') {
    this.move(evt);
  }
  else if (this.mode === 'resize') {
    this.resize(evt);
  }
}
```

Of course in this case we want to move.

```
pincher.prototype.move = function (evt) {
  if (!this.startingOffset)
    this.startingOffset = this.getPosition(evt);

  //move already assumes a single touch, so the zero-based indexing works.
  this.element.style.left = (this.touchInfo.touchArray[0].pageX - this.startingOffset.x) + 'px';
  this.element.style.top = (this.touchInfo.touchArray[0].pageY - this.startingOffset.y) + 'px';
}
```

The first thing we need to do is determine where in the element we are touching so we can subtract that offset from the final. Otherwise the element will visually jump the distance of that offset on the page. We get our position with this function.

```
pincher.prototype.getPosition = function (evt) {
  var pageX = this.touchInfo.touchArray[0].pageX;
  var pageY = this.touchInfo.touchArray[0].pageY;

  //This will get us the x/y position within the element.
  return {
    y: pageY - this.element.offsetTop,
    x: pageX - this.element.offsetLeft
  };
}
```

As the touch moves, the pageX and pageY values change, moving the element with the touch point. Move is now complete.

Resizing

When we are in resize mode, we need to start either resizing or rotating (or both). Let's start with resizing. It starts with the change method.

```
pincher.prototype.change = function (evt) {
  this.updateTouchEvent(evt);

  if (this.mode === 'move') {
    this.move(evt);
  }
  else if (this.mode === 'resize') {
    this.resize(evt);
  }
}
```

Both resizing and rotation have to set a starting state before performing their respective actions. The actions are cumulative, so the starting place is necessary. This means the resizing method is broken into two pieces, which call two different methods.

```
pincher.prototype.resize = function (evt) {
  if (!this.startingPointSet) {
    this.beginTransform(); //set our beginning state so we can begin
  }
  else {
    this.continueTransform(); //apply next change
  }
}
```

Resizing requires that we collect the distance between the initial touch points. As the distance increases, we make the image larger. As the distance decreases, we shrink it. But it starts with determining the original value.

```
pincher.prototype.beginTransform = function () {

  //setup initial values for resize
  var firstLength = Math.abs(this.touchInfo.touchArray[0].pageX - this.touchInfo.touchArray[1].pageX);
  var secondLength = Math.abs(this.touchInfo.touchArray[0].pageY - this.touchInfo.touchArray[1].pageY);

  this.originalDistanceBetweenTouchPoints = Math.sqrt((firstLength * firstLength) +
(secondLength * secondLength));

  //setup initial values for rotation
  //...

  this.startingPointSet = true;
}
```

Now that we have the original value, on subsequent moves we can use that to determine the new size. Here is that code.

```
pincher.prototype.continueTransform = function () {
  //calc rotation change
  //...

  //calc size transform
  var firstLength = Math.abs(this.touchInfo.touchArray[0].pageX - this.touchInfo.touchArray[1].pageX);
  var secondLength = Math.abs(this.touchInfo.touchArray[0].pageY - this.touchInfo.touchArray[1].pageY);

  var newDistance = Math.sqrt((firstLength * firstLength) + (secondLength * secondLength));
  this.activeTransformValue = newDistance / this.originalDistanceBetweenTouchPoints;

  //A new currentTransformValue will be set when the transform ends.
  if (this.currentTransformValue) {
    this.activeTransformValue = this.currentTransformValue * this.activeTransformValue;
  }

  //apply to element style
  this.element.style.webkitTransform = 'scale(' + this.activeTransformValue + ')';
  this.element.style.transform = 'scale(' + this.activeTransformValue + ')';
}
```

The size calculations should be relatively straightforward; but there are two things to note. First, we are using CSS transforms to change the size of the element. We could just change the height and width of the element, but we can't do that with rotating, so I'll use the transform for both to keep it consistent.

Second, once you resize, the next time you resize you need to start with the original size. We save that in the currentTransformValue variable. You won't know to save that value until the touch event ends. This happens in the end function, which you've already seen.

```
pincher.prototype.end = function (evt) {
  this.removeDeadTouches(evt);

  this.setMode();

  //If one of the two touches has ended, need to prep for the next time two touch and can resize
and rotate.
  if (this.touchInfo.touchArray.length < 2) {
    this.startingPointSet = false;
    this.originalDistanceBetweenTouchPoints = null;
    this.currentTransformValue = this.activeTransformValue;
  }
}
```

And at this point our resizing code is complete.

Rotation

Now on to rotation. We need to return to our beginTransform method but focus on the rotation aspect. We need to get our initial angle, because we'll use that when we execute our next move.

```
pincher.prototype.beginTransform = function () {

  //setup initial values for resize
  //...

  //setup initial values for rotation
  this.startPoint0 = { x: this.touchInfo.touchArray[0].pageX, y: this.touchInfo.touchArray[0].pageY };
  this.startPoint1 = { x: this.touchInfo.touchArray[1].pageX, y: this.touchInfo.touchArray[1].pageY };

  var xDelta = this.startPoint1.x - this.startPoint0.x;
  var yDelta = this.startPoint1.y - this.startPoint0.y;

  this.initialAngle = Math.atan2(xDelta, yDelta);

  this.startingPointSet = true;
}
```

So on each move re-calculate the angle and rotate the element accordingly.

```
pincher.prototype.continueTransform = function () {
  //calc rotation change
  var touch0 = this.touchInfo.touchArray[0];
  var touch1 = this.touchInfo.touchArray[1];
```

```
    var xDelta = touch1.pageX - touch0.pageX;
    var yDelta = touch1.pageY - touch0.pageY;

    var newAngle = Math.atan2(xDelta, yDelta);

    var rotationAmount = this.initialAngle - newAngle;

    //calc size transform
    //...

    //apply to element style
    this.element.style.webkitTransform = 'scale(' + this.activeTransformValue + ')';
    this.element.style.transform = 'scale(' + this.activeTransformValue + ')';

    this.element.style.webkitTransform += ' rotate(' + rotationAmount + 'rad)';
    this.element.style.transform += ' rotate(' + rotationAmount + 'rad)';
}
```

For those unfamiliar with the Math.atan2 method, it calculates the angle between the x-axis and the given coordinate. For more information, I recommend the excellent article on the function on Wikipedia [http://en.wikipedia.org/wiki/Atan2].

To accomplish the rotation, we are once again using transforms. The transform CSS property takes multiple transforms, so we are always applying scale and rotation styles, even if nothing changed.

Summary

If you follow the right techniques, you can create some nice, re-usable code for gestures and touch manipulations, despite the very different browser touch implementations. Doing complex touch interactions can get, well, *complex*, but if you work at it you can come up with some easy abstractions. Some of you might be thinking this is too complex and that you should use a library to make this easier. In some cases I agree; and in the next chapter I will discuss a couple of touch libraries I have found to be very useful. But this chapter and the previous one were about teaching the core principles, the things you need to know if the libraries don't give you what you need or if they have a bug you need to fix. Hopefully, these chapters will inspire you to put a little touch code in your next mobile project.

CHAPTER 12

■ ■ ■

Useful Libraries for Mobile

This book has thus far been about the skills you need to do mobile well without libraries (most of the time). This was intentionally done because we will always be better developers if we understand our medium well, even if we eventually decide to use libraries to make developing in that medium easier. But we've covered the basics, and it's time to start talking about some tools you can use.

Responsive Libraries

The first part of the book was dedicated to responsive web design, so it only makes sense to start with the same subject here. Here are a number of useful libraries to help our websites be more responsive.

Bootstrap

Bootstrap [http://getbootstrap.com/] is a flexible, responsive framework for quickly building responsive websites. A few of the templates in Visual Studio 2012 were responsive but didn't use any particular responsive library. In Visual Studio 2013 Microsoft switched the default MVC template to use Bootstrap 3.0. You get this by first creating a new project as you see in Figure 12-1.

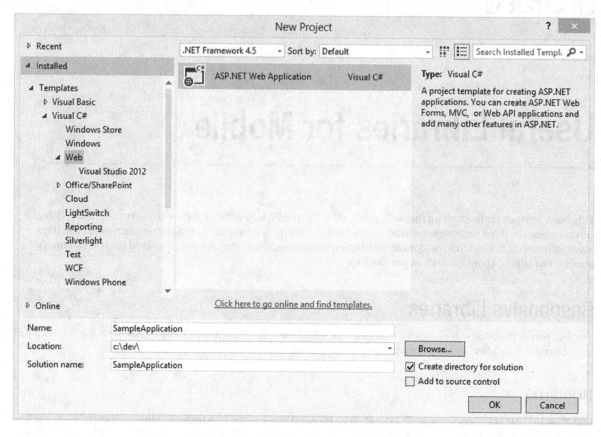

Figure 12-1. *The new web project dialog in Visual Studio 2013*

Once "ASP.NET Web Application" is chosen, a new dialog appears, shown in Figure 12-2, that lets you specify how the project is set up.

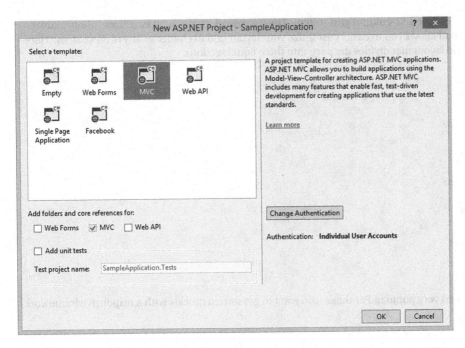

Figure 12-2. *If this option is chosen, a new ASP.NET MVC project using Bootstrap will be created*

This project comes with bootstrap pre-installed and integrated into the template. Bootstrap makes it easy to define a grid, create menus that collapse when the browser is narrow to preserve space, gives you standard sets of styles you can use, allows you to hide/show sections of a page depending on screen size and more. Here in Figure 12-3 is what the default template with Bootstrap looks like.

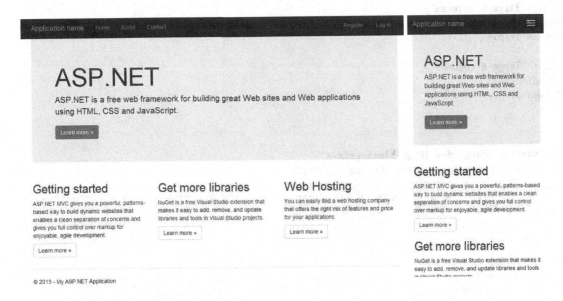

Figure 12-3. *The default ASP.NET MVC template with Bootstrap 3.0, large and small screen*

Layout is done using a CSS-based 12-column grid system. The framework comes with four sizes (phone, tablet, monitor, and large monitor) and allows you to easily customize your layout grid to change at any of these sizes. Here is an example of a row of a grid layout that divides the page into three equal sections.

```
<div class="row">
  <div class="col-lg-4">
    <h2>Heading</h2>
    <p>First column... </p>
  </div>
  <div class="col-lg-4">
    <h2>Heading</h2>
    <p>Second column...</p>
  </div>
  <div class="col-lg-4">
    <h2>Heading</h2>
    <p>Third column...</p>
  </div>
</div>
```

Bootstrap is easy to use and very popular. For those who want to get started quickly with a responsive framework, this is a good choice.

Zurb Foundation

Another popular responsive framework is Zurb Foundation [http://foundation.zurb.com/]. It's very similar to Bootstrap in many ways, and if you are shopping for a responsive framework, take a look at this one as well before deciding. Here is an example of some HTML with styling to create a two-column row over a four-column image grid.

```
<div class="row main-content">
  <div class="large-6 columns">
    <h2>Heading</h2>
    <p>Column 1</p>
  </div>
  <div class="large-6 columns">
    <h2>Heading</h2>
    <p>Column 2</p>
  </div>
</div>

<ul class="small-block-grid-2 large-block-grid-4">
  <li><img src="/content/images/dice_200.jpg" /></li>
  <li><img src="/content/images/ready_200.jpg" /></li>
  <li><img src="/content/images/greek_200.jpg" /></li>
  <li><img src="/content/images/bacon_200.jpg" /></li>
</ul>
```

FitText

Let's leave the realm of larger responsive frameworks and start solving individual problems. Have you ever needed headline text to expand as the browser width expands? If so, FitText [http://fittextjs.com/] will come in handy. With FitText you only need to do this to get an element to a size relative to the size of the viewport:

```
$(document).ready(function () {
  $('h1').fitText();
});
```

As for what this would look like, take a look at Figure 12-4. Note that the screenshot on the right shows a wider viewport and the header grows correspondingly.

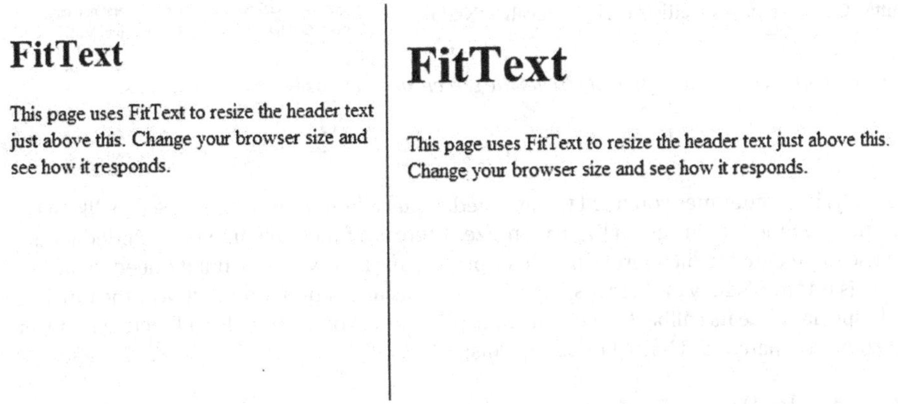

FitText

This page uses FitText to resize the header text just above this. Change your browser size and see how it responds.

FitText

This page uses FitText to resize the header text just above this. Change your browser size and see how it responds.

Figure 12-4. FitText applied to the header of this page

This can be quite a bit easier than using multiple media queries to tweak headers for various viewport sizes in your responsive implementation. But note that this is not even going to be needed in most cases since text is already flexible (as discussed in Chapter 5, "Flexible Content"). This is more for visual effect and aesthetics: but if that's something you are looking for, this library could be useful for you.

FlowType.js

FitText is for headline text but if you need something that is meant to work with body text, FlowType [http://simplefocus.com/flowtype/] is a good option. FlowType allows you to set minimum and maximum sizes and between those widths it will keep line-length pretty consistent. Once you include the library, this is how you would setup an element to use FlowType.

```
$(document).ready(function () {
  $('.main-content').flowtype({
    minimum: 500,
    maximum: 800
  });
});
```

Like with FitText, this can be an easier way to flexibly manage text sizes in your responsive sites. You can see an example of this in action in Figure 12-5.

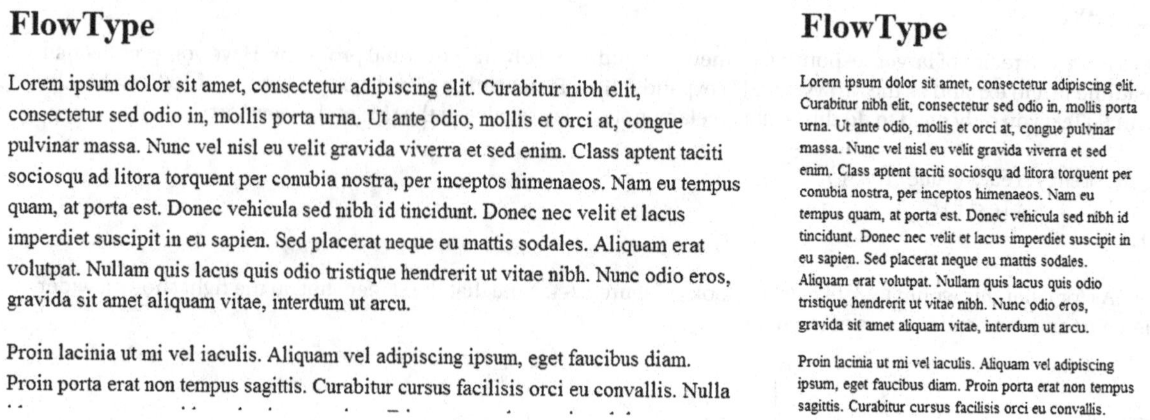

FlowType

Lorem ipsum dolor sit amet, consectetur adipiscing elit. Curabitur nibh elit, consectetur sed odio in, mollis porta urna. Ut ante odio, mollis et orci at, congue pulvinar massa. Nunc vel nisl eu velit gravida viverra et sed enim. Class aptent taciti sociosqu ad litora torquent per conubia nostra, per inceptos himenaeos. Nam eu tempus quam, at porta est. Donec vehicula sed nibh id tincidunt. Donec nec velit et lacus imperdiet suscipit in eu sapien. Sed placerat neque eu mattis sodales. Aliquam erat volutpat. Nullam quis lacus quis odio tristique hendrerit ut vitae nibh. Nunc odio eros, gravida sit amet aliquam vitae, interdum ut arcu.

Proin lacinia ut mi vel iaculis. Aliquam vel adipiscing ipsum, eget faucibus diam. Proin porta erat non tempus sagittis. Curabitur cursus facilisis orci eu convallis. Nulla

FlowType

Lorem ipsum dolor sit amet, consectetur adipiscing elit. Curabitur nibh elit, consectetur sed odio in, mollis porta urna. Ut ante odio, mollis et orci at, congue pulvinar massa. Nunc vel nisl eu velit gravida viverra et sed enim. Class aptent taciti sociosqu ad litora torquent per conubia nostra, per inceptos himenaeos. Nam eu tempus quam, at porta est. Donec vehicula sed nibh id tincidunt. Donec nec velit et lacus imperdiet suscipit in eu sapien. Sed placerat neque eu mattis sodales. Aliquam erat volutpat. Nullam quis lacus quis odio tristique hendrerit ut vitae nibh. Nunc odio eros, gravida sit amet aliquam vitae, interdum ut arcu.

Proin lacinia ut mi vel iaculis. Aliquam vel adipiscing ipsum, eget faucibus diam. Proin porta erat non tempus sagittis. Curabitur cursus facilisis orci eu convallis.

Figure 12-5. *An example of using FlowType to increase text size as the screen size increases*

Enquire.js

CSS media queries are very handy, but sometimes you need to have media query support in your JavaScript, like when you need to have different client-side functionality given the screen size. There is a function named matchMedia on newer browsers that you can use to execute media queries in JavaScript, and this is very handy: but if I need to do this, I would rather use enquire.js [http://wicky.nillia.ms/enquire.js/] because I prefer the API over the raw matchMedia JavaScript API. I especially like its callback mechanism, which allows you to provide callbacks whenever a media query matches or becomes unmatched. The API looks like this:

```
window.addEventListener('load', load);

function load() {

  enquire.register("screen and (max-width:500px)", {

    match: function () {
      $.ajax({
        url: '/thirdpartylibraries/smallerlibraries/enquirecontent',
        success: function (content) {
          console.log('got this', content);
          $('#put-content-here').html(content);
        }
      });
    },

    unmatch: function () {
      $('#put-content-here').html('');
    },

  });
}
```

In this sample the match function executes whenever the screen drops below 500 pixels in width and the unmatch function executes when it is 500 pixels in width or greater. Here I'm adding some content from the server when the page size drops below a certain value. That content could be an ad or a new widget. Or maybe you could enable/disable some functionality. Whatever your needs, if you need to execute some JavaScript when a page changes size, have a look at this.

Respond

What do you do if you need media query support in a browser that doesn't support it (like IE 6-8)? You can complain about it on Twitter, or you can polyfill it with Respond [https://github.com/scottjehl/Respond] by Scott Jehl. Respond adds the functionality for min/max-width media queries to these older browsers (and more). The only requirement is that you add the respond JavaScript file.

PictureFill

Another very useful library is PictureFill [https://github.com/scottjehl/picturefill], also created by Scott Jehl. This library is a polyfill for the proposed picture element [http://www.w3.org/TR/2013/WD-html-picture-element-20130226/]. Using background images in responsive web design works pretty well without a polyfill. What responsive techniques don't normally help with as elegantly are inline image tags. The picture element is designed to solve this problem, and you can use PictureFill to mimic it even though browsers don't support it yet. For more information and an example, see Chapter 5.

Touch Libraries

The following libraries are useful for your mobile touch development. We had two chapters on touch development, so we know that creating good touch applications can be difficult. Hopefully these will help.

Swipeview

Swipeview [http://cubiq.org/swipeview] is a very fast and fluid swipe control. We use it for our mobile website at Match.com for our photo gallery as well as a few other features. Figure 12-6 shows a picture of what it looks like though that doesn't do it justice. I would recommend trying it out on the live site.

Figure 12-6. Swipeview used for a photo gallery. Also, bacon

The only negative about Swipeview is that it doesn't work on Windows Phone 8. If this is not a device you plan to support, I would strongly recommend using it.

Hammer.js

When I'm not writing my own gnarly touch code and if I want gestures, I usually turn to hammer.js [http://eightmedia.github.io/hammer.js/]. Not only does it work well and works with both the touch event and the pointer event models, it also has a really awesome theme. And setting up gestures is a snap. Assuming you have a div on the page with an id of "touch-me", this is all you need to set up some simple gestures.

```
$(document).ready(function () {
  $('#touch-me').hammer().on('tap', function () {
    $('#touch-me').text('tapped');
  });

  $('#touch-me').hammer().on('swipeleft', function () {
    $('#touch-me').text('swiped left');
  });

  $('#touch-me').hammer().on('swiperight', function () {
    $('#touch-me').text('swiped right');
  });
});
```

This version uses jQuery, but they supply a version that is plain JavaScript.

Hand.js

In our touch chapters you probably noticed the differences between the Webkit/Gecko touch event model and Internet Explorer's pointer events. In Chapter 11 I showed one example of how to normalize the event models. But what if we could just give other browsers pointer events? That is the purpose of Hand.js [http://handjs.codeplex.com/], a pointer event polyfill. If you include the hand.js library into a page, you can start using unprefixed pointer events like this:

```
window.addEventListener('load', load);

function load() {

  var tapMe = document.getElementById('tap-me');

  tapMe.addEventListener('pointerdown', function () {
    tapMe.innerHTML = 'You have tapped using the pointerdown event.';
  });
}
```

This provides a nice alternative to handling the different events in your own code when it makes sense to do so, which is probably most of the time.

Device/Feature-Detection Libraries

The following two libraries are very useful for device and feature detection.

WURFL

WURFL (Wireless Universal Resource File) is a project headed up by Scientia Mobile [http://www.scientiamobile.com/] and is a library and database combination for server-side device detection. It is as useful for older devices like feature phones as it is for our new smartphones. The most useful feature is that it does User Agent parsing and detection, though they gather bits of information about the devices. The drawbacks are that it always has to be updated, it costs money to keep it updated, and that it doesn't tell you necessarily what the device can do. WURFL was described and put to use in Chapter 7, so see that chapter for more information.

Modernizr

Modernizr [http://modernizr.com/] is a library for doing client-side feature detection. While WURFL focuses on what the device is, Modernizr focuses on what the device can do by doing client-side sleuthing. In this respect Modernizr is much more future-friendly, in that the same feature-detections should continue to work as browsers advance while WURFL can go out of date. Modernizr was used in Chapter 7, so see that chapter for more information.

Mobile Application Frameworks

The other sections in this chapter examined special-purpose libraries and tools. The last libraries and tools we cover tend to be much more invasive to how you create your website, giving you guidance and delivering a wide variety of tools to help you along. These tools are also generally well tested on a wide range of devices, which is very valuable because cross-device debugging can be a large time and money investment.

jQuery Mobile

jQuery Mobile [http://jquerymobile.com/] is not the mobile version of jQuery (as many probably assume when they first hear the name of the project) but as I described above, a framework for creating mobile web applications across a wide variety of devices. This is a description of the library description:

> *A unified, HTML5-based user interface system for all popular mobile device platforms, built on the rock-solid jQuery and jQuery UI foundation. Its lightweight code is built with progressive enhancement, and has a flexible, easily themeable design.*

The sample app I created (which is a part of the downloadable source code) starts with a list page as can be seen in Figure 12-7.

Figure 12-7. *A simple list page using jQuery Mobile*

Here is the markup that created everything above.

```
<div data-role="page" class="ui-page ui-body-c ui-page-panel ui-page-active"
  tabindex="0" style="min-height: 728px;">

  <div class="ui-panel-content-wrap ui-body-c ui-panel-animate ui-panel-content-wrap-closed">
    <div data-role="header" class="jqm-header ui-header ui-bar-a" role="banner">
      <h1 class="ui-title" role="heading" aria-level="1">jQuery Mobile</h1>
    </div>

    <div data-role="content" class="ui-content" role="main">
      <ul data-role="listview">
```

```
        <li><a href="/link/to/food">Food</a></li>
        <li><a href="/link/to/humor">Humor</a></li>
      </ul>
    </div>
      <p style="font-size: .9em; font-weight: bold; margin-top: 30px;">This demo was created jQuery
Mobile 1.3.2.</p>
  </div>
</div>
```

The only thing in this markup that I had to create custom styling for is the note about the demo at the bottom. All the rest uses built-in jQuery Mobile CSS and JavaScript and is adapted from an actual jQuery Mobile demo. There are two things in particular that I want to point out. First, data-role="x" attributes are used throughout the markup to tell the framework the role a particular block of markup is playing in the page. Second, many of the classes end in things like –a, -b and -c, which are markers to indicate which built-in theme you want to use. If I change the header to use the ui-bar-c class and the panel content wrap to ui-body-a, I get a very different theme as can be seen in Figure 12-8.

Figure 12-8. *An example of what you can do with jQuery Mobile theming*

On the next page I used an accordion for showing the food choices, which you can see in Figure 12-9.

The markup for the accordion (no need to repeat the other outer markup as it is essentially the same) with a little Razor markup to build my page is as follows:

Figure 12-9. An example of the jQuery mobile accordion control

```
<div data-role="collapsible-set" data-theme="c" data-content-theme="d">
  @foreach (var image in Model.Images)
  {
    <div data-role="collapsible">
      <h3>@image.Name</h3>
      <p>@image.Description</p>
      <img src="@image.Url" style="max-width: 200px;" />
    </div>
  }
</div>
```

I found jQuery Mobile easy to get started with. The project also has a very active community, and it is easy to find help online. Much of the popularity is undoubtedly due to its association with jQuery. Another factor that has probably increased its popularity among ASP.NET developers is that it's used in the Mobile project template (as can be seen in Figure 12-10) for ASP.NET MVC 4.

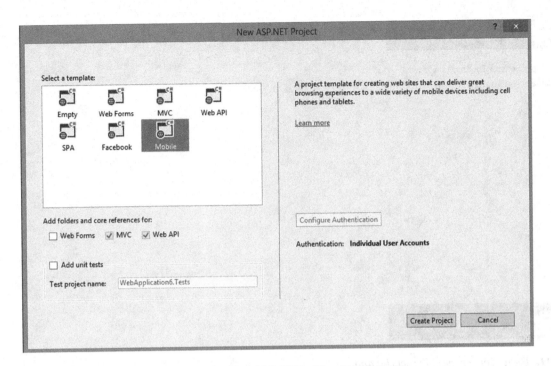

Figure 12-10. *The new project dialog for ASP.NET MVC in Visual Studio 2013*

Sencha Touch

Sencha Touch is another popular framework for building mobile web applications. As for the purpose of the framework, here is Sencha's own description from their website [`http://www.sencha.com/products/touch`].

> *HTML5 Mobile App Development*
> *With over 50 built-in components, themes for every popular mobile platform, and a built-in MVC system, Sencha Touch provides everything you need to create universal mobile web apps.*

It took me longer to get up and running and to get the core ideas of Sencha Touch than with either of the other two frameworks we are discussing in this section. It's also radically different in its approach. First of all, it has a command-line component to it, and this component requires Java and Ruby to be installed, which .NET developers may not have installed yet (though there is no harm in this). Second, the approach is **entirely JavaScript-based**, which will be quite different from the experience of most ASP.NET developers. As the Single Page Application model becomes more popular, this becomes less of a problem, but it's also not like any SPA that I have used, so it will still likely be foreign to most. You will see a sample shortly.

The most natural thing to do for my Sencha Touch demo was to have the whole demo on one page, though this isn't necessary. The app had three virtual pages, a welcome page, a blog page, and a gallery. Most of this was taken from or adapted somewhat from samples found on the Sencha Touch site, so it should at least be representative enough for you to get a basic feel for using it. Let's start with the welcome page, seen in Figure 12-11.

Figure 12-11. The welcome page of the Sencha app

The tab panel is set up by doing this:

```
Ext.create('Ext.tab.Panel', {
  fullscreen: true,
  tabBarPosition: 'bottom',

  //There are three things in this array, so there are three elements in the tab bar.
  items: [
    {
      //First tab
    },
    {
      //Second tab
    },
    {
      //Third tab
    },

  ]
});
```

This is simple enough. What about the content of the first tab?

```
{
  title: 'Welcome',
  iconCls: 'home',
```

```
    styleHtmlContent: true,
    scrollable: true,

    items: {
      docked: 'top',
      xtype: 'titlebar',
      title: 'Sencha Touch Demo'
    },

    html: [
        "This is a simple Sencha Touch demo. It was created with Sencha Touch 2."
    ].join("")
}
```

Hopefully you can see what I mean when I say that this is a JavaScript-based solution.

One element of their demos was the following blog list. Of course I changed the RSS feed to that of my blog!

```
{
  xtype: 'nestedlist',
  title: 'Blog',
  iconCls: 'star',
  displayField: 'title',

  store: {
    type: 'tree',

    fields: [
        'title', 'link', 'author', 'contentSnippet', 'content',
        { name: 'leaf', defaultValue: true }
    ],

    root: {
      leaf: false
    },

    proxy: {
      type: 'jsonp',
      url: 'https://ajax.googleapis.com/ajax/services/feed/load?v=1.0&q=http://feeds.feedburner.com/
ericsowell',
      reader: {
        type: 'json',
        rootProperty: 'responseData.feed.entries'
      }
    }
  }
}
```

As far as code goes, that's a fairly concise bit of code for fetching a blog's feed and displaying the results in a mobile-friendly manner. The result is what you see in Figure 12-12.

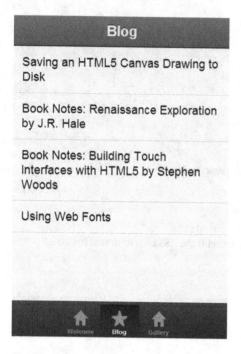

Figure 12-12. *A fairly simple list of blog posts using Sencha Touch*

So far so good. Creating a carousel is fairly easy to do as well.

```
{
  title: 'Gallery',
  iconCls: 'home',

  styleHtmlContent: false,
  scrollable: false,

  layout: {
    type: 'hbox',
    pack: 'center'
  },

  defaults: {
    height: 200,
    width: 200
  },

  items: [
    Ext.create('Ext.Carousel', {
      fullscreen: false,

      defaults: {
        styleHtmlContent: false,
```

```
    height: 200,
    width: 200
},

items: [ //Each image in the carousel is its own object.
    {
      html: '<img src="/content/bacon_200.jpg" />',
    },
    {
      html: '<img src="/content/css_200.jpg" />',
    },
    {
      html: '<img src="/content/dice_200.jpg" />',
    }

    ]
  })
 ]
}
```

The result from this is what you see in Figure 12-13.

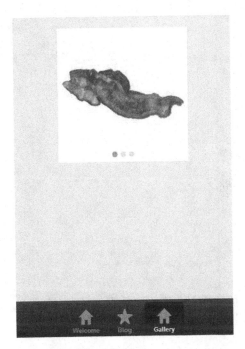

Figure 12-13. *The carousel of Sencha Touch. It works great and is even better with bacon!*

Sencha Touch provides an interesting approach to developing mobile web applications. Even though the development style is quite different than what most ASP.NET MVC developers would be used to, if you are looking for a framework to use, I would check it out anyway.

Kendo UI Mobile

Kendo UI by Telerik [http://www.kendoui.com/] provides another alternative for building mobile web applications. Kendo UI's mobile component takes an approach similar to jQuery Mobile, as you will see. For this sample I started with a simple list page, which can be seen in Figure 12-14.

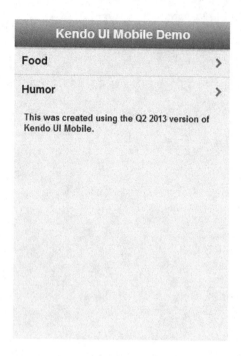

Figure 12-14. *A list page created with Kendo UI Mobile*

The code for this is as follows.

```
<div data-role="view" data-title="Kendo UI Mobile Demo" id="index">
  <header data-role="header">
    <div data-role="navbar">
      <span data-role="view-title">The Title</span>
    </div>
  </header>

  <ul data-role="listview">
    <li><a data-role="listview-link" class="km-listview-link" href="/link/to/food">Food</a></li>
    <li><a data-role="listview-link" class="km-listview-link" href="/link/to/humor">Humor</a></li>
  </ul>

  <p class="kw-text">This was created using the Q2 2013 version of Kendo UI Mobile.</p>
</div>
```

Like jQuery Mobile, Kendo UI uses data-role attributes to specify function, which the JavaScript and CSS of the framework use to build the page. The next page, which has an image gallery, (see Figure 12-15) is understandably more complex than the previous page.

Figure 12-15. An image gallery built with Kendo UI

```
<div data-role="view" data-title="@Model.Title" id="detail">

  <header data-role="header">
    <div data-role="navbar">
      <a class="nav-button km-button km-back"
        data-align="left"
        data-role="backbutton" href="" data-transition="slide:right" style="">
        <span class="km-text">Back</span>
      </a>
      <span data-role="view-title">@Model.Title</span>
    </div>
  </header>

  <ul data-role="listview" data-style="inset" data-type="group" class="km-listview km-
listgroupinset">
    <li class="km-group-container">
      <div class="">
        <div class="km-group-title">About @Model.Title</div>
      </div>
      <ul
        <li>This is the detail page for @Model.Title. It is rockin.</li>
        <li>
```

```
      <div id="scrollview-container">
        <div data-role="scrollview">

          @foreach (var image in Model.Images)
          {
            <img src="@image" class="photo" />
          }

        </div>
      </div>

    </li>
   </ul>
  </li>
 </ul>

</div>
```

Despite the added complexity, the Kendo UI gallery was very straightforward to implement. Alternatively, Kendo UI Mobile comes with some server-side components for generating the markup. Telerik distributes these through the Visual Studio Extensions gallery. Once installed, these components include project templates for getting it all set up.

Telerik has been investing heavily in the .NET community for some time. Those who already use Telerik products and need a mobile application framework like this would be well served. Those who have not now have a reason to try their products.

Summary

Mobile web development can be very difficult. Sometimes it's best to use third-party libraries to make development easier. There are of course many more out there, but these are all libraries that I have tried out myself. I tend to prefer the approach of using smaller libraries to solve my individual development needs; but some will prefer the larger frameworks, so pick the approach that works best for you.

Index

■ W, X, Y

■ Z

Get the eBook for only $10!

Now you can take the weightless companion with you anywhere, anytime. Your purchase of this book entitles you to 3 electronic versions for only $10.

This Apress title will prove so indispensible that you'll want to carry it with you everywhere, which is why we are offering the eBook in 3 formats for only $10 if you have already purchased the print book.

Convenient and fully searchable, the PDF version enables you to easily find and copy code—or perform examples by quickly toggling between instructions and applications. The MOBI format is ideal for your Kindle, while the ePUB can be utilized on a variety of mobile devices.

Go to www.apress.com/promo/tendollars to purchase your companion eBook.